GEORGIAN GARDENS
The Reign of Nature

The Grotto at Amwell.

GEORGIAN GARDENS

The Reign of Nature

DAVID JACQUES

BT BATSFORD LTD · *LONDON*

ISBN 0 7134 3457 0

Printed in Great Britain by
Butler & Tanner Ltd,
Frome, Somerset
for the Publisher,
B. T. Batsford Ltd
4 Fitzhardinge Street
London W1H 0AH

Frontispiece: Amwell, the
grotto.

When John Scott, the
Quaker poet, constructed
this grotto for himself he
was following the tradition
of eighteenth-century poets
in making their own
gardens. This vignette was
published with Scott's
Poetical Works of 1782.

Contents

List of Illustrations

Acknowledgements

The institutions that I have consulted in the preparation of this book are too numerous for a full list to be attempted. I hope that it is acceptable to all if I make special mention of just a few of the persons I have met who share my interest in garden history, and who have contributed some of their knowledge to this book. They are: George Carter of the Sainsbury Centre for Visual Arts; Patrick Conner, Keeper of Fine Art at the Royal Pavilion, Brighton; John Harris, curator of the Drawings Collection and Heinz Gallery of the British Architectural Library; the Hon. Mrs Jane Roberts of the Royal Library, Windsor Castle; J. C. M. Shaw, Local Studies Officer at the London Borough of Bexley; and Frederick Stitt, Librarian of the William Salt Library and the Staffordshire County Archivist.

I am much indebted to the many individuals who have given their own time. Patrick Bowe corresponded about John Webb, Timothy Connor about Goodwood and Peter Eden about Francis Richardson. I have exchanged much information on John Hill, Thomas White, John Webb and Adam Mickle with Peter Goodchild. Keith Goodway has been my chief source on William Emes. John Harris was a great help with the illustrations. John Harvey supplied names and dates for many of the royal gardeners. Heather Lawrence wrote about Francis Richardson. Justin Meath-Baker gave me some interesting facts about Walsingham. David Neave has contributed much on Thomas White, including the plan of Lumley Castle, and Judge Lyall Wilkes has helped with John Dobson.

The author and publishers acknowledge with thanks permission from the following to reproduce illustrations.
Roman numerals denote colour illustrations.

His Grace the Duke of Abercorn: V; His Grace the Duke of Beaufort: 28; Basilisk Press, 53; London Borough of Bexley, Libraries and Museums Dept: 35; Michael Bignal: 28; Bodleian Library: 2; British Architectural Library, RIBA: 45, 72; British Library: VII, VIII, X, frontispiece, 5, 12, 14, 21, 23, 31, 52, 57, 58, 61, 62, 65, 70, 73, 75, 76; British Museum: XI, 4, 41, 42; Sir John Carew-Pole: I; Sir Francis Dashwood: 48; T. Cottrell-Dormer: 9, 10; *Country Life*: 16, 27, 32, 34, 50, 68; Country Life Books: 1, 8, 10, 13; Courtauld Institute of Art: 7, 9, 30, 37, 38, 78; Devonshire Collection, Chatsworth: 7; Fitzwilliam Museum, Cambridge: 63; Christopher Gallagher: V; The Earl of Harewood: IX; John Harris: III, 11, 19, 20, 40, 48, 55, 59, 60; Peter Hayden: front cover, VI; Lancashire Record Office: IV; The Earl of Lichfield: 40; London Borough of Lambeth Archives Dept: XII; The Earl of Leicester: 13; Metropolitan Museum of Art, New York: 29; National Library of Wales: 47; National

Trust: I, 15; His Grace the Duke of Norfolk: 37, 38; Philipson Studios: 64; Public Record Office: 80; John Rea Studios: 46; Major Philip Riddell: 64; Royal Academy of Fine Arts, Stockholm: 40; Royal Library, Windsor Castle: 24, 33; Rutland Gallery: II; Kay N. Sanecki: 69; The Earl of Scarborough: 39; Sotheby Parke Bernet & Co.: 51; Staffordshire Record Office: 36; M. D. Trace: XII; Trustees of the Lonsdale Estate Trust: 30, 78; Trustees of the William Salt Library, Stafford: 43; University of East Anglia: 71; University of Hull: 39; Yale Center for British Art, New Haven: 18, 22, 25, 44, 79; Yale University Library: 20

Preface

This book was commissioned in the wake of the exhibition, 'The Garden', at the Victoria and Albert Museum in 1979. It is one of a series; one by John Harris, the editor of the booklet accompanying the exhibition, will be on the great formal gardens up to and including the time of Charles Bridgeman, whilst some of his former contributors are covering other periods of English garden history, John Harvey's book on *Mediaeval Gardens* has already appeared, as has Brent Elliott's on *Victorian Gardens*.

The division of English garden history into the periods selected is conventional, but this does not obviate the problems of dislocation, overlap and omission. Setting the period of this book between 1733 and 1825 inevitably creates some of these problems, but, I hope, keeps them to a minimum. The terminal date for the period is intended to denote the end of the great schemes of parkland improvement and the beginning of 'the gardenesque'. The year 1825 seems to meet these requirements. The date 1733 is more precise. In that year the Natural Style was first tried out by William Kent in small and more private parts of patrons' gardens.

Since the style started as a mere variation of the classical landscapes of the Palladians it is not easy to disentangle the references to these regular gardens from the references to those parts of gardens laid out by Kent 'without line or level'. This has led many historians to seek for the commencement of the Natural Style in the 1710s when there was much talk of Art and Nature. I am convinced that Joseph Addison and Alexander Pope both meant that bringing Nature into gardens was to apply Her precepts in *regular* gardens. Both John Harris and I have taken the view that most aspects of the highly interesting period from, say, 1713 to 1733 properly lies within the scope of his book on regular gardens. The major exception are the ideas on ornamental estate management suggested by Addison, sustained by Stephen Switzer, and which, in the guise of the *ferme ornée*, were to contribute so much to the development of the Natural Style.

I have set bounds on the scope of the book besides its dates. It is restricted to taste in English and Welsh gardens, although links to Scottish, French and other nations' gardens are treated where relevant. There are recent books on the Natural Style in Scotland, Ireland and France that can be referred to instead (see TAIT, 1980, MALINS & GLIN, 1976, and WIEBENSON, 1978, listed in the bibliography).

The period delimited above roughly coincides with the era in architectural history known as Georgian. This book is about matters of taste and design, and not a history of gardening. The distinction between the histories of gardens and of gardening was pointed out to me firmly by the late Peter Hunt. I had carelessly referred to the forthcoming *Oxford Companion to Gardens* as a companion to gardening. He rounded off his admonishment by stating, 'I am quite sure that you will agree that the two subjects are entirely different'. Whilst I wouldn't in fact go as far as this, I would refer the reader to the published histories of gardening and of plant introductions for more on those subjects.

The mention of taste introduces the social context of eighteenth-century improvement. A proficiency in matters of taste was a much prized accomplishment of the nobility and gentry. It could be exercised only by individuals with excess wealth, and ornamental improvement was a luxury amidst widespread rural poverty. This should not worry us today, as we must accept the eighteenth-century background without applying twentieth-century standards. However we should remember that status was largely determined by the ownership of land, that agriculture produced most of the income of the landed classes, and that the average nobleman's life revolved around London society during the winter months and on electioneering, building and improvement at country estates in the summer.

Although garden history is a well recognized subject, there has never been a fully satisfactory term to denote the making of gardens during this period. Richard Owen Cambridge recognized this deficiency when he wrote in *The World* of 1755 of

the modern art of *laying out ground* (for so we must call it, till a new name be adopted to express so complicated an idea).

Thomas Whately and Horace Walpole referred to it as 'modern gardening', but this will not suffice nowadays. Walpole later urged William Mason to think of a better term. Mason could only think of 'The English Garden'. Walpole himself thought of 'the landscape garden', but this did not catch on. Mason's friend William Gilpin distinguished 'embellished grounds' from natural landscape, and to others they were 'ornamental gardens'. The French spoke of 'le jardin Anglo-Chinois', but this will not be acceptable to any true Englishman.

The common term for those who laid out grounds was 'improvers', but 'improvement' is too general a term since it embraces agricultural and other forms of improvement besides the ornamental. Walpole called improvers 'gardenists', in the same way that some painters were 'landscapists'. Shenstone and Repton thought of 'landscape gardening', but as it was so closely identified with Repton its strict meaning is too limited. Any author who has agonized over a title will, I feel sure, spare me some sympathy at this point. However I kept returning to John Claudius Loudon's phrase 'The Natural Style'. He used it for the period of irregular gardens between Kent's time and his own, and it is succinctly descriptive of the prevailing purpose of garden and park design throughout the period. Hence the sub-title of this book.

As mankind inhabits the Earth and is part of the biology of its surface, it is perfectly understandable that some of its more civilized minds should strive to establish the proper relation between Man and Nature. This quest is strongly evident today, as conservationists, ecologists and landscape planners raise what they see as pertinent issues. However only the concern about the survival and treatment of other species is modern; the more general quest has frequently recurred through history. Much of the attraction of the Georgian era to historians of English gardens is that this quest was then conducted in large part through theories on garden design and the appreciation of natural scenery. It is not just the histories of architecture and horticulture with which the garden historian must become acquainted. The gardens of the period had connections with politics, psychology, poetry and painting.

The other side of the coin is that Georgian gardens are a difficult subject to treat in a balanced and authoritative manner. I must have read all the modern books relating to this subject, and despite their great number few have the same assurance that a number of recent books on architectural history display. One author sought to 'avoid art history', another concentrates on providing photographic illustrations, and numerous others treat the subject lightly as part of the garden histories of Great Britain or the world. In particular I have felt that biographies have deserved a better background. Batsford's request to me to write the sort of book that I felt was lacking was an offer I could not refuse.

An examination of the numerous writings on taste in gardens is bound to be bewildering. There were so many points of view, and so many different understandings of Nature. However I have found it helpful to divide all writers on taste into two camps. On the one side there were those who had a vision of an ideal form of Nature, and whose ideas centred around realizing their vision. The Natural Style was engendered by the ideal classical landscape of the Augustan age, but as the eighteenth century drew to a close fewer and fewer people subscribed to any such convictions. At last it was only the great romantic paradises of William Beckford and Thomas Johnes that maintained this line of thought as a creative inspiration.

In the other camp there were those who recognized that pleasure is derived from gardens and scenery, but who sought an explanation for this in the operation of the human mind. Edmund Burke's theory of the sublime and the beautiful identified the emotions as the source of the pleasure. This theory dominated this camp, though William Shenstone preferred to work on the premise that our greatest pleasures obtain from exciting the imagination, and Joseph Cradock looked to the exercise of our judgement based on the classical principles of fitness, harmony and utility as the essential criterion of taste. Despite a rearguard action by Mason these lines of thought had overrun the idealism of the other camp to such an extent that chief antagonists in the picturesque debate, Repton and Uvedale Price, were both professed followers of Burke.

It is easy to simplify the Natural Style as a single 'movement', whereas there were many conflicting viewpoints at any date, and the issues that were important to each succeeding generation differed from those of their predecessors. I have divided the period into enough chronological chapters to make some order out of the chaos, but without losing the detail. Six main chapters suggested themselves. There was the initial phase of the invention of the Natural Style. This was followed by a period of intense theorizing and experimentation from 1745 to 1760, and the style reached its zenith in the 1760s, with Lancelot Brown the dominant practitioner. The decade-and-a-half following the paper war of 1774 between William Chambers and Mason was a time of comparative inactivity in improvement, but also one of reassessment of theories of garden design. The fifth chapter begins with Humphry Repton's successful entry into landscape gardening, and continues with his involvement in the picturesque debate which flared up from 1794. The last chapter is referred to as Regency, although its duration has been stretched from 1804 to 1825. With the exception of Repton's work, garden design between these years has been given little attention by historians. However the reintroduction of geometric gardens and the new emphasis on the display of plants are of considerable interest.

Each chapter discusses the authors on taste as well as the work of contemporary improvers. The extent to which theory entered practice can then be judged. I have not confined myself to the major practitioners, Kent, Brown and Repton, but I have examined the work of the many and excellent private improvers as well. I have also set out what I have been able to glean about the minor improvers, and no doubt most readers will come across unfamiliar names in these sections.

No doubt every knowledgeable reader will consider that I have omitted some place or person which he thinks is important; however my concern has been to bring out those places which were important in their day, and so the fame that certain parks and gardens enjoy today was not germane. Also, the book is of limited length and so I had to be selective. No doubt further investigations by the many people currently interested in garden history will enable the overall picture to become clearer and the detail fuller.

1

The Birth of the Natural Style

Genius of the Place

The early part of the eighteenth century, and in particular the reign of Queen Anne (1702–14), has often been called 'the Augustan age'. It was marked by a deep reverence for the poetry and ideals of Rome in the day of Augustus, and the extraordinarily high standards set by English men of letters in emulation. The same attitude demanding intellectual rigour can be seen developing in painting, with the emphasis on connoisseurship; in architecture, with Palladianism; and in the theory of the Earth, with the belief in a concealed natural order.

There may be some truth in the notion that in every age there has been a tendency for a balance to be struck between control and freedom in the arts. Certainly in the Augustan age, if we take it as including also the reign of George I (1714–27), imagination and fantasy often accompanied an intellectual approach; indeed Joseph Addison's essays on 'the Pleasures of the Imagination' in *The Spectator* during 1712 were very influential.

A notable feature of the religion of ancient Greece and Rome had been the number of minor deities, or presiding spirits, that were supposed to populate the landscape. Of course, nobody in eighteenth-century England abandoned Christianity for those old beliefs, but the notion of the genius of the place was a convenient metaphor for characterizing its natural qualities. Consulting the genius of the place would reveal which assets should be enhanced and which deficiencies remedied. Thus Alexander Pope told Joseph Spence in 1728 that:

In laying out a garden, the first and chief thing to be considered is the genius of the place. Thus at Riskins for example, Lord Bathurst should have raised two or three mounts because his situation is all a plain, and nothing can please without variety[1].

On the other hand, springs were always an asset, and we find a number of water-nymphs living in grottoes constructed for them. The ancient deities were also invoked when a garden was laid out with an allegorical theme illustrating some moral or political point; hence the number of temples dedicated to Venus, Bacchus, or some other deity, or perhaps to some human quality such as fame, or friendship.

Occasionally, temples and other garden buildings would impart a message collectively. At Castle Howard, Yorkshire, the Earl of Carlisle's repeated references to his forebears[2] amounted almost to ancestor-worship. At Chiswick, Middlesex, Lord Burlington's garden buildings were an essay in Palladian architecture, whilst Alexander Pope was deeply immersed in the 'moral utility' of his statuary at his garden at Twickenham[3]. Two of the most extreme cases were Aaron Hill's ideas for an extensive rockwork garden[4], and Jonathan Tyers' famous grounds at Denbies, in Surrey[5]. Hill was visited at his

1   Castle Howard, view from the Temple of the Four Winds.

The temple in the distance had great significance to the third Earl of Carlisle as his family's new mausoleum.

town garden in Petty France, Westminster, in the autumn of 1733 by Pope, who showed an interest in an obelisk covered by 'Jersey shells'. In the late spring of the following year Lady Catherine Walpole, seeking ideas for a grotto of her own, called in and saw the beginnings of extensive rockworks, embellished by shells and pebbles. Hill considered this means of embellishment to be 'natural', even though he also used what he called 'Blue Stones', which were the glazed fragments of broken vessels from a glass kiln. This echoes Pope's view that *his* grotto was natural on the basis that most of his materials were found in nature.

Hill explained the design of his rockwork to Lady Walpole. It was merely a model of a garden that he intended for a country house. He envisaged a small, circular cloister within a larger, square garden. A Temple of Happiness was to stand on a mount within the cloister and be visible over the outer wall of the cloister from all parts of the garden. The mount was to be surrounded by an idyllic pastoral scene comprising cornfields, meadows and a cottage, and which was to be extended by frescoes on the inner wall of the cloister. In order to reach the temple, one had to choose the correct path through one of 12 grottoes outside the cloister. The four largest grottoes were dedicated to Power, Riches, Honour and Learning, but all ended in disappointment. It was only by taking a small pathway between statues dedicated to Reason and Innocence, and passing through the Grotto of Independence, that access to the cornfields could be discovered. The whole design was, therefore, merely a laboured and highly allegorical way for Hill to illustrate his controversial view that Man is essentially good, and that all he requires for happiness is the gift of reason.

Jonathan Tyers, on the other hand, considered that salvation came through true belief in Christ and a useful, upright life. Since 1728 he had been the proprietor of the most famous pleasure gardens in London, the Spring Gardens at Vauxhall. He had kept his less desirable customers out, and improved the gardens with an orchestra. They became enormously popular, and in 1734 Tyers was in a position to purchase the small estate called Denbies on the top of the North Downs near Dorking as a Sunday retreat.

The grounds, which were laid out sometime in the next ten years, were calculated to excite the very opposite emotions to those excited by the public gardens at Vauxhall. In the middle of an eight-acre grove called 'Il Penseroso'[6] there was the 'Temple of Death', designed as an encouragement to industry. Inside there was a monument to that paragon of diligence, Lord Petre, who Tyers claimed as a friend. On the walls, and in books chained to a desk, were writings on the theme, whilst a clock chimed every minute to remind one of the fleeing time.

The adjacent garden area was a natural amphitheatre, called the 'Valley of the Shadow of Death'. One entrance gateway was in the form of coffins on their ends topped with skulls, supposedly those of a celebrated courtesan and a noted highwayman. Inscriptions warned ladies to strive for virtue rather than beauty, and men to value wisdom rather than wealth or position. Another gateway provided an even more striking reminder that the moment of truth is death. A believer in Christ and an unbeliever were depicted in two large paintings within an alcove. As might be expected, the believer was dying blissfully with a Bible in his hand, whilst the unbeliever was dying in the agony of self-doubt, unable to find the answers in the books that had buoyed him up in his libertine life.

If, as Hill pointed out to Lady Walpole, 'It is the *imagination* that does all, in this amusement', then clearly garden features did not need to be absolutely realistic. Hill knew that his cornfields and frescoes would have fooled nobody as being Paradise, but he was assuming that visitors would be willing and able to involve themselves in the allegory. If they did so, then their imaginations would supply any deficiency in the physical representation; indeed they could raise far more powerful images than the most carefully contrived creations of Man.

This attitude pervaded the beginnings of the Natural Style, just as it did much of the gardening of the Augustan era. Many of William Kent's garden buildings were built on a toy scale. The arcade called 'Praeneste' at Rousham, Oxfordshire, was simply a few arches, but these and its name was enough to evoke the real Praeneste, a series of massive Roman terraces descending a mountain east of Rome. His cascades would have seemed ridiculous if placed side by side with those in nature or in gardens that he had seen in Italy, and the associated planting, just a few small conifers, was supposed to remind one of their Alpine setting. Succeeding generations regarded the gothic ruins and cascades of Kent's day as puerile, but then they had come to despise fantasy.

Kent was not sufficiently immersed in the classics to have more than a light-hearted approach to classical allegory, but Viscount Cobham was. He felt passionately about liberty and patriotism, and in the late 1720s he arranged a collection of busts of great English statesmen in front of a semi-circular hedge behind James Gibbs' building at his country seat, Stowe, in Buckinghamshire[7]. It was not unusual to make a collection of paintings or sculpture of one's heroes, and the arrangement was repeated by, for example, Lord Burlington for the exedra at Chiswick about 1734. However, Cobham likened his heroes to those of antiquity when he added an inscription to the building containing lines from the *Aeneid* which described the passage of blessed spirits to the Elysian Fields across the River Styx.

In 1733 Cobham added a small valley to the east of Charles Bridgeman's layout to the grounds, and diverted a road out of it. A cylindrical temple designed by Kent was already planned or under construction at the end of the Great Cross Walk and overlooking this valley. Although this valley had a somewhat irregular course, it had the advantage of springs towards its upper end. This acquisition occurred in the same year that Cobham resigned from Sir Robert Walpole's ministry, no longer able to stomach its financial policies.

Cobham saw that the quotation from the *Aeneid* at Gibbs' building could also express his conviction that a system of government with just and honourable policies would one day come about. He decided to create a River Styx and, beyond, the Elysian Fields to which the busts of his 'British Worthies' would be transferred. Near to the pure and graceful form of Kent's temple, to be renamed the Temple of Ancient Virtue, there was to be a contrasting ruined temple, satirically dedicated to Modern Virtue, and containing a headless statue representing the fate of vanity (some said it was of Walpole). The number of British Worthies was doubled with the addition of certain heroes of free trade, the military heroes King Alfred and the Black Prince, Inigo Jones and Pope, who 'employed the pointed Brilliancy of Wit to Chastise the Vices, and the eloquence of Poetry to exalt the Virtues, of human Nature'. The inclusion of Pope was perhaps thanks for the dedication of one of the *Moral Essays* to Cobham in 1731. All 16 busts were housed in a stone exedra designed by Kent in about 1735.

The *Ferme Ornée*

Bridgeman's vast gardens, admired as they were, could be enormously costly. His one-time fellow apprentice, Stephen Switzer, spent much of his career as a garden-designer and theorist trying to persuade the public that another way existed, which he called 'Rural Gardening'. The essence of this approach was that estate management, rather than the idle pleasures of gardens, is the key to both the pleasurable and the profitable enjoyment of the countryside. He still saw a place for regular gardening, but he felt that too much expenditure had gone into it, and not enough into the embellishment of whole estates.

Switzer's early career had included gardening works during the early stages of both Castle Howard and Blenheim, where he acted as Henry Wise's deputy[8]. He gravitated towards John Vanbrugh, whose ideas on grand simplicity he much admired. About 1710 he lost his connection with Wise, and followed Vanbrugh to Grimsthorpe, Lincolnshire, where he remodelled the gardens, along rather unconventional lines[9]. Rather than extending the formal gardens with more enclosed walks, basons of water and architectural features, he did his best to draw the occupants of the house out into the countryside. The wilderness acquired a number of military bastions that gave wide views over the fields, and an arm of the garden was taken along the ridge of the hill so that fields remote from the house could be viewed. Clearly his ideas on Rural Gardening were already developing.

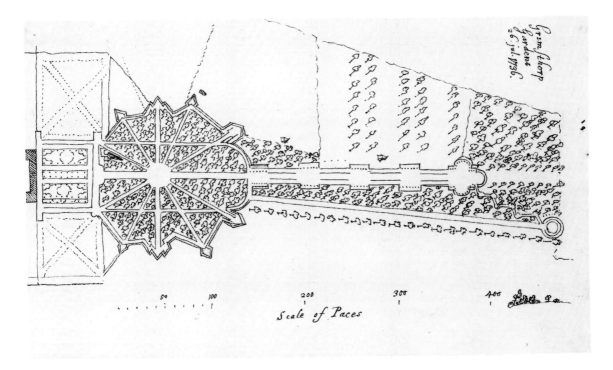

These ideas were first set down in *The Nobleman, Gentleman and Gardener's Recreation* (1715), which had the more descriptive subtitle 'An Introduction to Gardening, Planting, Agriculture, and the other Business and Pleasures of a Country Life'. This was written at Grimsthorpe, and was dedicated to its proprietor, the Marquis of Lindsey, shortly to be created Duke of Ancaster. In the Preface Switzer writes:

And since all agree, that the Pleasures of a Country Life cann't possibly be contained within the narrow Limits of the greatest Garden; woods, Fields, and distant Inclosures should have the care of the industrous and laborious Planter: Neither would I ... advise the immuring, or, as it were, the imprisoning by Walls, (however expensive they are in making) too much us'd of late; but where-ever Liberty will allow, would throw my Garden open to all View to the unbounded Felicities of distant Prospect, and the expansive volumes of Nature herself.

In the mean time I preserve some private Walks and Cabinets of Retirement, some select Places of Recess for Reading and Contemplation ...

This method I have propos'd, well manag'd, will, I hope, very much abridge the Expence of making and keeping Gardens, and will yet add very much to their magnificence, when, for the Enlargement of their view, all the neighbouring Fields, Paddocks, etc., shall make an additional Beauty to the Garden, and by an easy, unaffected manner of Fencing, shall appear to be part of it, and look as if the adjacent Country were all a Garden.

He was careful to find whatever encouragement and precedent he could from literature or gardening. Naturally he looked to the pastoral poets of all ages and found plenty of support. A passage from Horace's *Ars Poetica*—

Utile qui dulci miscens, ingentia Rura,
Simplex Munditiis ornans, punctum hic tulit omne

(translated as 'He that the beautiful and useful blends, simplicity with greatness, gains all ends')—was particularly appropriate, and he took it as a

2 Grimsthorpe, plan

The sketch, made in 1736 by Stephen Switzer's friend William Stukeley, shows bastions added to the wilderness and garden walks extended into the countryside.

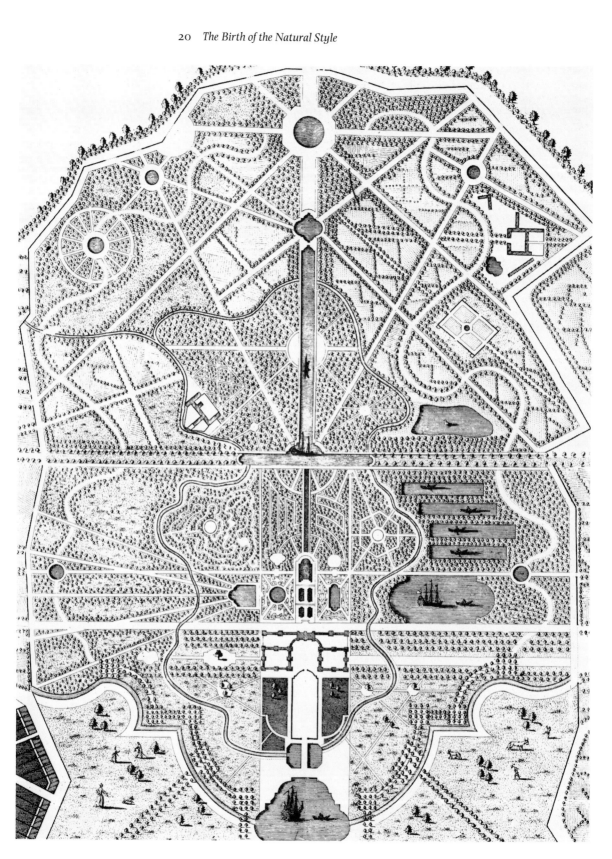

motto. He also quoted from Milton's *Paradise Lost* (1669), and Pope's *Windsor Forest* (1713). As to actual examples of his method, he pointed out Wray Wood at Castle Howard, the hillside woodland garden made by Laurence Hyde, Earl of Rochester, at New Park (part of Richmond Park), and the woodlands at Cassiobury. In a more general sense, following Addison's *Spectator* No. 414, he commended 'that Magnificence which is easily discoverable from the *French* Designs, which certainly yet very much excel ours', and which he said the French called 'La Grand Manier'[10]. Yet Switzer thought that English gardens, with their superior grass and gravel, could surpass the French.

This first book consisted mainly of a History of Gardening, essays on soil, the effect of the weather, and the circulation of sap, and directions for raising forest trees. Three years later Switzer added two more volumes, the second being concerned with surveying and containing plates of designs, and the third further agricultural matters. He gave the set the title *Ichnographia Rustica* to indicate that it gave

Directions for the Surveying and Distributing of a Country-Seat into Rural and Extensive Gardens, by the Ornamenting and Decoration of distant Prospects, Farms, Parks, Paddocks, etc.

One plan, of the imaginary 'Manor of Paston divided and planted with Rural Gardens', showed a garden with a greatly extended axial walk, and with peripheral bastions, much as he had made at Grimsthorpe, embedded in a well-wooded countryside through which numerous tracks ran.

Another plan, 'The Plan of a Forest or Rural Garden', seems to be remotely derived from Blenheim, and shows a large estate divided up into woodland and fields with straight rides and meandering estate roads. It must be confessed that the whole looks confused, but it shows that Switzer regarded neither the regularity of the parts nor the regularity of the whole as essential. As he said[11]:

If his Grounds were handsomly divided by Avenues and Hedges; and if the little Walks and Paths that ought to run through and betwixt them, were made either of Gravel or Sand; and if there were Trees for Shades with little Walks and purling Streams, mix'd and incorporated one with another, what cou'd be more diverting? And why, is not a level easy walk of Gravel or Sand shaded over with Trees, and running thro' a Corn Field or Pasture Ground, as pleasing as the largest Walk in the most magnificent Garden one can think of?

And, again:

Why should we esteem nothing but large regular Walks, the only Characteristicks of a noble seat? But, for diversity, should not rather mix therewith Serpentine Meanders; and instead of levelling Hills or filling up Dales, should think it more entertaining to be sometimes on the Precipice of a Hill viewing all round and under us, and at other times in a Bottom, viewing these goodly Hills and Theatres of Wood and Corn that are above us?

He was following Addison's ideas expressed in the *Spectator*:

Why may not a whole Estate be thrown into a kind of Garden, by frequent Plantations, that may turn as much to the Profit as the Pleasure of the Owner? ... Fields of Corn make a pleasant Prospect; and if the Walks were a little taken care of that lie between them, if the natural Embroidery of the Meadows were help'd and improv'd by some small Additions of Art, and the several Rows of Hedges set off by Trees and Flowers that the Soil was capable of receiving, a Man might make a pretty Landscape of his own Possessions.

However, Switzer found that he was unable to find many patrons interested in such rural embellishment at this date. Even the Palladians, who despised symmetrical layouts, required the parts of their gardens to be highly polished.

3   Design for a 'Rural and Extensive Garden'.

The plan is from Vol. III of Stephen Switzer's *Ichnographia Rustica* of 1718. It shows how a loose style of gardening could effectively turn a whole estate into a garden.

One notable exception was the grounds at Richmond Lodge—a commission that Switzer would have dearly loved but which Bridgeman obtained[12]. Richmond Lodge was granted to George Augustus, the Prince of Wales, in 1722, and he gave it to his newly crowned queen, Caroline, upon his accession as George II in 1727, by which time Caroline had already made several embellishments. The most noteworthy characteristic of Richmond Gardens, as they came to be known, was the sense of retirement to a country estate. There were woodlands, cut into walks, in which a number of visitors noticed birds singing, and fields of corn, said to have been introduced primarily 'for the benefit of the game'[13]. The boundary of the estate was planted with a belt, and there were clumps in the fields. Within the ornamental gardens there was a dairy, and, close to the Thames, a mount with wide views over the river and the countryside beyond. Everyone spoke of Richmond Gardens as a pretty rural retreat, and as a marked contrast to the more formal Kensington Gardens.

Whilst Bridgeman's fortunes rose, Switzer relied more and more upon his abilities as an agricultural improver. He kept writing, and his *Practical Fruit Gardener* (1724) was followed by a string of publications on husbandry. In 1727 he moved to London, and set up as a seed merchant in Westminster Hall[14]. Within a few years he had his own nursery at Millbank. This trade provided him with a regular business, so that he was no longer dependent on the unpredictable gains from writing and designing.

Upon this move to London, he found that he had some unexpected allies. Switzer's attitudes and those of his earlier clients were thoroughly Whig, and yet he dedicated his *Practical Kitchen Gardener* (1727) to Allen, Baron Bathurst, a notable Tory, whom he described as one of 'the best of Masters, and best of Friends'. Bathurst was a close friend of Viscount Bolingbroke, the leader of the Tories, who had been forced into exile for plotting with the Old Pretender when George I succeeded to the throne. Bolingbroke had affected the lifestyle of a rural philosopher at La Source, near Orléans[14], and plotted his return to British politics. At last, in 1723, he returned briefly after a pardon, and then in 1725 he bought Dawley, Middlesex, through the assistance of Bathurst, whose villa at Richings was only four miles distant. Bolingbroke gathered round him the remnants of the Tories, and joined forces with opposition Whigs in the production of *The Craftsman*.

They had a real and visible target—the 'vanity of expense' by the Whigs, a theme that Lord Cobham later took up when he went into opposition in 1733. Bolingbroke put the inscription 'Satis beatus ruris honoribus' above his door at Dawley and became ostentatiously engaged in the conversion of his 'agreeable sepulchre' into a suitably rustic retreat[15]. Dawley was previously an earl's mansion, and had grand gardens and a large park. Bolingbroke disparked the 373-acre park, and placed tenants on 135 acres of it. He renamed the place 'Dawley Farm' and Pope, who was drawn into his circle, reported to Jonathan Swift in June 1728 that 'I overheard him yesterday agree with a Painter for £200 to paint his country-hall with Trophies of Rakes, spades, prongs, etc'. However Bolingbroke's interest in husbandry was largely a political gesture— there was no desire to establish a new system of gardening.

To Switzer, though, Bolingbroke's campaign offered an opportunity to pursue the theme of Rural Gardening. He presented his novel ideas on 'Rural Kitchen Gardening' at Richings at the end of his *Practical Kitchen Gardener* (1727), and promised a plan, which eventually appeared in the second edition of *Ichnographia Rustica* (1742). Richings had a central canal, a network of diagonal allées and a circumferential ride. The plan was not a faithful representation, but 'a regulated Epitome', sufficient to illustrate his theme. It showed grass in the main avenues containing the entrance drives and the canal being grazed by sheep: 'the insides of the Quarters for sowing of Corn, Turnips, etc., or for feeding of Cattle'; and a 'cart, coach or chaise Road round the whole Plantation'.

Such rural gardening 'may serve as a specimen of what this and some other noble Lords have and are so judiciously doing on this head', Switzer assured his readers; and he cited Stowe and Dawley as further examples. His claim for Stowe was perhaps a little doubtful, but inclusion of the grazing land called the Home Park within the grounds by Bridgeman's perimeter ha-ha was perhaps what was meant. The text that accompanied the plate of the Richings 'epitome' was written about 1730[16], and mentions Richings and Dawley once again as places 'now a doing'.

By 1730 Switzer could claim that justification for his theories could be found in Robert Castel's *Villas of the Ancients* (1728). This described how Pliny's villas were partly laid out as 'Imitatio Ruris', which, though improved by Art, took 'the Form of a beautiful Country, Hills, Rocks, Cascades, Rivulets, Woods, Buildings, etc'. To Switzer it was clear that Rural Gardening had antique precedents:

That this was the Method used by the *Romans* of old, the curious Drafts and Accounts of the Ancient Villa's about that once Mistress of the World *Rome* fully evince.

Also, 'this Taste ... has for some time been the Practice of some of the best Genius's of *France*, under the Title of *La Ferme Ornée*.' It is probable that Switzer never went to France, but perhaps he had picked up this information from Bolingbroke or Bathurst.

Pope also wrote about Bolingbroke's and Bathurst's concern with husbandry. His *Moral Essays* appeared annually from 1731, and were successively dedicated to Lords Burlington, Bathurst, Cobham and Bolingbroke. In the first of these he explored the respective roles of Taste and Sense. Artists were not expected to exercise Sense—'Jones and Le Nôtre have it not to give'—but their patrons were, and he goes on to describe what Sense meant in gardening, in terms that could apply to Bathurst, Cobham and Bolingbroke:

> Who then shall grace, or who improve the Soil?
> Who plants like Bathurst, or who builds like Boyle?
> 'Tis use alone that sanctifies Expense,
> And Splendour borrows all her rays from Sense.
> His Father's Acres, who enjoys in Peace,
> Or make his Neighbours glad, if he increase:
> Whose cheerful Tenants bless their yearly toil,
> Yet to their Lord owe more than to the Soil;
> Whose ample lawns are not asham'd to feed
> The milky heifer and deserving steed;
> Whose rising Forests, not for pride or show;
> But future buildings, future Navies, grow;
> Let his plantations stretch from down to down,
> First shade a Country, and then raise a Town.

George Montagu, first Earl of Halifax of the second creation, was one of those who were at this time improving the soil and planting like Bathurst. Besides Horton, his seat in Northamptonshire, he had a small estate called Apps Court, in Walton-on-Thames parish in Surrey. He was also Ranger of Bushy Park, just across the river, and so was well placed to supervise the improvements that his tenants were carrying out. When Switzer came to bind up the *Practical Husbandman and Planter* (1733), a collection of essays by 'a Private SOCIETY of HUSBANDMEN and PLANTERS' of which Switzer was the 'principal Assistant', he dedicated it to Halifax, described as

a good Husbandman and Planter; in both which you have made such great Advances, that Posterity must recite it with Pleasure, and everyone of the fine Fields at *Houghton* and *Abbs Court*, must of Consequence perpetuate the Memory of their *Improver* to Generations yet to come.

Once again, Switzer likened such a patron to the '*Romans* of old', and although he gave little hint of the embellishment of Apps Court, he did describe it elsewhere as a *ferme ornée*[17].

Only one of the essays in the *Practical Husbandman and Planter* could be said to have given advice on layout, rather than husbandry[18]. In this Switzer advised planters to avoid placing plantations where they would block out views, even where this was at the expense of letting in winds, and

> it may be laid as a Rule certain, that Hills ought to be cloathed with Wood, but Vallies to lie open in Lawn and Meadow ... it being certain, that one Tree on a Hill adds more beauty to a Seat, and looks better than six, I had almost said ten, in a Bottom.

Then, in the 'Prooemial Essay' to the second edition of *Ichnographia Rustica* (1742) he mentions that a number of improvers had made circumferential rides or 'enfilades', around their estates, which

> ought to be six or seven yards wide at least, and should be carried over the tops of the highest Hills that lie within the Compass of any Nobleman's or Gentleman's Design, though it does not extend to the utmost Extremity of it; and from those Eminences (whereon, if any where, Building or Clumps of Trees ought to be placed) it is that you are to view the whole design.

Although regularity was seen as desirable, such common-sense rules were more so. Indeed, some of the less ambitious schemes of Rural Gardening to be

4   Woburn Farm, grounds south of the house.

The print of 1759 by Luke Sullivan shows cattle outside the ha-ha, and winding canals, a waterwheel, urns, a Chinese bridge and sheep (giving a fine texture to the grass) inside.

carried out by subscribers to Switzer's books were almost totally devoid of regular features[19].

One of the minor landowners to improve his estate in the late 1730s along Switzer's lines was a young Catholic, an acquaintance of Pope's, called Philip Southcote[20]. Marriage to a dowager duchess enabled Southcote to purchase a 116-acre estate with a gentleman's house near to Chertsey, Surrey, called Woburn, in 1735. It consisted of a hill with good views northwards over the Thames valley and lower grounds to the west and east. Southcote told Spence:

All my design at first was to have a garden on the middle high ground and a walk all around my farm, for convenience as well as pleasure: for from the garden I could see what was doing in the grounds, and by the walk could have pleasing access to either of them where I might be wanted.

If he had contented himself with these objectives, Southcote's estate would have been merely one of a number of the small *fermes ornées*. However Southcote had a number of helpers who had additional ideas to offer.

One was his kinsman, Lord Petre, who was only 22 in 1735, but already an accomplished botanist and planter. He made large collections of trees and shrubs, and of hothouse plants, at Thorndon Hall, his seat in Essex, which astonished even experienced collectors like Peter Collinson[21]. His early death in 1742 from smallpox was widely acknowledged as a great loss to botany. He helped Southcote with his flower garden, a rosary, and evidently taught him much about planting for effect. Southcote told Spence that Petre

understood the colours of every tree, and always considered how he placed them by one another.

Southcote became famous for the skills in planting design that he had learnt from Petre. His circumferential belt was of particular note. A thick thorn hedge with standard trees was supplemented on the inside by small trees and flowering shrubs. Between these and the five-foot-wide sand walk was a $2\frac{1}{2}$-foot flower bed[21]. In other places there were flower beds and groups of shrubs detached from the belt. All the species were thoroughly mixed with others that flowered at different times of the year, so that there was always, except in midwinter, some colour and interest. One might have had reservations upon whether it was worth so much effort to embellish a farm, but none disagreed that the effect was delightful.

Southcote's other helpers were from Lord Burlington's circle. At the furthest part of his hill Southcote erected a Palladian octagon summerhouse, probably to William Kent's design[23]. He was certainly visited by Pope and Kent, both of whom discussed the pleasing effects of parts of his grounds with him. His concern for the painterly effects of his improvements must have developed from these occasions.

Uniting the Arts

It became highly fashionable to be interested in paintings during George I's reign[24]. At the beginning of the reign the only serious book on painting available was John Dryden's translation in 1695 of *De Arte Graphica* (1668), by the Frenchman Charles-Alphonse Du Fresnoy. One of the first Englishmen to obtain an appreciation of painting that was as scholarly as Du Fresnoy's was the third Earl of Shaftesbury, whose collection of essays, published as *Characteristicks* (1711), did much to place the word 'Taste' on everyone's lips. He was soon after followed by the painter Jonathan Richardson with *The Theory of Painting* (1715), which introduced the term 'connoisseur' to the

English language. Richardson pleaded for painting to be seen as a liberal art, like poetry, and not just a mechanical art: in other words, that it could contribute to intellectual enlargement and refinement, and that its study was thus a proper pursuit for gentlemen.

Du Fresnoy and Richardson both graded types of painting. The most liberal form was 'history painting', the purpose of which was usually to illustrate instructive scenes from classical history. Next came portrait painting which was liberal to some extent in that it could reveal character. Most English painters at this time, including Richardson, were portrait-painters. Then came landscape painting, which pretended to no intellectual content.

The elevation of painting to the ranks of the liberal arts invited comparisons with them, and the notion of a fraternity of arts. Dryden had translated Philostratus to say: 'The Art of Painting has a wonderful affinity with that of Poetry'. As a young admirer of Dryden, Alexander Pope had been immensely impressed with such ideas. By 1713, he had made the acquaintance of Charles Jervas, a young and fashionable portrait-painter, and was spending much time in his studio[25]. He wrote at this period:

> Like friendly colours, our kind arts unite,
> Each from their mixture gathering strength and light,
> Their forms, the features in resemblance strike,
> As twins they vary, and as twins are like.

Pope had commenced the translation of Homer's *Iliad* into English, and was thereby doing his best to resurrect the classical world. When his *Iliad* was published in parts from 1715, it was evident, from his frequent use of painters' terms, and the explanation of passages as if they were pictures, that Pope was committed to the ideal of uniting the arts. He hoped that Jervas would turn to history painting, but in vain; although they both contributed to a new edition of Dryden's translation of Du Fresnoy in 1716. An issue of *The Free Thinker* of 1718 shows that the notion of a fraternity of arts was gaining in popularity. It put the case very forcibly when discussing the strong images that poetry could excite in the reader's mind:

The Perfection of a Master Painter is, to be able to perform the same wonders by Colours which a Poet commands by Language.

A generation being educated by Shaftesbury and Richardson to understand painting readily grasped the parallels.

However Pope was not content with uniting just poetry and painting. He was a great admirer and friendly critic of the regular but asymmetric gardens of the time, such as those at Chiswick, Down Hall and Sherborne[26]. Evidently he held the art of garden design in much esteem. He told the Earl of Oxford in 1724 that Charles Bridgeman was

of the Virtuoso-Class as well as I; (and in My notions of the higher class, since Gardening is more Antique, and nearer God's own work than Poetry)[27].

He had a hand in the design of the vast scheme of improvement in Cirencester Park, Gloucestershire, by Lord Bathurst in the late 1710s. Probably he had Cirencester in mind when composing a poem on gardening in about 1720. This eventually appeared, much expanded, as the *Essay on Taste* (1731)[28]. He advised the gardener to consult the genius of the place, clearly a painter and gardener as well as a poet, and who

> Calls in the Country, catching opening glades.
> Joins willing woods, and varies shades from shades,
> Now breaks, and now directs, the extending lines;
> Paints as you plant, and, as you work, designs.

When Pope acquired his own garden at Twickenham in late 1718 he wanted to see whether he really could unite poetry and painting with gardening. He wrote nothing on his own garden except in letters to friends, but his gardener, John Serle, published 'A Plan of M.ʳ Pope's Garden as it was left at his Death', i.e. in 1745. This shows a garden of the Chiswick type, with *allées*, 'rooms', groves and plenty of statuary. It also shows some unusual features for this date—a mount, a grotto and a curious sequence of groves and greens between the mount, and an obelisk (erected in 1735) to the memory of his mother.

His letters provide a rough chronology. In the winter of 1719/20 he was having 'a vast deal to do with Gardeners' and bowers, avenues and a rising mount are mentioned. In 1721 the gardens were sufficiently advanced for Pope to encourage visitors to view his 'Great Walk', a 'Green', and the Mount, and John Gay congratulated him in verse on the finishing of them. Then from 1722 there is increasingly frequent mention of the grotto, which provided a subterranean connection between his house on one side of the road to Hampton and his five-acre garden on the other. Its embellishments were a spring discovered during construction, porches at each end, closing doors to create a *camera obscura* when closed, and a cockleshell floor that extended to an open temple studded with shells standing close to the mount. In the year of the grotto's completion, 1725, Charles Bridgeman came with a detachment of men from the Princess Caroline's works at Richmond Gardens and laid out a small 'Bridgemannic' theatre.

The grove-and-green sequence had not been seen before. Pope himself hinted in a letter of 19 March 1722 that it was a composed view: 'I will carry you up a Mount to show you in a point of view the glory of my little kingdom.' This view would have been a spacious bowling green flanked by solemn groves. A similar arrangement was repeated beyond on a smaller scale, producing the effect of increased apparent distance. Pope remarked on this effect to Spence:

You may distance things by darkening them and by narrowing the plantation more and more toward the end, in the same manner as they do in painting, and as 'tis executed in the little cypress walk to that obelisk.

Tricks of perspective had been tried in bosquets in France in the seventeenth century[29], but the only other garden design in England that seems to have attempted them was Bridgeman's plan for Gunton, in Norfolk, in which the view towards a garden temple from a mount is composed of terraces of diminishing width and then a narrowing walk[30].

There is more than a simple device of perspective in the grove-and-green sequence, though. Pope told Spence that 'the lights and shades in gardening are managed by disposing the thick grovework, the thin, and the openings.' This concern for lights and shades was shared by history painters, and Du Fresnoy expended much of *De Arte Graphica* in advising upon the composition and execution of a compact group of figures in the centre of the canvas, in the 'Great Light'. Any landscape was dark background designed to make the central group stand out. The field of the centre should be clean, free and light, and 'terre verte' was, conveniently, suitable. The change from the 'Shadows that bound the sight' to the Great Light should, Du Fresnoy advised, be 'imperceptible, that is by degrees of Lights into Shadows'. So it looks as if Pope's bowling green was his Great Light, and the bowlers the central group.

It is not known how closely Kent followed Pope's ideas of using painting techniques, although Southcote told Spence that 'Mr. Pope and Mr. Kent were the first that practised painting in gardening', and Horace Walpole was quite

5   Pope's garden at Twickenham, plan.

Although this garden was a typical Palladian's in many respects, the twice-repeated grove-and-green sequence shows that Alexander Pope was experimenting with painting techniques of perspective and composition.

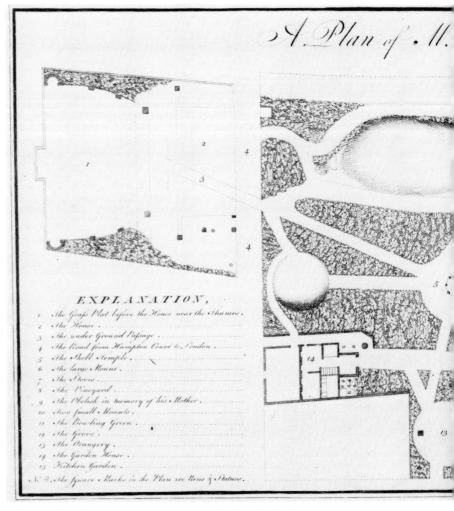

definite when he wrote in his *Essay on Modern Gardening*:

The great principles on which he worked were perspective, and light and shade.

Fortunately, though, Joseph Spence recorded numerous remarks by Philip Southcote about 1752, and, from the examples he gave of 'attracting' and 'distancing', it is clear that he was using the principles of perspective at Woburn.

Southcote was also conscious of the picturesque advantages of framing views. He distinguished between 'perspective' and 'prospect':

By perspective he meant looking *under* trees to some farther object (under-view); by prospect, looking *by* trees, but the line open at top (clear-view).

Directing long distance views could be done too:

There should be leading trees, or clumps of trees, to help the eye to any more distant clump, building, or view.

Pope and Southcote also seem to have agreed that gardening could be seen through the eyes of the landscape painter. Pope told Spence in 1734 that

All gardening is landscape painting . . . just like a landscape hung up,

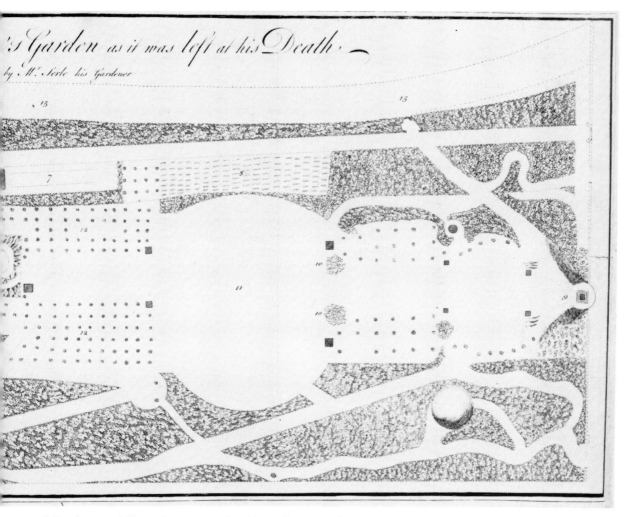

's Garden as it was left at his Death.

by Mr. Serle his Gardener

and Southcote told him about 1752 that ''Tis all painting'.

On the other hand, Pope never identified the use of painting principles with an irregular natural style, whereas Southcote did. He told Spence that

Lord Cobham began in the Bridgeman taste: 'tis the Elysian Fields that is the painting part of his gardens.

Like Kent, Southcote had realized the benefits from using painting techniques with an irregular style of gardening.

Beautiful Nature

The Augustan way of thinking led to subjugation of emotions to the intellect. Consequently Augustan literature tended to be rather dry and intellectual, though Pope could leaven his moral themes with very effective satirical wit. As the 1720s neared their end, it is apparent in retrospect that the public lacked the poetry to arouse sentiment or emotion. Pastoral poetry was not catering for the moods that warm and sleepy summer evenings induce; whilst the opposite extreme, of horror aroused by Alpine scenery, was barely explored despite the flood of English tourists to Italy after the end of the wars with France in 1713.

This is not to say that all Englishmen were unimpressionable. In 1714 George Berkeley, who had crossed the Alps, advised Pope that it may

be worth a poet's while to travel, in order to store his mind with strong images of Nature. Green fields and groves, flowery meadows and purling streams, are no where in such perfection as in England; but if you would know lightsome days, warm suns, and blue skies, you must come to Italy; and to enable a man to describe rocks and precipices, it is absolutely necessary that he pass the Alps[31].

However Pope never left lowland England, and so, even if he had wished to follow Berkeley's advice, he was unable to do so.

During the mid 1720s two young poets, John Dyer and James Thomson, furnished themselves with the images of mountains in Wales and Scotland respectively. The prevailing wisdom was that mountains were the rubbish of creation. Instead of finding this distasteful, though, they revelled in the fear and wonder of such natural features, and in the strange beauty of the striking effects of light and colour to be found in them. In addition James Thomson was adept at giving thanks for Nature's annual miracle amongst the fields and orchards of England's farmland.

Neither Dyer nor Thomson felt it incumbent upon them to provide moral themes in poetry; their chief purpose was simply to give pleasure to their readers through portraying scenes romantically. Despite differing from Pope in this respect, they readily took up the theme of the sisterhood of arts. They made frequent use of painterly terms, described colour (by such phrases as 'purple hills', and 'gilded by the sun'), and even gave hints as to the composition of their scenes.

Thomson's *Seasons* were issued from 1726, when 'Winter' appeared. At first they attracted little attention, but even before the last season, 'Autumn', was published with the rest in 1730, they were already a great success. Many years later Joseph Warton reflected that

The *Seasons* of Thomson have been very instrumental in diffusing a general taste for the beauties of *nature* and *landschape*[32],

and this may indeed have been true, in so far that the taste can be explained. It is certain that heeding Nature was of central concern to theories on garden style from this time.

Pope's advice to gardeners not to clip trees, but to let them grow naturally, was being heeded, with increasingly disastrous effects upon regular gardens. A few places persisted in clipping until late in the century. For example, the best known regular gardens in England, those at Hampton Court, were probably still being clipped when Lancelot Brown was appointed in 1764 to maintain them[33]. Nevertheless, Bridgeman had not been introducing any new topiary in his schemes[34], and Switzer and Kent dispensed with high clipped hedges as well. Revulsion against clipping was becoming widespread by the early 1740s. Whilst Daniel Defoe had described the Hampton Court wilderness as

perfectly well kept, and the Espaliers fill'd exactly, at Bottom to the very Ground, and are led up to proportion'd Heights on the Top: so that nothing of that kind can be more beautiful . . .

in his *Tour Thro' the Whole Island of Great Britain* of 1724, the editor of the 1742 edition thought that he should alter this to say that nothing could be more disagreeable than to be 'immured between hedges, so as to have the Eye confined to a straight walk'.

Thomson's appreciation of Nature was almost a personal relationship: he saw Her as a bounteous yet careless goddess particularly associated with spring. Pope, on the other hand, held to his more intellectual view of Nature as

6   Merlin's Cave,
Richmond Gardens, section.

Merlins' Cave was built in
1735 by William Kent for
Queen Caroline to house
Stephen Duck, the thresher
poet, and his library. Trees
grew on top of the structure.

the guiding hand of creation, and argued that Her forms should therefore be respected. Despite this difference, Pope's advice to follow Nature was adopted uncritically by those sharing Thomson's viewpoint. Spence's observation that 'the making of pleasure-grounds is an imitation of "beautiful Nature'" was pretty conventional by the time that he made it about 1752; and the Nature he was referring to was the wild and irregular Nature assumed by Thomson and Kent. Pope's ordered but concealed Nature had been forgotten.

It is difficult to know what Pope felt about Thomson and Kent. At a personal level he seems to have been cordial with both, but he wrote little about Nature or gardening after the mid-1720s. Perhaps this speaks for a decline of his interest in these subjects anyway, as his interest in politics and, consequently, rural gardening, rose. Besides his interest in Richings and Dawley, he was intrigued by the *ferme ornée* at Bevois Mount. A loose arrangement of paths and paddocks was being laid out there in the early 1730s by his friend Lord Peterborough[35]. These gave access to two hilltops with panoramic views of Southampton and its water. He was also friendly with the Apps Court tenants, one of whom contributed spas to his grotto[36]. He mentioned that place in his *Imitations of Horace* (The Second Epistle of the Second Book) (1737):

> Delightful Abs-court, of its fields afford
> Their fruits to you, confess you its lord:

For political reasons, Pope was severely critical of Merlin's Cave, in Richmond Gardens, which was designed by Kent for Queen Caroline in 1735, and which was intended to house the thresher/poet Stephen Duck with a small library. Pope's only reference to Kent's gardening was in the *Epilogue to the*

Satires (1738). He mentioned Esher 'where Kent and Nature vie for Pelham's love'. This implicitly distinguishes Kent's work from Nature's, and so perhaps some ambiguity was intentional. However it was widely taken as marking Pope's approval: this was important for the new taste, as Pope's authority was immense.

An example of the changing taste is provided by Lady Hertford, to whom Thomson had dedicated 'Spring'. Lord Hertford bought Richings in 1739 from Lord Bathurst. Pope, alluding to the sheep grazing its lawns amongst the matured regular grounds, called it 'his Lordship's *Extravagante Bergerie*' in his letters, published in 1735. Lady Hertford wrote to a friend about the sound of the sheep-bells, a cave, arbours and 'seats under shady trees disposed all over the park' which carried inscriptions. She summed up this *Extravagante Bergerie*:

The environs perfectly answer that title and come nearer to my idea of a scene in Arcadia than any place I ever saw[37].

She was clearly far more interested in the romantic qualities of the place than in rural gardening. Shepherdesses, dairies, hermitages and all the accompaniments of pastoral romance were in the ascendant.

Mr Kent's Notion of Gardening

Sir Thomas Robinson wrote to his father-in-law, the third Earl of Carlisle, on 23 December 1734 to say that:

There is a new taste in gardening just arisen, which has been practised with so great success at the Prince's garden in Town, that a general alteration of some of the most considerable gardens in the Kingdom is begun, after Mr. Kent's notion of gardening, viz., to lay them out, and work without either line or level ... The celebrated gardens of Claremont, Chiswick, and Stowe are now full of labourers, to modernise the expensive works finished in them, even since everyone's memory[38].

This statement might appear to place the date and authorship of the Natural Style of gardening beyond question, but a number of questions arise. For example, what did these gardens look like? There is considerable uncertainty as to exactly what took place when.

The Prince's garden in town was the small Carlton House garden which had once been the Privy Gardens to St James's Palace. It had been Lord Carleton's by lease till his death in 1725 when it passed to his nephew Lord Burlington. Frederick Louis, Prince of Wales, acquired it in 1732, and Burlington was asked to modernize the house and garden[39]. Over the next two years Henry Flitcroft refaced the garden front of the house, and Kent revised the garden, which ran across the southern face of the house. He built a domed Palladian temple at right-angles to the house and from which there was a vista almost the length of the gardens. Half-way down was a large circular flower garden surrounded (except for the vista) by an arbour. Towards the end of the vista, where there was a pool, the outline of the groves became increasingly irregular[40]. This is the only part of the garden which could be fairly described as laid out 'without line or level'.

Kent's alterations to Kensington Gardens seem to have been in a secluded quarter adjacent to the Serpentine and enclosed by some of the walks of Bridgeman's great layout[41]. Here the Queen's Temple was erected to Kent's design in about 1734 in the angle between two walks and backed with irregular planting, whilst the vista down to the recently filled Serpentine was opened out by largely removing the rows of trees along its bank.

At Chiswick the works of 1733/4 seem to have been the removal of all but a few standard trees from the bosquet between the west façade of the villa and the cascade. Designs for remodelling the latter in a rusticated manner had been prepared[42]. The result was similar to Kensington—a broad vista interspersed by only a few irregularly placed trees down a grassy slope to the water's edge.

Judging from these three cases, from Stowe and from Kent's other early gardens, the much vaunted Natural Style had quite modest beginnings. The areas concerned were small, and usually either at a villa or, if at a mansion, in the more secluded parts. The distinguishing feature was irregularity in the planting, which was arranged as the setting to Palladian or rusticated temples, grottoes, or cascades. No gravel paths or flowering plants were permitted.

Other features of the style were not entirely new. Some Palladian villas already had grass settings, for example Sir Thomas Robinson's villa at Rokeby in Yorkshire, and the Countess of Suffolk's Marble Hill in Twickenham[43]. Grass parterres had been used by Vanbrugh at Castle Howard, Yorkshire, and advocated by Stephen Switzer and Batty Langley, whilst many houses in sporting country had always been set in grass. Uppark in Sussex was an example of this. Nor were serpentine rivers entirely new. The Serpentine at

7 Chiswick house grounds from the cascade.

George Lambert's painting of 1742 shows the serpentine river and the grassy slope made down to it in the mid-1730s. Chiswick was known as one of the first gardens where the Natural Style was tried.

Kensington Gardens and the river at Chiswick[44] both pre-dated Kent's use of the Natural Style. Sir Thomas Robinson informed the Earl of Carlisle of 'a pretty rivulet cut in a winding and irregular manner' at Euston[45], Suffolk, in 1731, and the Earl himself had the river dug below the Temple of the Four Winds at Castle Howard in 1732–4[46]. Kent left few hints as to the inspiration for his style, and so telling what these early gardens were intended to represent is guesswork. Perhaps they were an attempt to imitate Chinese gardens, which had been a matter of curiosity since Sir William Temple reported what he had heard about them[47]. It is possible that sets of prints of one of the Emperor's hunting preserves beyond the Great Wall at Jehol, engraved in China by the Jesuit missionary Matteo Ripa in 1713, reached England before or during the 1730s, and that Burlington acquired one of them[48]. However these show extensive lakes, bare and craggy landscapes and the flimsy wooden buildings which are characteristic of Chinese gardens, and it is hard to believe that they could have been directly responsible for the leafy Elysiums in the Home Counties.

More likely, Kent had in mind the relaxed, pastoral landscape of Paradise. There had been many versions of Paradise invented over the previous 200 years in literature, painting and the theatre. There had been a strong Dutch tradition of representing Paradise as an irregular, natural, landscape abounding with the fruits of the Earth and teeming with every species of animal, all of which lived in perfect harmony. There were a number of such paintings by Jan Breughel the elder and Rubens in English country houses that Kent must have seen[49]. He must also have seen stage designs by Inigo Jones[50], Sir James Thornhill and Filippo Juvarra. Juvarra, who was in England in 1720[51], evidently drew upon Claude Lorrain's classical landscapes for his sets, whereas Jones pictured the settings of Philip Sidney's and Edmund Spenser's stories of the imaginary classical heroes of some unrecorded Golden Age in which magic and chivalry had flourished. Arcady, a pastoral district of ancient Greece populated by shepherds, was a popular location for the poems and plays of Jones' time. There were, then, a number of images of Paradise or blessed landscapes upon which Kent could have drawn.

In fact, he is reported to have told people that he had Spenser's *Faerie Queene* in mind when devising his garden designs[52]. This may have been so; he certainly decorated the interior of the Temple of Venus at Stowe with scenes from this book. However, his vision of such scenes was his own. Some impression of his vision can be discovered from the elaborate bookplates that he devised for John Gay's *Fables* (1727) and Thomson's *The Seasons* (1730). A few years later he made a drawing of Phaedria's Island, for a bookplate for the *Faerie Queene*, republished 1751, and this shows a Palladian mansion on an irregular hillside with irregularly disposed trees, many of which were cypress or pine. These all seem to stem from Kent's vision of a natural, classical landscape.

The influence of his patron, Burlington, should not be overlooked. Southcote told Spence that both Burlington and Kent thought of themselves as the introducers of the Natural Style. It was Burlington who commissioned Kent to edit the *Designs of Inigo Jones* (1725), and who liked Kent's ideas enough to experiment with them at Carlton House and Chiswick. Some impression of Burlington's thoughts on gardening may be gathered from Robert Castel's *Villas of the Ancients* (1728) dedicated to Burlington. Castel's purpose was to reconstruct Pliny the Younger's villas, as described in his letters. Although Castel's plans were mostly imaginary, the accompanying text was scholarly and had great appeal to those who, like the Palladian enthusiasts in architecture, sought an intellectual approach to gardening.

Castel speculated that the ancients practised three distinct styles of gardening, although they might all have been found together at one place. The first, and most ancient, style was to leave the ground as found, and merely to plant choice trees where they would best grow. The second style was invented by 'those of a more regular and exact Taste' who preferred layouts 'by the Rule and Line' to the rough manner of the first style. The third style, which he called 'Imitatio Ruris' was a combination of the first two. The greatest art was used in creating the same amenities that could be found in the most regular gardens, whilst maintaining the agreeable disorder of Nature. The purpose of Art, in this style, was to imitate Nature so that it was not apparent in the rocks, cascades, or trees.

Castel remarked that this third style was 'the present Manner of Designing in China'. Whether this information was derived from Sir William Temple's or Matteo Ripa's accounts is unclear as it seems that Burlington and Castel either did not see, or took no notice of, Ripa's engravings. It does seem likely, though, that Burlington agreed with Castel that the ancients practised the 'Imitatio Ruris'. He would then have recognized that the irregular layout with regular parts for which Chiswick was famous lacked this third style which an authentic Roman villa would have had. This would have been his reason for turning some part of his gardens over to a natural style. Kent explained his ideas with the aid of drawings, and Burlington must have recognized that they were sufficiently close to his own notions on classical landscape for him to trust Kent's taste.

The Progress of the New Taste

Kent's involvement in gardening was a consequence of his interest in architecture, and especially garden buildings. From about 1730 he was providing designs for a variety of temples, at Stowe, Richmond Gardens and Claremont. These were mainly in the Palladian style of his patron Burlington, but he also designed 'rustic' stone or timber hermitages and cascades for Romantic effect. He frequently drew the elevations of his designs, and added a background landscape in order to show them in their intended setting. Early examples were various schemes for Chatsworth in Derbyshire, the rustic cascade and the exedra at Chiswick, the Temple of Ancient Virtue at Stowe, and the garden area adjacent to the south front at Holkham.

Many of Kent's garden buildings were to be placed on the axes of formal gardens, and the planting was therefore often rather symmetrical. At the same time the sketches clearly owed much to the mountain scenery of Italy. He showed cypress and stone pine, or the equivalent forms available in England, seemingly larch and a broadleaved deciduous tree such as beech[53]. Generally the spiky form of the conifer predominated behind any feature to which he wished to draw attention.

Rustic or tumbledown buildings came to be one of Kent's specialities. Buildings like the hermitage in Richmond Gardens, built for Queen Caroline in 1730, and the Temple of Modern Virtue at Stowe, built about 1734, actually had conifers planted on top of the structure. Other rustic structures, in particular cascades such as those at Chiswick, Claremont, Stowe and Rousham probably owe much to grander examples that he had seen in Italy, just as the hermitages derive from caves.

Another feature of Kent's layouts was the contrast, where possible, between the more retired areas, replete with shady walks and statuary, and the illusion that one was roaming at will through a pastoral scene. This contrast had

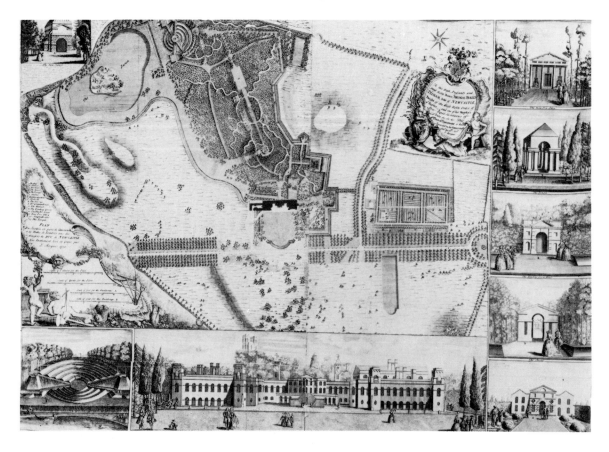

8   Claremont, plan.

John Rocque's plan of 1738 shows William Kent's recent alterations. They included breaking the avenue, extending the bason, digging the ha-ha and turning the wilderness into groves.

already been achieved with the Home Park at Stowe through the use of extensive ha-has. However the ha-has at Claremont and Esher, where Kent first tried out such ideas, were quite unlike those at Stowe. First, they were taken away from the walks and out into the fields, which made them much less obvious. Second, they were not built in straight lines. They snaked through the grassland according to Kent's whim or convenience. Bridgeman's circular bason below the amphitheatre at Claremont was enlarged into an irregular shape by the addition of a loop, the foremost ranks of woodland thinned, and the ha-ha redug in a serpentine line further out into the grazing land and around the enlarged pool.

Although all the buildings in the Elysian Fields at Stowe were designed by Kent, neither he nor Bridgeman seems to have been directly responsible for the layout or planting, and these must be attributed to Lord Cobham himself[54]. An irregular Paradisiacal scene was chosen for his Elysian Fields, and in this, and in the planting design, Cobham's ideas were so similar to Kent's that it is highly likely that both men were fully conversant with what the other thought. The buildings were placed irregularly; the River Styx, and indeed all the water bodies in the Elysian Fields and Hawkwell Field to the east, were dug as serpentines; and the encircling groves were loosely and irregularly planted. The first significant change to the regular gardens themselves was the removal of the earthworks and arbour walks of the *parterre* under the south front in 1740.

The most admired of Kent's designs was that for Rousham[55]. As at most of his other schemes, Kent was remodelling a regular layout, and this accounts

for it still being semi-regular after the alterations of 1738–41. The bulk of the garden lay beyond and to one side of the bowling green which fronted the house. Beyond this green was a slope down to the River Cherwell. This river serpentized naturally, forming a narrow neck of the garden near the green, and then swinging out again to define one side of the main garden area. The estate boundary at a road was the other. Within this area there were already square pools, from the bottom of which an elm walk ran to the furthermost part of the garden.

Early in 1738 there was a great deal of earthworks under way to remove the straight parapet along the river, to clean out the river and the ponds, and to turn the slope below the bowling green into a concave slope. This was followed by the construction of the arcade called Praeneste at the neck of the garden, and the conversion of the square pools to 'Venus's Vale'. The owner, General James Dormer, was a close friend of Lord Cobham, and these classical allusions seem to owe more to Stowe than Kent's other gardens. Certainly some of the architectural features were borrowed. The Praeneste was an enlarged version of the cold bath that stood near the Elysian Fields, and the cascades added to the pools were similar to the Shell Bridge which stood at the upper end of the River Styx.

Unlike the confined Elysian Fields, though, the views over the countryside were opened out, and embellished. Kent added Gothic ornaments to a cottage to make it seem like a mill, placed an eyecatcher on the skyline, and took in land further down the river bank in order to open out views of the genuinely

9 Rousham, Venus' Vale.

The drawing by William Kent nicely illustrates his vision of pastoral scenes enclosed by loose groves. A hint of decayed ancient splendour is given by the rustic cascades.

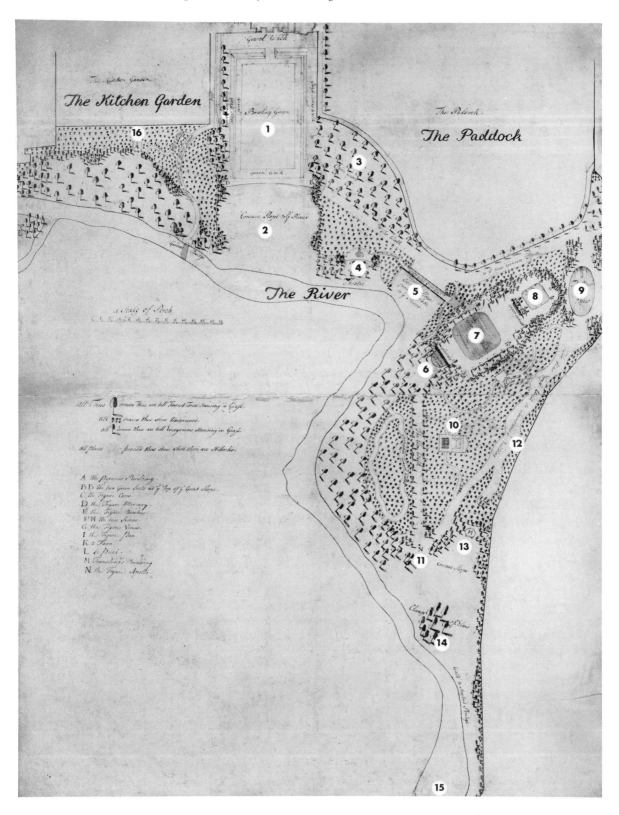

medieval Heyford Bridge. He also thinned out the planting around the pools and intermingled the survivors with pine and spruce trees to form a grove-like appearance. A circuit around the garden was devised. From the further end of the elm walk Praeneste could be seen, and this happy accident caused Kent to have some trees cleared away to reveal more of the view. The problem of masking the boundary wall was solved in 1741 by planting flowering shrubs along this section of the circuit. This is the only case of Kent using such planting. It was reminiscent of the dense boundary planting at Woburn Farm, and indeed Southcote afterwards claimed to have 'prevailed on Kent to resume flowers in the natural way of gardening'.

About the time that Rousham was being laid out, Henry Herbert, the ninth Earl of Pembroke, was remodelling his own gardens at Wilton with the assistance of his clerk of works, Roger Morris[56]. The famous garden laid out a century before had been much simplified already, and the remaining cedars, the earliest in Britain, were already magnificent[57]. In 1737 the River Nadder, which flowed through the garden, was dammed downstream to form a lake. This raised the water level in the old garden, and the much admired Palladian Bridge was constructed to allow communication with the garden beyond the river. Over the next few years the whole garden was finally grassed over entirely, and the only vestiges of the old layout were lines of mature trees. As William Chambers reported about 1756:

The garden's ... principal beauty consists in a fine river that flows through it ... and in a great deal of old planting, particularly many fine Cedars of Lebanon ... Some of the old

10 Rousham, plan.

Drawn possibly by the estate steward, William White, in about 1738, this plan shows: *1* Bowling Green; *2* Concave Slope to ye River; *3* Open Grove; *4* Theatre; *5* Praeneste; *6* Bason to ye cascade; *7* Great Pond; *8* Upper Pond; *9* The New Pond; *10* Cold Bath; *11* the Figure Apollo; *12* The New Grass Walk to Townshend's Building; *13* Townshend's Building; *14* Clump of Elms; *15* Heyford Bridge; *16* the Pyramid Building.

11 Wilton, south front.

The gardens of Wilton, from Luke Sullivan's engraving of 1759 date in this form from the late 1730s. The Palladian bridge, (built 1736–7), was the model for others at Stowe and Prior Park.

12   Nostell Priory, design for the estate.

This layout of the early 1730s was one of Stephen Switzer's 'Rural and Extensive Gardens'. Lord Petre's layouts were similar but even more elaborate.

planting judiciously taken away, some few alterations by any skilful hand, could render the thing very perfect, as all the ingredients for composing a fine landscape are there.

Kent's first few experiments with his version of informal pastoral scenes appealed to a variety of romantic sensibilities. Support from such influential men of taste as Cobham and Pembroke was probably a major reason for the success of the taste. The *Gentleman's Magazine* commented in 1739 that

Every Man now, be his fortune what it will, is to be *doing something at his Place*, as the fashionable Phrase is; and you hardly meet with any Body, who, after the first Compliments, does not inform you, that he is *in Mortar* and *moving of Earth*; the modest terms for Building and Gardening. *One large Room*, a *Serpentine River*, and a *wood*, are become the most absolute Necessaries of Life, without which a Gentleman of the smallest Fortune thinks he makes no figure in his Country . . .

and in the same year Philip Miller, the curator of the Chelsea Physic Garden, brought out a new edition of his *Gardeners' Dictionary* in which the recommended style of gardening had changed from regularity to serpentine walks and the opening out of areas of the countryside.

Not all would-be possessors of a garden in the natural taste had Kent's ability to manipulate scenes in a seemingly relaxed manner. The only book claiming to tell them what to do in detail was Batty Langley's *New Principles of Gardening* (1728)[58], and elaborately serpentine walks through bosquets to either side main vista became exceedingly common during the 1740s[59]. Kent, Cobham, Pembroke and Southcote were virtually the only exponents of a true Natural Style until the mid-1740s.

Parkland

About 1730 a number of garden-designers were using the sort of geometry that Le Nostre had used for some of the later bosquets at Versailles in about 1680[60]. These bosquets were outdoor 'rooms', treated architecturally with walls of clipped hedges. Their plans were composed from intersecting shapes and are reminiscent of the plans of Baroque churches. Although symmetrical about their axes, they varied in width and shape possibly with the intention to give optical or theatrical effects. Juvarra was laying out similar bosquets in Italy in about 1730[61] but his gardens were dwarfed by some grandiose layouts in England at about the same time.

Apart from Switzer's unexecuted design for Nostel Priory, Yorkshire, of the early 1730s[62], the few layouts in England reminiscent of French bosquets are associated with French designers. The outstanding examples are Thorndon, in Essex, the seat of Lord Petre[63], and Worksop Manor, in Nottingham-shire, the seat of his kinsman and fellow Catholic, the ninth Duke of Norfolk[64], both laid out by Lord Petre assisted by a surveyor and draughtsman, Peter Bourginion. The Thorndon plan was drawn prior to 1734 and the Worksop plan is dated 1737. They share numerous characteristics with contemporary layouts by Bridgeman, such as their axial but asymmetric layouts, turfed ramps and mounts, and intricate winding paths through densely planted areas. However they could not be mistaken for Bridgeman's designs because of their paucity of diagonals and cross axes, the tremendous variety of shapes and sizes of their features, their menageries, the extension of the same geometry on a larger scale into the parks and the huge lawns or parades in front of the houses. Whilst they lack the coherent organization of Bridgeman's layouts the intricate geometry of the parts is more highly contrived.

Admired as Petre's park layouts were, though, the increasing concern in the 1740s for the park landscape largely passed them by. Of more significance for the future were the few tentative steps taken by Kent in translating his ideas on

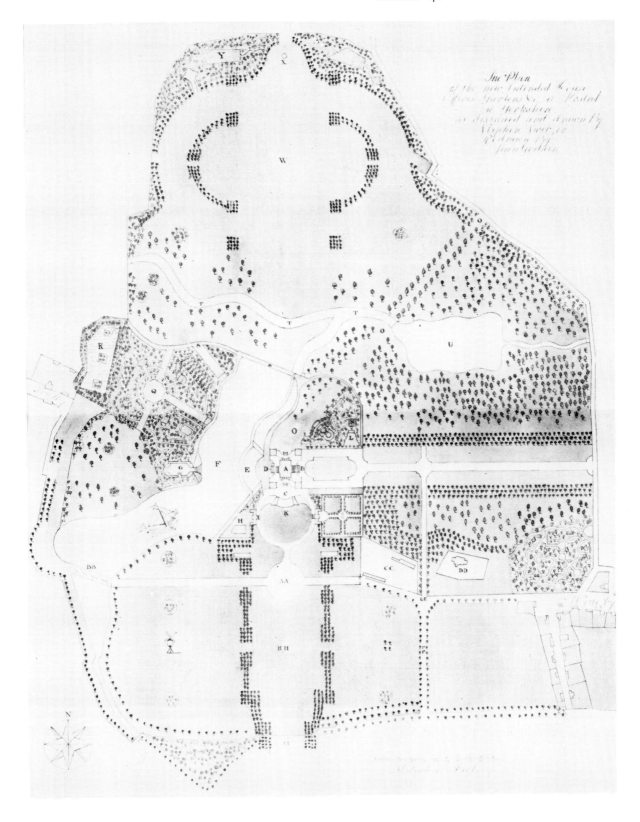

gardening to the scale of a park. His most used device was the clump, though he was not the first to use it. For example there were some large ones at Blenheim by 1709[65], and Castle Howard had acquired a large number, probably for sporting reasons, by 1727[66].

A number of Kent's sketches of park landscapes survive to show that he liked open ground varied only with clumps and buildings. As Walpole justly wrote:

He felt the delicious contrast of hill and valley changing imperceptibly into each other, tasted the beauty of the gentle swell, or concave scoop, and remarked how loose groves crowned an easy eminence with happy ornament[67].

Kent's ideas for turning this vision into reality were very successful where the hills and valleys were small in scale, as at Claremont and Esher where an intricate landform naturally gave a great variety of views and viewpoints. His clumps could be used to provide backdrops to buildings, emphasize knolls, constrain views, or merely to vary the surface of too large an expanse of lawn.

However when Kent had to work with a broad scale of landform he continued to suggest clumps as a means of varying the surface and of creating grand vistas. Walpole thought that the effect of such planting was 'puny', and he much preferred to see extensive old woods than

Mr. Kent's passion, clumps—that is sticking a dozen trees here and there till a lawn looks like the ten of spades. Clumps have their beauty; but in a great extent of country, how trifling to scatter arbours, where you should spread forest[68].

13 Holkham Hall, north front.

The sketch, of the early 1740s, shows William Kent's idea of parkland planting. Horace Walpole disliked it, and likened such clumps to the ten of spades.

The notable examples of Kent's layouts with clumps are the north lawn at Holkham[69] and the unexecuted scheme for remodelling Euston[70]. These were some of his last schemes, dating from about 1740. When Walpole was about to visit Holkham in 1743 he wrote to Lord Lincoln,

I go to Holkham tomorrow for two or three days ... I have the comfort of not having it the first time of my being there, and so need not be dragged to see clumps ...,

although he may have been disappointed in this because Kent was at Holkham during his stay, and setting out yet more clumps.

The Progress of Taste

Chinoiserie and Gothic Revival

Chinese porcelain, lacquer work and screens were no novelty to England in the 1730s and the scenes depicted on such manufactured articles were already familiar. Despite this, very little was known of the way of life, the manners, the customs and the arts of this sophisticated but alien culture. An irresistible fascination attached to these questions in Europe and any authentic record on the subject could not fail to have aroused much interest. When the Jesuit missionary Jean-Baptiste Du Halde published a book entitled *Description géographique, historique . . . de l'empire de la Chine* in 1735, translations appeared in England in succeeding years and in 1738 Samuel Johnson wrote an essay eulogizing the Chinese way of life for *The Gentleman's Magazine*[1].

Du Halde's book was a collection of essays; one of which, the recollections of a Jesuit called Gerbillon of his travels with the emperor in 1688–91, included some information on Chinese gardening:

The Beauty of their Houses and Gardens consists in a great Propriety and Imitation of Nature as Grotto's, Shellwork and craggy Fragments of Rocks, such as are seen in the wildest Desarts. But above all they are fond of little Arbors and Parterres, enclosed with green Hedges which form little Walks. This is the Genius of the Nation. The Rich lay out a great deal of Money in these sort of Whims . . .

Sir William Temple had warned that Chinese gardening rested on a skill in

contriving Figures, where the Beauty shall be great, and strike the Eye, but without any Order or Disposition of Parts, that shall be commonly or easily observ'd . . . But I should hardly advise any of these Attempts in the Figure of Gardens among us; they are Adventures of too hard Achievement for any common hands; and tho' there may be more Honour if they succeed well, yet there is more Dishonour if they fail and 'tis Twenty to One they will[2].

Gerbillon would have made Chinese gardening seem far less formidable; after all, it sounded as if it was virtually indistinguishable from the irregular garden layouts advocated by Batty Langley.

As a result, anyone who had a Batty Langley-type layout could call it Chinese[3], provided, of course, that the garden buildings were Chinese too. Perhaps the earliest Chinese building in England was a small 'Chinese House', erected on stilts in the Alder River at Stowe in 1738[4]. The Chinese style quickly became a fashion after the example of the Honourable Richard Bateman, who had a villa called Grove House at Old Windsor, in Berkshire. His portrait of 1741 shows a Chinese porch in the background. This porch and numerous pavilions, kiosks, bridges and arches, in both Gothic and Chinese styles, adorned his small *ferme ornée* in conjunction with a profusion of circular flower beds scattered along the circumferential walk.

14   Wroxton, plan.

The number of Chinese and Gothic garden buildings at Wroxton was remarkable, as can be seen on this undated plan by Francis Booth. Most of them date from the late 1740s.

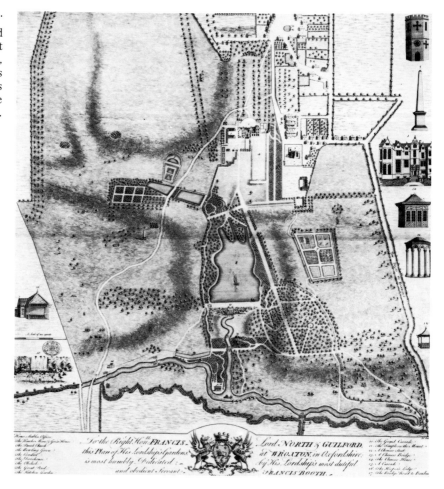

Bateman was one of the patrons of the painter Thomas Robins, who specialized in views of villas with borders of flowers and butterflies, between the late 1740s and the early 1760s[5]. Although Robins could be highly accurate as a topographical artist, he also captured that sense of fantasy in ornament so prevalent at the time. Based at Bath he travelled throughout the Midlands and Thames Valley to paint such places as Honington, Warwickshire, the seat of Joseph Townshend, and Grove House and Woodside at Old Windsor.

Another early garden with Chinese architecture was at Wroxton, Oxfordshire, the seat of Lord North, who was created the Earl of Guildford in 1752. Sanderson Miller was making alterations at Wroxton in the Gothic style from the mid-1740s, and, given that in 1749 he advised Joseph Townshend on the layout of the grounds at Honington[6], it seems likely that it was he that was responsible for altering the garden layout at Wroxton, its Moorish temple on a mount, the lake with a 20ft cascade and numerous Chinese buildings and bridges. The Chinese features were confined to the lower end of the garden where a serpentine canal was dug. From the examples of Wroxton, Honington, and other places, it seems that, if Chinese gardening existed at all, it was particularly associated with lakes and canals, although at one place at least, the Skell valley at Studley Royal, the Chinese temple was placed above crags; and there were a number of instances where a Chinese building was the centrepiece of a flower garden.

The architectural characteristics of the Chinese style were upswept eaves, often hung with bells, and trelliswork of discontinuous diagonals and verticals forming intricate patterns in bridge railings, fencing, windows and glazed doors. Despite the Chinese House at Stowe, architectural chinoiserie was at first more a matter of decoration than of building form. Pagodas had such striking forms that small garden pavilions had only to be octagonal with upswept eaves to remind one of them, and be called 'Chinese'.

Probably the first true pagoda in England was at Shugborough, in Staffordshire. This was the seat of Thomas Anson, brother of George Anson who arrived at Spithead in 1744 after a near-four-year journey around the world, during which he had visited Canton and captured a Spanish treasure ship off Manila. Shugborough benefited, because by 1748 the house had been extended to designs by Thomas Wright, and a Chinese house had been built on an island in the old moat along the lines of one sketched in Canton by Anson's lieutenant. This was reached by Chinese bridges, and in the moat was a Chinese boat. Further away from the house, in the midst of what Philip Yorke, the son of the Lord Chancellor, Lord Hardwicke, described as a 'ferme ornée'[7], the hexagonal six-storeyed pagoda was erected astride a brook in 1752[8].

Few Chinese buildings were as authentic as those at Shugborough, though. The vast majority were cheap and bad conversions of older buildings. Architectural pattern books furthered the debasement of genuine Chinese architecture. The first was William Halfpenny's *Rural Architecture in the Chinese Taste* which appeared in parts from 1750. This showed, ridiculously enough, various buildings of a Gothic nature with Chinese decorations applied, which he called 'partly in the Chinese Taste'.

Few people took the idea of Chinese gardening very seriously: Chinese architecture was merely another craze after the revival of Gothic in the

15 Shugborough, panoramic view from the south-east.

Nicolas Dall's painting of 1769 shows the pagoda built in 1752 and the triumphal arch and other Grecian garden buildings of the 1760s.

fashionable parts of the Home Counties. However Joseph Spence did not let the opportunity provided by a full description of one of the Ch'ien-lung Emperor's gardens go by without citing it as support for the Natural Style. In 1749 a letter from another Jesuit missionary in China, called Jean-Denis Attiret, was published in Paris. The garden in question was the Yuan Ming Yuan ('Garden of Perfect Brightness'), which was a few miles north west of Peking. It was an entire artificial landscape of hills and lakes with accompanying buildings and bridges, and had been created at vast cost. Attiret particularly noticed the bridges, some of which were zig-zag, as if spanning between imaginary rocky outcrops. The letter could be compared to a set of 40 views of the Yuan Ming Yuan, commissioned by the Emperor and undertaken by two Chinese artists. These were sent to Paris in 1749 and engraved[9].

Spence wrote to a friend in 1751 that:

I have lately seen thirty-six prints of a vast garden belonging to the present Emperor of China ... there is not one regular walk of trees in the whole ground, they seem to exceed our late best designers in the natural taste almost as far as those do the Dutch taste, brought over into England in King William's time[10].

So impressed was Spence with the parallels between Chinese gardening and the Natural Style in England that he published a translation of Attiret's letter under the pseudonym of Sir Harry Beaumont. One passage was translated as:

They rather choose a beautiful disorder, and a wandering as far as possible from all the Rules of Art,

and another as:

so much Art that you would take it to be the work of nature;

Spence had, in his zeal for the Natural Style, freely rendered the translation to be compatible with Castel's description of *Imitatio Ruris* supposed by Castel to have been 'the present Manner of Designing in China'.

Most men of taste, though, already felt that the novelty of Chinese architecture did not offset its lack of rules, and that it was therefore bad taste. Horace Walpole later said of Spence's translation:

I have looked it over, and except a determined irregularity, can find nothing in it that gives me any idea of attention being paid to nature[11].

In Walpole's eyes, Dutch gardening was no more deviant from Nature than the Chinese. He added sarcastically:

Methinks a straight canal is as rational at least as a maeandring bridge.

The World contained numerous criticisms. In 1753 an issue written by William Whitehead, who had clearly seen Halfpenny's pattern book, complained that:

everything is Chinese, or in the Chinese taste: or, as it is sometimes more modestly expressed, *partly after the Chinese manner* .... every gate to a cow-yard is in T's and Z's, and every hovel for the cows has bells hanging at the corners.

He did not decry the Chinese nation, though. He blamed the excesses of the style upon English invention:

not one in a thousand of all the stiles, gates, rails, poles, chairs, temples, chimney pieces, etc, which are called Chinese, has the least resemblance to anything that China saw[12].

To many architects, the Chinese taste was as abhorrent as the revival of the Gothic taste in the late 1730s had been. Robert Morris dismissed the Gothic as 'rude', and the Chinese as 'unmeaning', and reasserted that Palladian

architecture was the highest pitch of taste, and therefore the only style that should be contemplated[13]. A correspondent of *The World* remarked in 1755 upon how 'this Chinese and Gothic spirit has begun to deform some of the finest streets in this capital'[14], and others said much the same. However, Gothic architecture had one great quality that the Chinese lacked; it was native to England and therefore appropriate to the rising mood of medieval romanticism in literature and a reawakened interest in English constitutional history in politics. For this reason it transcended its rather frivolous beginnings when the fashion for Chinese architecture dwindled in the 1760s.

The beginnings of a more serious approach to Gothic architecture are associated with gentlemen antiquaries and men of letters. The first was Sanderson Miller, a Warwickshire squire, a keen student of history and an amateur architect. His house, Radway Grange, lay under the scarp of Edge Hill, famous for the Civil War battle. In 1745 Miller erected on Edge Hill a smaller version of Guy's Tower at Warwick Castle (to where Charles I had been obliged to fly after the battle) where it served as an eyecatcher. George Lyttelton was so impressed with its apparent authenticity that he asked Miller to design a larger castle to be placed on some high land at Hagley, his seat in Worcestershire. This was built in 1747[15]. Even the ever-critical Walpole was impressed: this is the castle of which he remarked, 'it has the true rust of the Barons' war'[16]. The third of Miller's famous castles was designed at Lord Hardwicke's request in 1749 for Wimpole Hall, Cambridgeshire, although built only in 1772[17].

16 Wimpole, mock castle.

Sanderson Miller's sketch of about 1750 for a ruined castle at the end of the northern avenue at Wimpole. It was similar to one at Hagley built in 1747.

Hard on the heels of Sanderson Miller was Walpole and his circle of friends. Walpole was encouraged in antiquarianism by the poet Thomas Gray, who combined the desire for atmosphere in poetry with considerable erudition in the study of Gothic architecture. His understanding of the periods and forms was excellent for the time, and Kent's and Langley's Gothic pained him: the latter 'has published a book of bad Designs'[18].

Walpole's interest in Gothic architecture was to revive it as the native style. He did not think it compared to the 'rational beauties of regular architecture', yet its romantic appeal to Englishmen, and its not inconsiderable intrinsic merit, made it appropriate in many situations[19]. Thinking that he could interest the Society of Antiquaries in recording the best of Gothic architecture and thus in contributing to the improvement of taste, Walpole joined it in 1753. He resigned in 1773 after an episode concerning Dick Whittington's cat convinced him that the Society was ridiculous. More fundamentally, though, he felt that it was too concerned with archaeology:

I have no curiosity to know how awkward and clumsy men have been in the dawn of arts or in their decay;

and that his own aims had been thwarted:

I endeavoured to give our antiquaries a little wrench towards taste—but it was in vain[20].

17   Strawberry Hill, south view.

This engraving of 1775 is based on a drawing by Paul Sandby. It shows the view from Horace Walpole's Gothic villa over the Thames at Twickenham.

The main practical outcome of Walpole's antiquarianism was the embellishment of Strawberry Hill[21]. He purchased this villa with five acres by the river in Twickenham in 1748. As time progressed he purchased more land and sought to extend the villa to house his library and to provide more living space. In 1751 he decided that he would use the Gothic Style, and started to assemble authentic Gothic designs which would be applied as fireplaces, ceilings, and so forth. The first extension was in 1753, and this and subsequent extensions in 1760 and 1776 gave a completely unsymmetrical ground plan—a startling idea at that date.

Walpole's personal reputation as a critic contributed much to the success of the Gothic revival. He was particularly proud of his conversion of Richard Bateman to Gothic architecture in the late 1750s:

I preached so effectually that his every pagoda took the veil[22].

Another convert was Philip Yorke's wife, the Marchioness Grey, who in 1756 confessed herself 'almost tired of the Chinese', and preferred the Gothic of 'Mr. Horry Walpole' at Strawberry Hill[23]. Walpole was not afraid to suggest designs, for example a Gothic building for Wentworth Castle, Yorkshire, for his friend Lord Strafford, based on Chichester cross. Nor was he afraid to criticize:

Aug. 22 1761. Went again to Mr. Charles Hamilton's at Payne's Hill near Cobham, to see the Gothic building and the Roman ruin. The former is taken from Batty Langley's book (which does not contain a single design of true or good Gothic) & is made worse by pendant ornaments in the arches.... The Goths never built summer-houses or temples in a garden. This at Mr. Hamilton's stands on the brow of a hill—there an imitation of a fort or watchtower had been proper[24].

Beyond the parallel between the irregularity of Walpole's planting and the ground plan of his house, though, the revival of Gothic architecture had no direct bearing on gardening style. Yet it did change the atmosphere of natural gardens, for the antiquarian interest in genuine Gothic buildings, and the new found skills in designing new ones, ensured that a high proportion of garden buildings were henceforward to be Gothic. Such buildings lent a sense of history and continuity to gardens and parks that encouraged Englishmen to think of the Natural Style as a rediscovered national characteristic.

Gardening Taste

The leaders of taste in gardening in the 1720s and 1730s, such as Alexander Pope, Lord Burlington and Lord Cobham, were highly revered even 20 years later. Visitors flocked to see Pope's garden before and after his death, and a few wrote carefully composed accounts of it, for example one printed in the *Newcastle Magazine* in 1748. On Pope's death his gardener, John Serle, thought it worthwhile to have *A Plan of Mr Pope's Garden at it was left at his Death* (1745) printed for the benefit of these visitors.

Visiting the great showplaces of England was becoming a popular pastime with the gentry during the 1740s. Antiquarians were already no strangers to tours, but the emphasis on country houses and their gardens increased greatly after Daniel Defoe's *Tours in England* (1724), and was given further encouragement by the publication of Pope's letters in 1735.

Some idea of the relative popularity of gardens close to the capital is given by the series of engraved plans by John Rocque paid for by subscription. He started with Richmond Gardens (1734) and followed this with Wanstead (1735), Chiswick (1736), Hampton Court (1736), Esher (1737), Claremont (1738), Windsor (1738), and others, and then, after a gap, with Richmond Gardens again (1748), Claremont again (1750) and a few more. Although he engraved maps of places outside the Home Counties, Wilton for instance, these were few by comparison.

However, indisputably the most popular gardens were those at Stowe, which had already been represented in views and a map published in 1739 by Charles Bridgeman's widow. In 1744 a local bookseller called Benton Seeley published his *Description of the Gardens of Lord Viscount Cobham at Stow*, and in 1750 he found himself in competition with an engraver called George Bickham whose *Views of Stowe* included 16 excellent engravings and a superb map from 1753. Seeley's guide was repeatedly reissued with improvements into the next century[25].

It was fortunate for the reputation of Stowe that Lord Cobham's successor, his nephew Richard Grenville, Earl Temple from 1752, took a keen interest in the gardens, and continued with improvements from Cobham's death in 1749, till his own 30 years later. In the spirit of the times, the hedges and avenues had not been clipped or pleached, and so one of Temple's tasks was to devise thinning or clearance to prevent the gardens becoming swamped by vegetation. His early alterations included the removal of the internal ha-ha around the Home Park, and the irregularization of the lake in the Home Park.

There was also the Grecian Valley to complete. This had been begun in 1747 by Lord Cobham with the assistance of his head gardener, Lancelot Brown. It was a continuation of the narrow valley in which the Elysian Fields had been made, and so at its start was a natural depression, although the location of an extension north-eastwards was determined more by the boundaries of the grounds. Much earthmoving in the first couple of years created the desired form and smoothness, and this was followed, after much deliberation, by extensive planting.

Once again Cobham had created something new, for nothing on this scale had been tried in the Natural Style before. Its name suggests that it was Cobham's own vision of how a Greek Valley would have appeared in antiquity. It had a broad, flattish bottom and as the sides sloped upwards they were met by irregular drifts of planting descending downwards from the rim. A track ran around the rim of the valley, here cutting through the planting, there along the upper edge of the lawn. The effect was to pass in and out of woodland, so that at each opening the scheme had altered. Unlike a garden by William Kent, which was designed around a number of principal objects and views, the Grecian Valley was best appreciated as an ever-changing scene as one moved around it.

The finished state of the Grecian Valley, though, was Lord Temple's responsibility[26]. It was he who erected the architectural counterpart to the valley's planting, the Grecian Temple, to be renamed the Temple of Concord and Victory later in the 1750s. This was closely modelled on actual Greek temples. It was the forerunner of a vogue for an archaeological approach to design which was followed by, for example, James Stuart, who added a number of Greek buildings to Shugborough in the early 1760s[27]. Amongst Temple's relations were an astonishing number of men of taste, and he frequently sought their advice. His brother-in-law was William Pitt, later to be Prime Minister, but also an accomplished layer-out of gardens, and amongst his cousins there was George, Baron Lyttelton, and Thomas Pitt, the former famous for patronage of James Thomson, and the latter an accomplished amateur architect.

With the great amount of publicity given to Pope's garden at Twickenham, to Stowe and to Woburn Farm, it was perhaps inevitable that ambitious improvers should wish to emulate them, and perhaps make improvements.

Allegory, which had inspired the Elysian Fields at Stowe, was again the theme in the much larger scene at Stourhead, and the most celebrated *ferme ornée* of all, The Leasowes, was inspired by Philip Southcote's Woburn Farm. Meanwhile the Palladians' formula of a grassy slope down to water, as seen at Chiswick in 1733 and at Stowe in 1740, became popular at gentlemen's villas. Two of the most admired of such scenes to be created in the 1750s were The Vyne in Hampshire, the seat of Walpole's friend, John Chute[28], and White-knights, Berkshire, the seat of Sir Henry Englefield[29].

Richard Cambridge was making similar improvements to his family seat in Gloucestershire, Whitminster, in the previous decade[30]. He was a schoolfellow of Thomas Gray and Horace Walpole at Eton, and shared many of their interests in adulthood. However, upon marriage in 1741 he removed himself from his circle of friends in London to Whitminster. This was situated in the Vale of Berkeley not far from the Severn estuary.

By judicious felling and placing of his buildings and plantations he revealed views of the Cotswolds, and nearer the house he made an open lawn down to the River Frome which ran through the grounds. His chief recreations at this time were boatbuilding, making the Frome navigable, making tours with his family on horseback, and composing a poem after the manner of Pope to be

18 The Vyne, view across the lake.

The painting by Johann Muntz of 1756 shows the new lawns and lake made by John Chute at his house, The Vyne.

called *The Scribbleriad*. His friend the poet William Whitehead, described Cambridge's life at Whitminster:

> You spread the lawn, direct the flood,
> Cut vistas through, or plant a wood,
> Build China's barks for Severn's stream,
> Or form new plans for epic fame . . .

Cambridge's greatest triumph here, though, was a visit in July 1750 by the Prince of Wales. Prince Frederick had been staying with Lord Bathurst, who well knew of Cambridge's improvements at Whitminster, and for a day's excursion from Cirencester Cambridge was asked to pick up the Prince at the navigable head of the Frome and convey him to the Severn after showing him Whitminster.

Although small country houses and villas like Cambridge's were perforce modest, there was nothing modest about Henry Hoare's mansion and garden at Stourton, Wiltshire, named 'Stourhead' to signify its being the source of that river. Hoare's father had died in 1725, having just built the huge Palladian Villa, and Henry moved into it himself in 1741 upon the death of his mother[31]. At that time the house was surrounded by conventional regular gardens, though he had already made a terrace walk from the gardens and around a hill overlooking the deep valley called the Six Wells Bottom. That is where the springs that gave rise to the Stour were to be found.

Hoare's early intention was to form a lake which, with various buildings around its perimeter, could illustrate the founding of Rome from *The Aeneid*. His architect for these works was Henry Flitcroft who, having formerly been in the employ of Lord Burlington, naturally executed them in the Palladian style. Flitcroft also seems to have designed the head of the substantial lake in 1744. An indication that Hoare was at this time following in Burlington's and Kent's style of gardening was his planting mix of firs and beech. Planting was undertaken at Stourhead on a massive scale, and by the 1770s he had quite literally converted an agricultural scene to one of woods and water.

Flitcroft's first building at Stourhead was the temple of Flora, built in 1745, and just below it, on the bank of the lake, was a small rock arch in which was placed a statue of the River God. Despite the dedication of the temple above to Flora, it seems that the rock arch was intended to mark the entrance to the underworld, which would mean the lake was Lake Avernus, across which Aeneas passed in order to reach Hades. Across the other side of the lake a copious spring was converted in 1748 into a substantial grotto, intended, perhaps on a suggestion by Pope, as the home of a sleeping water nymph. The inscription on the pediment associates it also with the cave near which Aeneas landed in North Africa after his flight from Troy.

William Shenstone was an aspiring poet, and felt that a poetical genius should be complemented by a gardening one. He had inherited a small estate called The Leasowes, situated near to Hales-Owen, Shropshire. It was on the side of a hill with views out over the Severn Valley towards the Clent Hills and the Welsh mountains. Two dingles ran down the hill meeting at the bottom, and were watered by small streams. Shenstone took this estate in hand in 1743[32], and applied himself to the question of how it should be improved.

Being a man of modest means and property Shenstone realized that the most practical way to achieve his gardening ambitions was to combine profit with pleasure. He already knew a *ferme ornée* at Mickleton, Gloucestershire, belonging to the family of his friend Richard Graves. Shenstone followed the *ferme ornée* model, and embellished The Leasowes with small pools and waterfalls, planted the dingles, and ran paths through them and around the periphery of the estate.

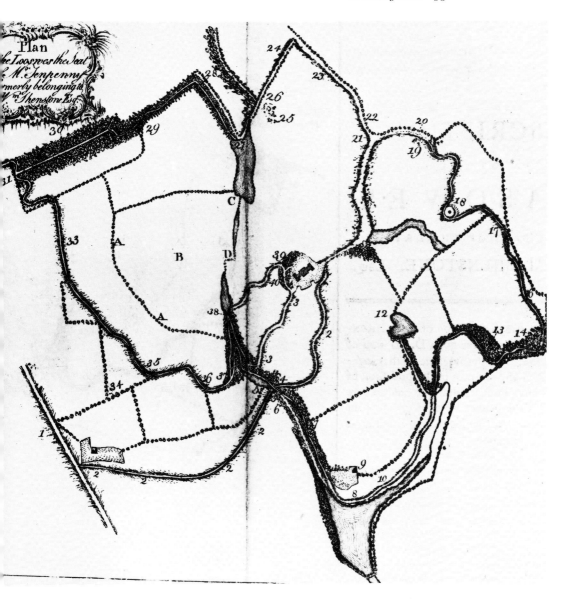

19 The Leasowes, plan.

The plan was attached to Robert Dodsley's *Description of The Leasowes*, published by him with *The Works . . . of William Shenstone, Esq.* (1764). The numerals indicate the suggested circuit.

He did not share Kent's or Hoare's visions of classical landscapes. However, he fervently believed in the pleasures of the imagination, and in Pope's dictums on variety, and following Nature. He understood this last principle to refer to common Nature, and although this was not Pope's intention, Shenstone's resulting theory of improvement was none the less tenable and, for Shenstone at least, successful in practice.

He acknowledged that unimproved common Nature is generally insipid, but he also noticed that different parts of a property would usually display mildly different characters. The aid of Art was thus required to enhance these different characters to give the property a variety of distinctive scenes. His own saying was that taste in gardening was the

collecting, or collecting into a smaller compass, and then disposing without crowding the several varieties of Nature[33].

20   Dean Paul's garden.

One of a number of
drawings made by Joseph
Spence for the gardens of his
friends from the 1740s. This
one dates from 1765.

Shenstone liked to keep a clear distinction between Art and Nature. Ground, woodland and water are the province of Nature, and so any alterations to these should be carefully concealed. On the other hand he contrived some scenes to appeal to the imagination through their artificially given associations, through names and urns and seats with inscriptions. By 1746 he had named part of the northern dingle 'Virgil's Grove', and planned a model of Virgil's tomb, an obelisk and some mottoes from Virgil to would give it a pensive air.

It was not long before the Lytteltons, whose mansion at Hagley was just over the county boundary in Worcestershire, took an interest, and brought James Thomson to see this *ferme ornée* in 1746. Ten years later The Leasowes's fame had spread and an anonymous visitor wrote some 'Verses written at the Garden of William Shenstone, Esq; near Birmingham. 1756' which appeared in the first issue of *The Annual Register* in 1758:

> ... And while, quick-shifting as you stray,
> The vivid scenes on fancy play,
> The lawn of aspect smooth and mild;
> The forest ground grotesque and wild;
> The shrub that scents the mountain-gale;
> The stream rough dashing down the dale,
> From rock to rock, in eddies tost;
> The distant lake, in which 'tis lost;
> Blue hills, gay beaming thro' the glade;
> Lone urns that solemnize the shade;
> Sweet interchange of all that charms
> In groves, meads, dingles, riv'lets, farms. ...

Like Shenstone, Joseph Spence wished to combine a fame in gardening with excellence in poetry, although by profession he was a clergyman. Not being very wealthy or well paid either, he had to content himself with devising layouts for friends' town gardens until 1747 when his poem *Polymetis* was financially successful. At the same time Henry Fiennes Clinton, ninth Earl of Lincoln, with whom he had once travelled on the continent for three years, offered to lease him a house with about 17 acres of land at Byfleet, Surrey, situated on the Oatlands Estate[34]. During 1748 Spence made a number of designs for a grove with serpentine paths running through it, which was to incorporate a great number of fruit trees, some already existing. The next year he had turned his attention to his meadows for which he designed a circumferential walk.

As Byfleet is only a few miles from Woburn Farm it is not surprising that Spence was drawn towards Southcote. He was enchanted by the place, and referred to it as a modern Paradise. Despite his own pretensions in garden design, he deferred to Southcote's views hardly without question. In the year that they came to know each other, 1750, Spence altered his plans of improvement according to Southcote's advice; and whereas Spence had been assiduous in recording Pope's remarks about gardening for his *Anecdotes*, he now recorded Southcote's.

When asked in 1751 by a friend, the Rev. Robert Wheeler, how he should lay out his garden, Spence took the opportunity to set down what rules he thought might be helpful, although he warned that 'nine parts in ten depend upon the application'. For the most part these rules repeated what he had been told by Pope. The first rule was the well known instruction 'to consult the Genius of the place', which he explained meant 'to study the ground thoroughly'. He explained Pope's advice to 'follow nature' thus:

Gardening is an imitation of 'Beautiful Nature' and therefore should not be like works of art.

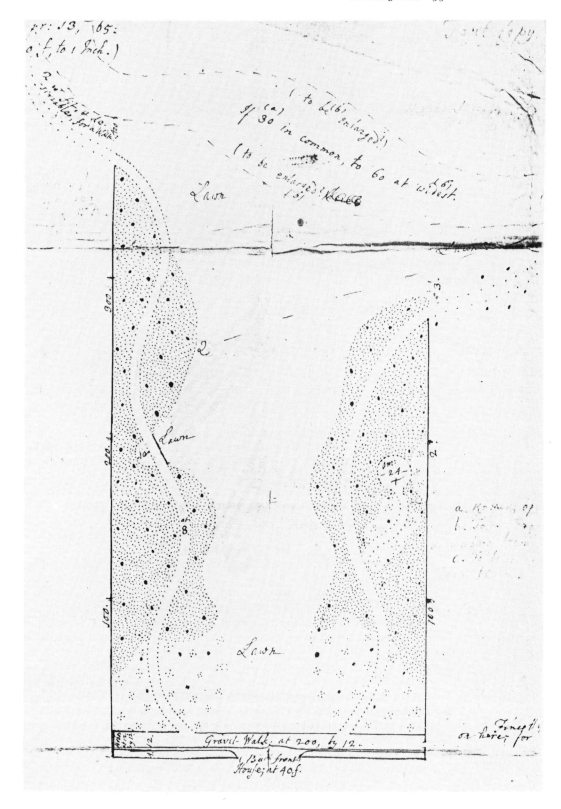

Although he did not define 'Beautiful Nature' to Wheeler, he jotted down elsewhere that[35]:

The chief aim of our best designers ... is TO IMITATE NATURE. Not like the Dutch painters, who often choose to copy nature in her lowest and most disagreeable works, nor like Michael Angelo Caravaggio who takes to her indifferently as he finds her, nor like Guido Reni who often hides or disguises her with a profusion of grace and beauty, but like Raphael, who follows her always with a careful judgement and a happiness of choice.

In accordance with this interpretation of imitating nature, the following rules followed:

To correct or conceal any particular object that is disagreeable.
To open a view to whatever is particularly agreeable.

His other main themes followed Pope's *Epistle to Burlington* in giving ways to surprise, to vary and to conceal the bounds. He discussed types of fencing, uniting the country with the garden, and the painterly techniques of attracting, distancing and mixing lights and shades.

Spence's understanding of the implications of imitating Nature were that:

I should almost ever prefer serpentinising walks to straight ones, and round off the corners of groves instead of pointing them.

Such a view was buttressed by William Hogarth's theories on beauty, finally published in *The Analysis of Beauty* (1753), but which he had been promoting for some years beforehand[36]. He believed that waving and serpentine lines were the *Lines of Beauty* and *Grace* respectively, and that all the best painters had been drawn to the same conclusion through close imitation of the beauties of Nature. However, such views, although seemingly analytical, provided no explanation of the relation between Art and Nature. Southcote must have felt that they were wide of the mark, for he added to Spence's draft as a more appropriate adage:

Wherever art appears, the gardener has failed in his execution.

Spence clearly took great trouble over his letter to Wheeler, for besides soliciting this and other comments from Southcote, he went through four drafts seemingly with a view to publication. Probably it was to be part of a book to be entitled *Tempe: or Letters Relating to Gardens in All Ages: and More Particularly to the Method of Making the Grounds and Country Pleasing All Round One, so Happily Introduc'd of Late Among Us*[37]. However, his next literary project was to be the translation of Attiret's letter about the Emperor of China's gardens in 1752. Also in the same year he was spending much time with a number of local gentlemen and in particular the new parson of Byfleet, who happened to be Stephen Duck, the one-time 'librarian' to Queen Caroline in Merlin's Cave in Richmond Gardens. For one reason or another Spence never completed *Tempe*.

Meanwhile another literary project, the magazine *The World*, which ran from 1753 to 1756, took the forefront in discussions of taste in gardening. The editor was Edward Moore, a protégé of George Lyttelton. Most of his contributors spoke from a certain amount of experience. One of the most prolific was Richard Cambridge. In 1748 he inherited from an uncle, surnamed Owen, whose name he then took. He was already feeling somewhat isolated from his circle of friends in London, and the extra money enabled him to spend his winters there. Then in 1751 a villa at Twickenham, in full view of Richmond Hill, was put up for sale and he bought it[38]. At that time the River Thames was shut out from the house by walls, fences and avenues. As at

Whitminster, he created a grassy slope down to the river and backed the house with plantations. Twickenham Meadows, as he called it, presented a very 'cheerful' scene from Richmond Hill, and was widely acknowledged as an excellent advertisement for that style of improvement.

Another frequent contributor was Horace Walpole. At the same time as he was making Gothic alterations to his villa, he was adapting his gardens to his own taste. He described them in 1753:

This view of the castle is what I have just finished, and is the only side that will be at all regular. Directly before it is an open grove, through which you see a field, which is bounded by a serpentine wood of all kind of trees, and flowering shrubs, and flowers. The lawn before the house is situated on the top of a small hill, from whence to the left you see the town and church of Twickenham encircling a turn of the river, that looks exactly like a seaport in miniature. The opposite shore is a most delicious meadow, bounded by Richmond Hill, which loses itself in the noble woods of the Park to the end of the prospect . . .[39].

Other contributors included William Whitehead, Joseph Warton and another amateur poet, the Reverend Francis Coventry.

For the most part these contributors discussed only the most general precepts, and gardening style was introduced only in order to ridicule the obviously inappropriate or nonsensical. They were primarily concerned with the rules of taste. As Whitehead stressed in his number[40]:

TASTE, in my opinion, ought to be applied to nothing but what has strict rules annexed to it, though perhaps imperceptible by the vulgar . . . People may have whims, freaks, caprices, persuasions, and even second-sights if they please, but they can have no TASTE which has not its foundation in nature, and which, consequently, may be accounted for.

21 Twickenham Meadows, south view.

The house beside the Thames by Richmond Bridge became Richard Owen Cambridge's in 1751. The engraving was published with his *Works* in 1803.

This idea that taste had its foundation in Nature was an important theme delivered by numerous contributors. Horace Walpole, in an early number[41], reflecting upon the increasing realism of stage effects in the theatre, noted also that:

In gardening, the same love of nature prevails. Clipt hedges, avenues, regular platforms, straight canals have been for some time very properly exploded. There is not a citizen who does not take more pains to torture his acre and half into irregularities, than he formerly would have employed to make it as formal as his cravat.

Not long after Francis Coventry wrote that William Kent,

truly the disciple of nature, imitated her in the agreeable wildness and beautiful irregularity of her plans, of which there are some noble examples still remaining, that abundantly show the power of his creative genius[42].

Joseph Warton discoursed on the theme of simplicity[43], which he saw as the characteristic of nature that made it noble and magnificent. He was not advocating dullness, but he objected to useless and extravagant decoration. Clearly he did not share Walpole's love of Gothic details:

A multiplicity of minute ornaments, a vast variety of angles and cavities; clusters of little columns and a crowd of windows are what distinguish MEANNESS OF MANNER in building from GREATNESS; that is, the Gothic from the Grecian.

22   The Hermitage, North End Road, London.

This painting of about 1770 is by Theodore de Bruyn. It shows the sort of garden that Francis Coventry mocked when he described 'Squire Mushroom's villa'.

Richard Owen Cambridge felt that strength and convenience were more important than magnificence, and advocated that people should be more willing to learn the lessons of practical experience in such matters[44]. He was backed up by other contributors who bemoaned the public's taste for novelty.

As a whole these papers were light-hearted. In one, the builders of follies were congratulated for their unselfishness in providing the public with amusement, whilst in another it was proposed that young men should make the Grand Tour to China rather than Europe. There were also some amusing parodies of the Batty Langley-style gardens that were so common. Francis Coventry observed that 'GARDENING, being the dress of nature, is as liable to the caprices of fashion, as are the dresses of the human body', and proceeded to investigate the rage for serpentine lines[45]. 'A great comic painter', he continued, meaning Hogarth, 'has proved, I am told, in a piece every day expected, that the line of beauty is an S'.

Coventry went on to invent the tale of Squire Mushroom, who turned a farmhouse into a villa with new gardens of less than two acres:

At your first entrance, the eye is saluted with a yellow serpentine river, stagnating through a beautiful valley, which extends near twenty yards in length. Over the river is thrown a bridge, *partly in the Chinese manner*, and a little ship, with sails spread and streamers flying, floats in the midst of it.

The squire's garden also had a hermitage called 'St. Austin's cave' in the midst of a wilderness and a temple, for no particular reason, dedicated to Venus.

Despite their humorous vein, these papers had the serious intent of improving Taste. They were in fact highly influential in removing some of the absurdities of the new taste and in directing a new generation towards more appropriate principles of taste in gardening.

The Scenery of Nature

Once the notion of a fraternity of arts was established, there was no reason to confine oneself merely to the principles of painting in gardening. During the 1740s the analogy was extended to the full, with Nature coming to be regarded as a painter in the creation of the landscape. The impression made on human eyes by the works of that great master, Nature, was the same, if not superior, to that made by the works of Nature's imitators on canvas, and gave pleasure for the same reasons.

In some respects the analogy was particularly apt. The different moods of Nature could be conveniently compared to the styles of certain painters. Claude Lorrain was identified as representing the beautiful scenes of Nature, and Salvator Rosa the terrible and sublime. On the other hand certain scenes in Nature were very dull, and this needed some explanation. The usual one was that Nature could work on such vast scales that humans could not comprehend the whole design.

The analogy was so persuasive to many that it sufficed as a working hypothesis in the absence of any fully adequate theory on the important question of the cause of beauty. Also, there was no need to believe that mountains were the rubbish of creation, as their irregularly and variety (which characterize good landscape painting) must always have been intended by the Creator in Nature. As one of Spence's friends put it:

God could never have been so bad a gardener as to have made Eden all on a flat[46].

Another effect of the analogy was to undermine Shaftesbury's belief that the perception of beauty is intellectual. It would have been a form of blasphemy to deny that the scenery of Nature was beautiful, and since there can be nothing intellectually pleasing about wild scenery, its appreciation must be an automatic reaction that it is in the nature of men to make.

Pope had once hinted that Nature used painterly techniques[47], and so had Thomson, when he had written 'who can paint like NATURE?' in 'Spring' (1728). Thomson's 1744 edition of *The Seasons* contained some excellent painterly descriptions, one of which was of the prospect from Hagley Park:

> Meantime you gain the height, from whose fair brow
> The bursting prospect spreads immense around;
> And snatch'd o'er hill and dale, and wood and lawn,
> And verdant field, and darkening heath between,
> And villages embosom'd soft in trees,
> And spiry towns by surging columns mark'd
> Of household smoke, your eye excursive roams:
> Wide-stretching from the hall in whose kind heart
> The hospitable Genius lingers still,
> To where the broken landscape by degrees,
> Ascending, roughens into ridgy hills;
> O'er which the Cambrian mountains, like far clouds
> That skirt the blue horizon, dusky rise.

On the other hand, one Cambrian mountain, Penmaenmawr, which rises straight from the sea, was 'heap'd hideous to the sky', and Thomson was still admiring the Bridgeman layout at Stowe, where 'all beauteous Nature fears to be outdone':

> Oh lead me to the wide walks
> The fair majestic paradise of Stowe . . .

If Thomson's vision of Nature as a painter was somewhat half-hearted, the conversion of men of taste generally was even less perceptible. The hallmark of this conversion was not persuasion by a brilliantly constructed theory, but a gradual change in the way that people looked at the real landscape. As the fashion for painting progressed from connoisseurship to the enjoyment of visual qualities, the landscape itself came to be appreciated for its composition, colouring and mood. The first people to find themselves with such pictorial appreciation found that their emotions often contradicted their understanding. In 1738 the Bishop of Bangor, Dr Thomas Herring, was 'agreeably terrified with something like the rubbish of creation' during his journeys in North Wales[48], and the next year Horace Walpole and Thomas Gray also discovered the strange attraction of the sublime in their crossing of the Alps[49].

The most convenient way to describe these emotions was to liken the landscape to a painting. Dr Herring remarked that the crags, woods and foaming stream, together with the flocks, herds and peasants, in a valley he had seen,

put me much in mind of Poussin's drawings, and made me fancy myself in Savoy, at least, if not in Rome.

Walpole at various times identified the Alps with Salvator Rosa[50], Esher Place during a musical evening with Watteau[51], and a well under a wood at Hagley with Nicholas Poussin[52]. However the commonest identifications were with Claude and Salvator Rosa. For example Mrs Elizabeth Montagu described an outing in the vicinity of Tunbridge, Kent, in the following terms:

After we rambled about for an hour, seeing several views, some wild as Salvator Rosa, others placid, and with the setting sun, worthy of Claude Lorrain[53].

As people gained confidence in excercising their painterly appreciation of scenes, they ceased to have patience with gardens that demanded an intellectual involvement and the use of imagination. The gardens at Stowe, being the epitome of Augustan gardening, were frequently the subject of criticism. Dr Herring thought that the sight of them after the mountains of Wales would have made him smile. Ten years later a young clergyman called William Gilpin wrote *A Dialogue upon the Gardens . . . at Stowe*[54]. In the guise of Polython, a tourist, Gilpin explored the differences between 'moral beauties' and 'picturesque' qualities by discussing his reactions to the various scenes at Stowe. Why, for instance, are ruins particularly attractive features when they denote only ruin and decay? Then he mocked Dido's cave because, being made of hewn stone, it was untruthful to the eye.

Also in 1748 Jemima, Marchioness Grey, complained that Stowe was 'so crowded with Buildings that as you see them at a distance seem almost at Top of One Another that each loses its Effect'[55]. It was not to her the scenery of Nature. Although Gilpin had appreciated the meaning of the Temple of Modern Virtue, he joined Horace Walpole in having 'no patience at building and planting a satire'[56]. The make-believe world of Augustan gardens had become unpalatable to the younger generation brought up to use their eyes and for whom their elders' concerns held little interest.

On the other hand the younger generation was awaking to the pictorial charms of the countryside. Polython extolled the scenery to be found in the North of England and nearly all those to see Nature as a painter, from Dr Herring onwards, were tourists in open country.

The recurrent discoveries of sublime qualities in Nature are striking. The idea of sublimity was discussed by Mark Akenside in his *Pleasures of the Imagination* (1744). He differentiated 'three sister-graces, whom the painter's hand, the poet's tongue confesses; the *sublime*, the *wonderful*, the *fair*'. Feelings of sublimity could be caused by vastness, but were most readily evoked by a degree of danger and mild terror. Precipices, beasts of prey and violent weather could all contribute.

Lord Lyttelton was fascinated by the sublime. He must have discovered its feeling early in life on the shaggy hillside behind Hagley and seeing the immense prospect towards Wales. In 1756 he undertook a journey into North Wales purely for pleasure, and made a journal of his observations. At Wynnstay, Denbighshire[57], for example, he felt that the Williams-Wynn's had missed an opportunity by not including the gorge of the River Dee within the park:

If the park was extended a little farther, it would take in a hill, with the view of a valley, most beautifully wooded; and the river Dee winding in so romantic and charming a manner, that I think it exceeds . . . any confined prospect I ever beheld.

His protégé, Dr John Brown, wrote to him not later than the same year about Derwentwater, Cumberland, near where he was a vicar:

The full perfection of Keswick consists of three circumstances, beauty, horror and immensity united . . . To give you a complete idea of these three perfections, as they are joined at Keswick, would require the united powers of Claude, Salvator and Poussin. The first should throw his delicate sunshine over the cultivated vales, the scattered cots, the groves, the lake and wooded islands. The second should dash out the horror of the rugged cliffs, the steeps, the hanging woods and foaming waterfalls; while the grand pencil of Poussin should crown the whole, with the majesty of impending mountains[58].

Sublimity is not a quality that is easily introduced into pleasure grounds, but Lyttelton's remarks on Wynnstay suggest that thoughts were turning that way. If walks or ridings are extended for great distances to encompass the crags, the wooded slopes and the viewpoints of a line of cliffs or a large gorge, then one might indeed be able to display the sublime from within one's

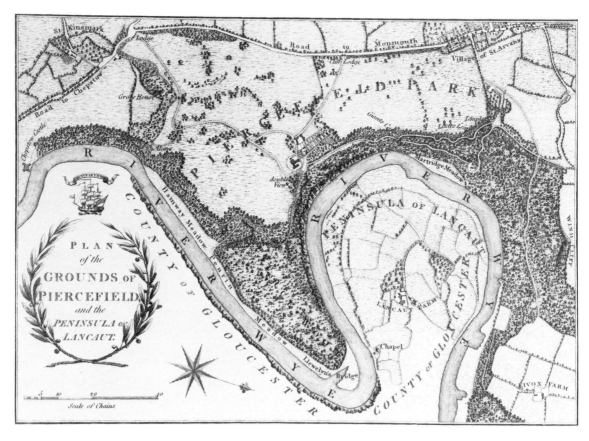

23   Piercefield, plan.

The plan was published in William Coxe's *Historical Tour Through Monmouthshire* (1801). The grounds had been laid out 50 years before by Valentine Morris, and had changed little except for a new approach made by Adam Mickle in the 1790s.

pleasure grounds. Philip Yorke was shown over Studley Royal in 1744, two years after William Aislabie had succeeded his father. Aislabie's new improvements were to be in a wild and rocky section of the Skell Valley, and Yorke was clearly taken with the idea:

Imagine rocks covered with wood, sometimes perpendicularly steep and craggy ...

Four years later he saw the much more impressive three-quarters-of-a-mile-long terrace at Hawkstone, Shropshire, the seat of Sir Rowland Hill, where a line of sandstone crags rose abruptly from the surrounding plains:

This place has great rude beauties and the owner is continually improving it. The rocks are more frequent and wild than at Studley and the prospect more extensive and various. The principal defect is in water, there being nothing wanting to complete the romantic wildness of the landscape but a torrent or cascade gushing out and tumbling down the precipices[59].

The most spectacular was Piercefield, Monmouthshire[60]. From near the house there was view of Chepstow Castle and the River Severn to the south, whilst to the east the River Wye meandered at the base of its precipitous gorge. The Wye gorge was one of the first natural wonders to be admired by those tourists seeking the works of Nature the painter. Richard Cambridge had made excursions on horseback from Whitminster with his wife or his guests to the River Wye, and in 1748 he even treated for the purchase of Piercefield[61]. About this time the Reverend Dr John Egerton, Rector of Ross,

caused a pleasure boat to be built to enable his guests to enjoy excursions by water and scenery which could not fail to delight and surprise, and in about 1750 the Duke of Beaufort had the ruins of Tintern Abbey tidied up for the sake of the tourists[62].

Piercefield was not sold, though. Instead, its young owner, Valentine Morris, took up residence there upon his marriage late in 1748 and, with Cambridge's assistance, laid out paths along the rim of the gorge to take the best advantage of the views. Besides the natural features along these paths, for example the Lovers' Leap, a sheer drop of 180 feet, there was a Giant's Cave, named after the giant in stone crouching over its entrance, and, at the end of a path descending from the rim, there was a Cold Bath fed by a spring. Morris refused to let visitors tip their guides, and he entertained them lavishly. As a result Piercefield quickly found its way onto tourist itineraries.

Like Piercefield, Hackfall in Yorkshire is a gorge with wooded sides[63]. Being only a few miles from Studley Royal, it was used by the Aislabies as a retreat. The main building, called Mowbray Point, was merely a kitchen and dining room suite perched on the rim of the gorge of the River Ure. Visitors had no inkling of the setting until the doors were thrown open and the scene revealed to their terror and amazement. Those strong of resolution and body could then take one of the paths down towards the river. Half-way down there were a rustic hut built of massive stone blocks, a circular pool with a central fountain and a grotto in view of a 40-foot cascade. There was a temple named after the Aislabies' gardener, William Fisher, and with William Aislabie's initials and the date 1750. A glance up to the rim would reveal Mowbray Point, which appeared from this direction as three massive ruined Roman arches.

These examples of the sublime in gardening were rare, though. Few places could boast crags or torrents, though many had milder beauties, and there the purpose of art was to refine and polish Nature to bring out the inherent landscape beauties:

> *Nature* the Pallat holds, the Canvas spread,
> Filled with *her* colours, *art* the Pencil guides[64].

This was an optimistic belief: it meant that a real landscape could be improved to provide an endless series of pictures. A few men who had whole landscapes at their disposal sought to turn this vision into reality in the 1750s; amongst them was Henry Hoare, who had already embarked on creating allegorical scenes at Stourhead, and Charles Hamilton, who had been transforming his heathland at Painshill, Surrey, into productive farmland.

Henry Hoare's early improvements soon took on a painterly aspect, and their allegorical purpose became indistinct. The Claudian qualities of Stourhead would have become apparent to a cultured man such as Hoare. However the scene lacked an object of view on the far bank of the lake, and so Flitcroft designed a Pantheon for a suitably conspicuous spot which was being constructed in 1753[65]. Nine years later Hoare had decided to add a bridge modelled on Palladio's at Vicenza:

The Bridge is now about . . . When you stand at the Pantheon the water will be seen thro the Arches and it will look as if the river came thro the village and that this was the Village Bridge for public use; the view of the Bridge, Village and Church altogether will be a Charming Gaspard picture at that end of the water.

Hoare's pains in building and planting were already paying off. Horace Walpole pronounced at the same date that:

The whole composes one of the most picturesque scenes in the world[66].

Charles Hamilton acquired a lease of Painshill[67] in 1738, and throughout the 1740s seems to have been chiefly employed there in agricultural improvement and the cultivation of exotic plants. This bore fruit with the vineyard, which was in cultivation by 1748, and the very wide range of conifers that he planted. He was particularly interested in American species that were suitable for his acid soil, and was to grow some of the first rhododendrons and azaleas introduced into England. The further improvement of Painshill into a picturesque scene took place in the 1750s. In 1754 a visitor remarked on the lake with islands, and the water wheel that supplied it with water from the River Mole, and in 1760 William Woollett engraved a view of this lake which showed that the Gothic Tower, the Turkish Tent and the Roman Mausoleum were built.

None of these features was aligned on avenues or other axes, but they were disposed around a circuit. It seems that Hamilton aimed at a succession of scenes each invoking a different mood. It is probable that he studied the Grand Masters for the express purpose of gaining hints for his scenes[68]. The lake was made about 1750 in irregular form with islands no doubt in conscious imitation of lake scenes in paintings. There is even a suggestion that the plantation of spruce and pine on the steep hill at the far end of the layout was intended to have a Salvatorial air. Here was a hermitage hidden deep in the dark woodland, which itself appeared to be wild, although it was in fact planted about 1750. It reminded Horace Walpole of Alpine scenery, and he designated it a 'forest or savage' garden[69].

Improvement

Both Hoare and Hamilton had shown great confidence in handling a whole landscape. Like-minded persons were called 'improvers', a term that had come into currency to describe agricultural improvers. As the distinction between agricultural and ornamental improvement was far from sharp, the term also came to include those who planted tree belts and clumps and erected new buildings in the landscape for purely ornamental reasons.

Richard Owen Cambridge teased improvers in *The World*[70], maintaining that they were constantly unsettling their visitors by talk of what is to be, and by enforced tours of alterations:

I remember the good time, when the price of a haunch of venison with a country friend was only half an hour's walk upon a hot terrace; a descent to the two square fish-ponds overgrown with a frog spawn; a peep into the hog-stye, or a visit to the pigeon-house. How reasonable was this, when compared with the attention now expected from you to the number of temples, pagodas, pyramids, grotto's, bridges, hermitages, caves, towers, hot-houses &c. &c.

One of the grandest schemes of improvement at this time was that in Windsor Great Park by William Augustus, Duke of Cumberland[71]. He moved to the Great Lodge as the recently appointed ranger in succession to Sarah Churchill, Duchess of Marlborough, between crushing the Young Pretender in 1746 and taking command of the campaign against the French in Flanders in 1747. His architect for various garden buildings was Henry Flitcroft. Attention was soon after turned to the southern end of the park. Large payments were made to Thomas Greening, a nurseryman, probably for the plantations installed on the brows of the hills overlooking the valley of a stream called the Virginia Water. In 1749 a dam was built to impound this stream.

As a concession to the rage for Chinoiserie a 50-ton ship's hulk was fitted up as a magnificent 'Mandarin Yacht', and a large Chinese pavilion erected on one branch of the lake. In 1752 Flitcroft built a triangular Gothic belvedere on a hill to the south called Shrubs Hill, overlooking the lake, and a single-arch

Palladian bridge over part of it about the same time. The dam was embellished by some of the earliest rockwork truly in the Natural Style: the cascade 20 feet in height was joined by a grotto in 1754. Although the various features around Virginia Water had parallels at Stourhead, the scale at the former was immense, as befitted the country's largest park. The lake was the largest artificial piece of water in its day, and the bridge had an unprecedented span of 165 feet. Thomas Sandby, the artist, became the Duke's deputy ranger in 1764.

The proprietors of the great country houses already with large formal gardens were, quite understandably, reluctant to alter them to the Natural Style at first, but by 1750 many were beginning to feel that they should. Wentworth Castle, in Yorkshire, was amongst the first to change. There was already a sham castle called Stainborough Castle on a prominent hill by 1730, and a Doric temple modelled on the Temple of the Sibyl at Tivoli had been started in 1739 on the far side of the park[72]. William Wentworth, fourth Earl of Strafford, succeeded in 1739, and by 1752 he had removed the avenue, gates and octagonal pool with fountain that lay in front of the house to create a long and graceful slope down to the bottom of the valley[73]. A lengthy canal was dug there that, with the aid of artfully placed groves of oak, really did look like a meandering river, and beyond the river on a low hill and backed by woods there stood the completed Tivoli temple.

Lord Petre had, together with Peter Collinson, been importing exotics from America via John Bartram, a Quaker farmer from Philadelphia, since the 1730s, while Archibald Campbell, third Duke of Argyll, had been amassing an extensive collection of citrus fruits and exotic conifers at Whitton Place, Middlesex, for 40 years before his death in 1761[74]. Other lords caught the enthusiasm of these two, and in 1740 Charles Lennox, second Duke of

24 Windsor Great Park, bridge over Virginia Water.

Paul Sandby made this engraving in 1754 from a drawing by his brother, Thomas. The huge Palladian bridge was built in about 1750 by Henry Flitcroft, and had parallels at Stourhead and Ditchley.

Richmond, Edward Howard, ninth Duke of Norfolk, and John Russell, fourth Duke of Bedford, joined them to add to their plantations at Goodwood, Worksop and Woburn respectively.

When Petre's collection of 219,925 trees, shrubs and evergreens was sold in 1746 many went to Goodwood and Woburn. Collinson built up his own substantial collection once he had moved to Ridgeway House at Mill Hill, Middlesex, in 1749, and acted for the Duke of Richmond at the sale of Petre's collection and subsequently, so that soon after the Duke's death in 1750 there were at Goodwood 'thirty different kinds of oaks, and four hundred different American trees and shrubs'[75]. Goodwood became particularly famous for its vast plantations of cedar.

Schemes of planting by lesser landowners were also underway at about the same time. Joseph Spence wrote to a friend in 1751 about St George's Hill, near his West Byfleet home in Surrey:

God help us, we live in the neighbourhood of one of the most dreary, sandy heaths in Europe ... All the hither line of it I have planted here and there with clumps of firs, which in a few years will make it part of my garden[76].

At first this planting was fairly modest, but Spence made plans for planting on many parts of the Oatlands estate for his patron, Lord Lincoln, and within a few years the whole face of the country around Weybridge and Byfleet was changing.

This was celebrated by Stephen Duck in *Caesar's Camp* (1755). The title alluded to the popular misconception that the Celtic fort on St George's Hill was Roman. The main part of the poem was spoken through the mouth of a Druid captured by Caesar's army who prophesied:

> I see those future times—I see, with joy,
> Those who can faster plant than thou destroy.
> Thy lamp, where now embattled legions shine,
> Shall bear the spreading beech and tow'ring pine.

Duck went on to speak of Spence at West Byfleet, Hamilton at Painshill, Cobham Park, Claremont, and Esher Place, Southcote at Woburn Farm, Lord Lincoln at Oatlands and numerous other places in the locality.

Caesar's Camp was amongst the earliest of the topographical poems celebrating the spirit of improvement in the latter half of the eighteenth century. Although often very exact topographically, such works were generally tepid as poetry. One such example is Richard Jago's *Edge-Hill*, published in 1767, but in preparation for many years previously. Jago was rector of Snitterfield, Warwickshire, a close friend of Shenstone, and an acquaintance of Sanderson Miller. The poem celebrated the limestone hills straddling Oxfordshire and Warwickshire, the most prominent of which is Edge Hill, and the rivers Avon and Cherwell that drain them.

The poem commences with thanks to Miller for his plantations along the brow of Edge Hill, his castle, and the walks and steps he laid out. Jago then progressed to the creation of the earth. He rejected the view that it was created flat, as Thomas Burnet had thought, and pointed out the signs of the violent creation of the earth in its first two days, and the subsequent modelling of the surface by the waters, and its vegetation, on the third. The flood in which Noah's family alone survived followed, and caused fossils to be formed and further earthquakes. This was an attempt to relate the new science of geology to the biblical story of the creation. Then Jago listed the country seats of note, including Wroxton, Compton Wynyates, Ragley, Warwick Castle, The Leasowes, Stowe, Newnham Paddox and numerous others.

In Leicestershire, the rector of Church Langton, William Hanbury, was making planting 'conducive to the Glory of God and the advantage of Society'[77]. His enthusiasm for planting and gardening had started in childhood and increased at university. In 1751, whilst only 26 and two years away from being rector, he had commenced extensive plantations. He had been in correspondence with the best English nurserymen and with contacts in North America to obtain seeds of the rarer plants. His intention was to raise capital from these plantations for philanthropic purposes, for example a hospital. In 1758, when his *Essay on Planting* was published, he gave the value of his plantations as £10,000, and he was apparently on his way to fulfilling his purpose.

Public regard to planting schemes like Hanbury's was growing, and before long found a means of expression in the Society of Arts[78]. This Society was founded in 1754 'for the Encouragement of Arts, Manufactures, and Commerce', and marked its admiration of technical achievement by awarding a monetary premium, a silver medal or a gold medal[79]. Very soon it offered premiums or medals for planting, and the first gold medal was awarded in 1758 to Henry Somerset, fifth Duke of Beaufort, for having sown 23 acres with acorns at Hawkesbury on the Badminton estate. Perhaps the greatest of the earliest achievements was Dennis Rolle's 101,394 Scots pine at Bicton House, Devon, for which he was awarded a gold medal in 1761[79].

25 Warwick Castle gardens from the south.

Francis Harding's painting of about 1760 shows the scattering of transplanted trees that replaced the walled gardens in 1749.

26   Warwick Castle Park, plan.

This reconstructed plan shows the park in about 1758. Lancelot Brown's style of clumps and belts is evident, although he did not remove all the old avenues.

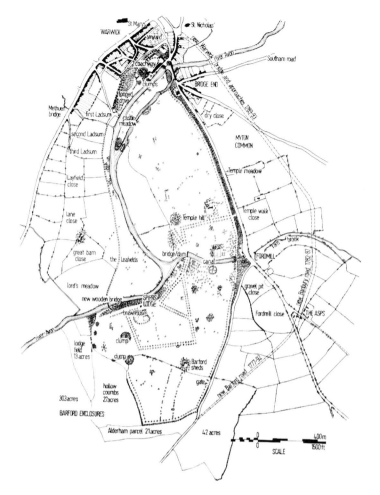

The time was right for a new type of ornamental gardener who could both operate on a large scale and who would keep the economic aspects of improvement in sight. One man quickly rose to the challenge. This was Lancelot Brown, Lord Cobham's head gardener at Stowe since 1741. Brown was not just a competent kitchen gardener, but had experience in improvement[80] and aptitude for it. Cobham was engaged in laying out Hawkwell Field and the Grecian Valley. Brown must have acquitted himself well enough in assisting with these works for Cobham to be happy to lend him to friends and relations to carry out their schemes. So, whilst still head gardener at Stowe, Brown assisted Richard Grenville in the early 1740s in the grounds at Wotton, Buckinghamshire, in making lakes in the grounds at Newnham Paddox, Warwickshire, in 1745, and at Wakefield Lodge, Northamptonshire, in 1748.

By 1749 Brown was receiving attention for his own sake, rather than as the executor of Cobham's schemes. He saw a lot of Sanderson Miller, both at Stowe and at Radway, and then two events occurred which precipitated him into conducting business on his own account. The first was Cobham's death in September, and the second was an invitation from Francis Greville, Baron Brooke, to lay out the gardens at Warwick Castle in the Natural Style. For this he was given workmen, a team of horses and a waggon, and in December he started to receive substantial payments for his pains rather than just gratuities[81].

Further commissions arrived in 1750: Packington Hall, Warwickshire, and then, through the agency of Sanderson Miller, Croome Court, Worcestershire, the seat of George William Coventry, Lord Deerhurst. Brown remained as head gardener at Stowe until the autumn of 1751, but then moved to Hammersmith near London.

Brown soon became very businesslike. When Sir James Dashwood decided late in 1751 to employ Brown to lay out Kirtlington, Oxfordshire, Brown drew up a plan and a contract. Similarly, when Charles Wyndham, second Earl of Egremont, expressed an interest, Brown went to Petworth, Sussex, in October 1751 with a surveyor in order to measure up for the plans he drew, and he charged all his expenses and a fee[82]. A contract followed in 1753. In this year Brown decided to try to put his continuing work at Warwick onto a more formal basis and persuaded Lord Brooke to sign contracts. This was to be the pattern of his work from now on. His clients knew from the plan what Brown was promising them, and knew from the contracts how much it would cost, and the certainty of it all may have suited the richer ones.

Brown was clearly very reliable and trustworthy once he had started a scheme. As his reputation spread, so did his business. Moor Park, Hertfordshire, for Lord Anson and Belhus, Essex, followed in 1753, followed by Burghley, Northamptonshire, in 1754, Longleat, Wiltshire, in 1757, and Wrest, Bedfordshire, in 1758, besides numerous smaller ones. By 1758 he was already the foremost layer out of grounds with a considerable body of satisfied customers and admirers. Some of these banded together in an unsuccessful attempt to obtain for him the post of Royal Gardener at Kensington Gardens as successor to Thomas Greening.

It would not be fair to attribute all his success to business acumen, for he certainly had an ability to comprehend the lie of the land quickly, and to see what it needed for ornament. He was the first professional designer since Vanbrugh and Switzer to think at the scale of a whole landscape, and this does not exclude William Kent, whose faltering use of clumps Brown much improved upon. He would have agreed with Richard Jago and Richard Owen Cambridge that the earth was created irregular and various, and that improvement should seek to return it to a state of nature. This meant the classically inspired abode of heroes and shepherds that Cobham had latterly striven for in grass and groves at Stowe, rather than wild and untamed Nature. Unavoidably, park landscapes by Brown were seen as the equivalent of Claude Lorrain paintings. Although Brown is not known to have had any connoisseurship in painting, nor a painterly approach to improvement[83], his supporters never tired of the comparison.

Brown had not been without rivals. The most formidable was Greening, whose experience and public position Brown could not at first match. Greening was a nurseryman in Brentford, Middlesex, at least from the late 1720s[84], and by 1738 he was the Duke of Newcastle's gardener at Claremont[85], where he would have come across William Kent. In 1738 he was appointed the Royal Gardener at Richmond Gardens in succession to Charles Bridgeman and in 1751 he took on Kensington Gardens and St James's Park as well. This meant that he was the Royal Gardener for all the Royal Gardens near the capital with the exception of Hampton Court, where George Lowe remained till his death in 1758. Moreover, Greening had some ambitious sons who were Brown's age and looked likely to succeed their father in his appointments.

Greening provided designs for gardens in addition to giving horticultural advice. He provided one for Kirtlington by 1746 and not long after one for Paul Methuen for Corsham Court, Wiltshire[86]. In 1753 his son Robert produced some alternatives for modifying the northern gardens at Wimpole[87]. These

27   Wimpole, design for
the gardens

Robert Greening's design of
about 1752 was essentially
a continuation of the style
popularized by Batty
Langley, but it shows some
influence of William Kent's
ideas.

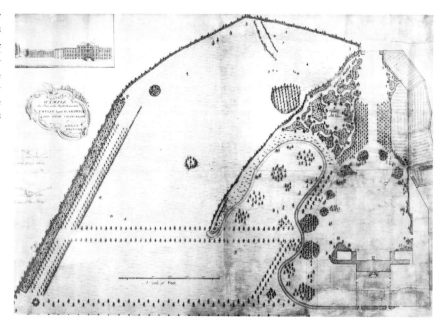

27   Wimpole, design for the gardens

showed that he favoured elaborate irregularity in his planting, although he
formed formal and symmetrical spaces and vistas with it. Brown's bolder
conceptions were a more convincing version of natural gardening, and it is not
surprising that they were favoured on merit. Sir James Dashwood preferred
Brown's ideas for Kirtlington very early in Brown's independent career, and
Methuen's successor at Corsham employed Brown from 1759. The Greenings
suffered a blow when both Thomas and his eldest son Thomas died in 1757[88],
but nevertheless, it must have been clear already to them that they could not
impede Brown's progress.

A second rival, Thomas Wright, had rather more claim to assuming Kent's
mantle than had either Greening or Brown, and succeeded him at Badminton
directly after his death[89]. If Wright had a profession it was astronomy, which
he taught to the aristocracy as a kind of working house guest. He added
architecture and garden design to his repertoire about 1742. He did design
some house fronts and even a Palladian villa, but his most noteworthy efforts
were his whimsical garden buildings. Like Kent he enjoyed the Gothic and
rustic styles. He designed a thatched, rustic, cold bath for the Marchioness Grey
at Wrest about 1748, an alcove for Shugborough slightly later, a root house
called 'The Hermit's Cell', a 'ragged castle', 'The Castle Barn' and other
buildings for the Duke of Beaufort at Badminton about 1750, a summer house
in miniature Gothic style for Sir Charles Sedley at Nuthall about 1754 and
numerous others. He published sets of six engravings of *Arbours* in 1755 and
Grottos in 1758.

Wright very often made suggestions for planting and handling water as well
as buildings at these places. He had no more fixed a style in laying out grounds
than he had in architecture. Some of his designs and sketches of arbours and
grottos show intimate scenes amongst complete irregularity. In other designs
he was like Spence and Greening in advocating irregular planting which was,
however, usually disposed axially and often with some degree of symmetry.
Lastly, as befits an astronomer, he could design a complicated geometrical
figure, as he did for a rosary at Beckett Park in the early 1750s.

Wright's most elaborate layout was for the remodelling of the woodland

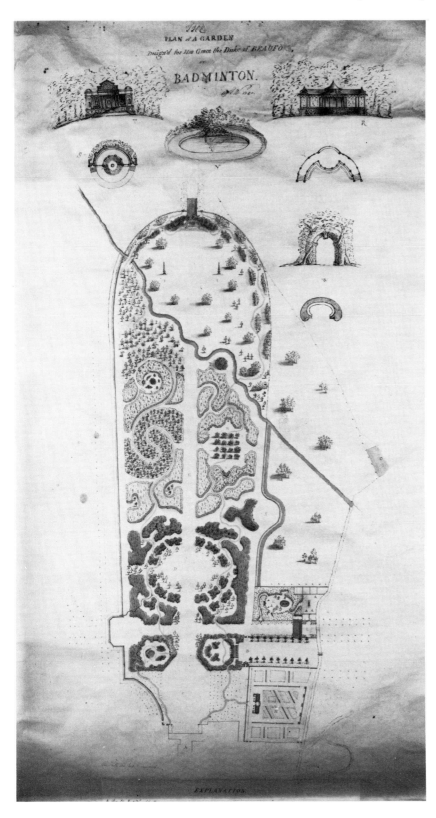

28 Badminton, design for the gardens.

Thomas Wright's drawing is dated 1750. The divergence between this layout, clearly made by art, and the ideas being developed at Stowe at the same date is marked.

garden opposite the east front of Badminton, the drawing for which is dated 1750. The side axis of the house was reflected in a vista down the length of the garden to a Doric Temple of Manly Fortune, and along it were an oval lawn surrounded by evergreens, some groves with highly contrived serpentine paths, and an open area with two obelisks ringed with small clumps at the end. Numerous features were incorporated into the layout such as a flower garden with a Chinese Temple for the Duchess, a rosary with a Gothic Temple, a 'magical grove' consisting of a grid of 16 clumps planted with such numbers of trees that the same number (34) could be counted in 14 different lines, a menagerie, arbours, and 'a variegated thicket of all the curious kinds of plants mix'd into the flowering Shrubs, Holyhocks, Heliotropes, &c'. The layout was unmistakeably a garden made by Art, and so although both Brown's and Wright's styles derived from Kent's, they mark entirely opposite tendencies.

Until 1762 Brown's only commissions north of the Trent were Chatsworth, Derbyshire, and Alnwick, Northumberland, both of which date from about 1760. Until that time the most respected voice in the north on laying out grounds was that of Joseph Spence, who was appointed prebendary of Durham Cathedral in 1754[90]. He took no money for his services but was willing to provide plans and advice to his bishop for the grounds of Bishop Auckland Castle in 1754, and for Raby Castle in 1755, besides continuing to assist his southern friends such as Robert Dodsley, the bookseller, at his home at Richmond, Surrey and Robert Montagu, third Duke of Manchester, at Kimbolton, Huntingdonshire, in 1757.

There was also a professional improver in the north in the 1750s. This was Francis Richardson, who drew at least half a dozen designs for places in and between Nottinghamshire and Northumberland in that decade. He would present a patron with a survey, and then with a plan showing his intended improvements, both drawn with exquisite draughtsmanship.

Richardson's early design style had much in common with that of Lord Petre, whose design for Worksop he had drawn out in 1738. However, his schemes approached Brown's style of belts and clumps as time progressed. An early one, Lowther, Westmorland, drawn for Sir James Lowther in 1754, shows the gardens remodelled into elaborate geometrical spaces and numerous winding paths through the dense surrounding woodland[91]. Terraces and bastions surround them. Long rectangular clumps and small round ones, like vast flowerbeds, alternate to form the new avenue and a cup shaped lawn in front of the house. The park behind the house was shown as dotted with irregularly placed clumps.

Richardson gave two designs for Hale, Lancashire[92], one involving replacing the house so that it would have better views of the sea. Both designs followed Brown's practice of setting the house in the parkland, rather than dividing house and park by a planted garden area, and used belts and clumps extensively. There was, however, a hint of the cup shape in the disposition of the parkland clumps. This last vestige of regularity was dispensed with in the design dated 1759 for Atherton, Lancashire[93]. Here the old avenues and walks were shown as entirely replaced by clumps, belts, natural looking woodland, and a sinuous lake with its ends curling round to lose themselves in plantations.

The Heyday of the Natural Style

Royal Patronage

The Whig political principles of liberty and free trade held by Lord Cobham and his nephews, Lord Temple of Stowe and his brother George Grenville, William Pitt and Lord Lyttelton, were buoyed up by a vision of Man in his perfect state—that is when living as a simple shepherd in some Arcadian free state. Nature herself was, by analogy, also perfected when complying with this vision. This was a metaphysical conception to which visual qualities such as texture, colour and contrasts were largely immaterial. Lancelot Brown was the practitioner *par excellence* of turning this conception into reality. His version of perfected Nature was flowing hills, capped with irregular groves, watered by serpentine rivers and emanating gentle serenity. His landscapes provided more of an intellectual atmosphere than a feast to the senses.

The attitude towards Nature that Brown represented did not go unchallenged. As might be expected, few Tories subscribed to them. Authors such as Dr Samuel Johnson and Dr Oliver Goldsmith were concerned with morals in a more down-to-earth way. They regarded the notions of liberty and patriotism as specious, hated wars fought merely to preserve free trade, and condemned the arrogance in turning out cottagers and tenants in order to fulfil some notion about improving Nature.

By the late 1750s the attitudes of the future George III to government was becoming clear. Under the strong influence of his mother, the Dowager Princess Augusta, he wanted to wrest power from the great Whig nobles and restore the royal prerogative. They found that the Tories were their natural allies, and it is not surprising that they differed from the Whigs in their interests in gardening too. Their chief adviser on political matters was John Stuart, third Earl of Bute. Coincidentally, Bute was a keen improver and botanist, as befitted a nephew of Archibald, third Duke of Argyll. He thus had a large hand in the improvements at Princess Augusta's home, Kew.

Kew had been leased by Prince Frederick in about 1731 as an already well-known garden under the care of John Dillman[1]. By 1736 William Kent had built Frederick and Augusta a Palladian mansion, and other building work and planting continued steadily thereafter. Frederick met Lord Bute in 1747. In 1750 Bute 'has already settled a correspondence in Asia, Africa, America, Europe and everywhere he can'[2] to fill a 300-foot hothouse at Kew then under construction. Despite the Prince's death in 1751 and Dillman's partial retirement in 1752, Bute continued to direct the improvements.

Bute was the chief patron and perhaps co-author with Dr John Hill in the publication from 1759 of *The Vegetable System*. Hill was a versatile but erratic character, trained as an apothecary. Despite being banned in 1744 from the Society of Apothecaries' physic garden at Chelsea for over-zealous taking of

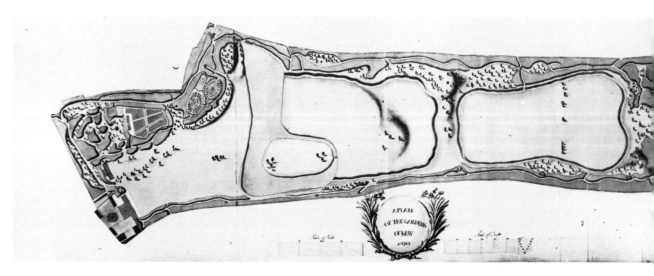

29   Kew Gardens, plan.

Despite William Chambers' liking for Chinese gardens, this plan of 1763 shows that the layout that he gave Princess Augusta was not very extraordinary except for the great number and variety of garden buildings.

cuttings[3], he worked for both Lord Petre and the Duke of Richmond in helping to establish their plant collections[4], and in 1751 he acquired his medical doctorate. He was a prolific author in a variety of subjects which included gardening.

His first notable book on this subject was *Eden* (1757). In this he advised his readers to set aside a flower garden in the Natural Style apart from the pleasure ground:

No edge becomes a Flower-piece like that of the Grass walk, and they never appear so well as when they follow Meander, and rise in little Clumps and Clusters. This, modern Taste has found . . .

Hill evidently shared Joseph Spence's taste for the beautiful wildness of Nature:

Let us again refer for the Rule of our Conduct to Nature, she is never so charming as where wildest. There is an easy Freedom and a pleasing Negligence in her Disposition, which charms because it is not regular.

In imitating Nature

It is an Air of Irregularity we advise, not irregularity itself; there requires more Art by far in this distribution than in any other; and there requires afterwards the great additional Labour of concealing it . . . Everything we see should be chosen for its place, though it seem the result of Accident.

He was also aware, presumably as a result of his contact with Lord Petre and his circle, of the value of autumn tints:

Good painters in Landscape call Autumn the most agreeable Season . . . it is one of those Beauties in Nature we can easily improve by chusing for this Plantation such as have the finest Tincts and the greatest Diversity of them.

This concern for the senses rather than the intellect was shared by William Chambers, another beneficiary of Bute's patronage. Chambers, a merchant's son, had been brought up in Sweden, and in his early twenties he visited Canton twice as an employee of the Swedish East India Company. He acquired a reputation as a sinologist and in 1749 was introduced to Prince Frederick as such[5]. He did not stay long in England, though, but spent the years 1750–55 in Rome studying classical architecture. Returning to London at the end of this period, he found little work, and so devoted his time to publishing his *Designs for Chinese Buildings* (1757). Samuel Johnson, who had a long-standing interest in Chinese customs and manners, contributed a few sentences at its beginning[6] to the effect that the Chinese are of interest as an entirely independent civilization.

A piece towards the rear of the book entitled 'Of the Art of Laying Out Gardens among the Chinese' received most interest. The most striking point (and perhaps the one that owed most to Chambers' own interpretation) was that the Chinese regarded a garden as a place to excite the emotions and senses. Chambers identified diversity and contrast as the two overriding themes, and categorized the scenes in Chinese gardens into three types. One scene might be 'enchanted', with strange plants, echoes, the sound of running water and so forth creating surprise and wonder in the beholder. Another might be 'horrid', with impending rocks, dark caverns, cataracts, misshapen trees, ruined buildings and huts indicating the wretchedness of the scene's inhabitants. This would be quickly followed by a 'pleasing' scene, where delicious contrasts of forms, colours and shades, and boundless prospects were heightened by being seen so soon after the 'horrid' scene. Chambers warned his readers against imitation of such a mode of gardening as it 'requires genius, judgement, and experience, strong imagination, and a thorough knowledge of the human mind'.

He also gave some interesting descriptions of common garden features, which are for the most part quite recognizable as typical of contemporary Chinese gardens. He mentioned how small many of the gardens were, and their emphasis on water. There were islands and rocks in most large pools, and the rivers were serpentine with hidden terminations. Where the situation permitted, the Chinese loved cascades of water and simple wooden bridges crossing roaring torrents. He also described how the Chinese treasured wave-worn rocks and made caves and grottoes out of the larger and less valuable ones.

The essay on garden design was instantly popular with editors and authors; it was published in the *Gentleman's Magazine* in May 1757, in the *Annual Register* in 1758, translated into French in 1757, and referred to obliquely or directly by numerous authors including Robert Dodsley and Henry Home, Lord Kames. The reason was that, whether Chambers' description of the intended effects upon the mind and imagination of the observer were authentic or not, a considerable body of opinion was moving towards examining the operation of the human mind for an explanation of beauty and the rules of taste.

The editor of the *Annual Register*, who had written about Chambers' article that it 'is much the best which has ever been written on this subject', was Edmund Burke, whose own *Philosophical Enquiry into the Origin of our Ideas of the Sublime and Beautiful* was published in 1756. This book made the case for the human mind being controlled by two predominant impulses—self-preservation and self-propagation, caused instantaneously by the sublime or the beautiful respectively. Obscurity, vastness, horror and terror were all attributes of the sublime. Astonishment, when 'all motions were suspended, with some degree of horror', was the reaction to the sublime in Nature. By contrast clarity, smallness, smoothness, and delicacy were attributes of the beautiful. Burke thought that

most people must have observed the sort of sense they have had, on being swiftly drawn in an easy coach, on a smooth turf, with gradual ascents and declivities. This will give a better idea of the beautiful, and point out its probable cause better than almost anything else[7].

Burke was a close friend of Johnson and Joshua Reynolds, and with others of their circle in 1764 they formed themselves into a club which came to be called 'The Literary Club'. The *Philosophical Enquiry* was ignored by Walpole, Lyttelton and other Whigs whose interest centred around Nature, but was well received by Johnson, who called it 'an example of true criticism'[8].

Certain passages in Hill's *Eden* (1757) showed that he was so persuaded by Burke's and Chambers's views on the emotional causes of beauty that he considered that:

there are in Nature objects of Disgust and Horror, which yet may be introduced happily; burnt Hills and blasted Heaths and barren Rocks and the wild waste of Commons afford a contrast . . . These objects therefore will be sure to please, but they must be introduced with a sparing Hand . . .

He considered that the artificial 'rock dell' at Goodwood, which seemed to be 'Rocks rent by an earthquake and earth sunk by a catastrophe', was 'the Sublime in Gardening; which as a late ingenious author had shown on other occasions, has its great source in Terror'[9].

Johnson's and Chambers' fascination with the Chinese way of life was shared by Hill, and by Johnson's admirer, Oliver Goldsmith. In one of his *Citizen of the World* letters, originally written in 1760 for a magazine called *The Public Ledger*[10], Goldsmith took up the question of laying out grounds. Writing as though he were a Chinese visitor, he commented that the English had begun to imitate Chinese gardens:

Yet still the English are far behind us in this charming art; their designers have not yet attained a power of uniting instruction with beauty. An European will scarcely conceive my meaning, when I say that there is scarcely a garden in China which does not contain some fine moral, couched under the general design, where one is not taught wisdom as he walks, and feels the force of some noble truth, or delicate precept, resulting from the disposition of the groves, streams or grottos.

He then proceeded to describe some imaginary 'gardens at Quamsi'. A walk leading from a house was bordered by impenetrable hedges, broken only by two gates. On the one hand there was the gate of Vice, made easy and alluring to enter. Beyond, the paths were gradually perplexed into a labyrinth in a horrid garden with impending rocks, heaps of unburied bones, terrifying sounds caused by unseen waters, and so forth, replacing the gay and luxuriant garden near the gate. On the other hand the gate of Virtue was decidedly uninviting, but the scene improved further on with beds of flowers, trees loaded with fruit or blossoms, and cascades, alongside the path which ascended to an arbour in the midst of a delightful scene with wide prospects. The moral, of course, was that the road to Virtue terminates in Happiness. The parallels with Jonathan Tyers's actual garden at Denbies are striking, and it is no coincidence that many of the descriptions of Denbies date from around this time.

Though Burke had no connection with Lord Bute, and indeed entered parliament as a Rockingham Whig in 1765, Chambers and Hill were both employed by Bute at Kew. Hill was asked to superintend the botanical garden[11] which was still expanding, and which in 1759 acquired a new head gardener in place of Dillman's successor, Robert Greening, who had died the year before. This was a young Scot called William Aiton who was sent from the Chelsea Physic Garden upon the recommendation of its director, Philip Miller.

Chambers was appointed architect to Princess Augusta in 1757. He had learnt how to be an excellent classical architect during his long training in Italy, and he was perhaps uneasy at being known for his attachment to the Chinese style. In the same year as his appointment at Kew he built the Kew

Orangery, and this, and the stables at Goodwood of about the same date, were in a restrained and noble classical style; so were the domed temples of Solitude, Eolus, Bellona, Victory and the Sun, all built at Kew in the next four years[12]. Anyone hoping that his task of converting the Kew estate to parkland and pleasure ground would produce horrid or enchanted scenes were disappointed.

Nevertheless there were certain characteristics of the Kew layout that distinguished it from Brown's work. Chambers treated it as a vast garden of over 100 acres (and indeed they were from the first called 'Kew Gardens') that was private and inward-looking. The land was flat and had uninteresting views, yet Brown would surely have tried to make something of them. Although its planting and lake were naturalistic, the chief delights of Kew Gardens were not Nature's, but frankly artificial. There were 25 separate garden buildings including the famous pagoda and other strange oriental ones. The botanical gardens and menagerie at the start of the circuit were laid out formally[13].

The improvements at Kew went ahead in earnest in 1759 when Princess Augusta acquired the freehold. A new 'Exotic Garden' was laid out in 1759 and 1760, being stocked by Aiton under Bute's and Hill's superintendence. In the same years the farmland was being improved, the lake dug and the plantations made under Bute's knowledgeable eye. Chambers was building the Ruined Arch, which served as a bridge to take livestock over the circumferential walk to the farmland, and various temples along the walk and on spoil raised from the lakes. Horace Walpole saw these improvements in late 1760 and wrote disparagingly:

There is little invention or Taste shown. Being on a flat, Lord Bute raised hillocs to diversify the ground, & carried Chambers the architect thither, who built some temples, but they are all of wood and very small[14].

Fortunately for Kew, the Duke of Argyll died in 1761 and many choice plants were moved there from Whitton[15]. Many of Argyll's most treasured trees were also transferred the next year[16], and more still upon the sale of the house in 1765. The exotics and trees at Kew were rapidly overtaking the Chelsea Physic Garden as the nation's foremost botanical collection, and in 1768 Hill made this obvious by publishing a catalogue called *Hortus Kewensis*, dedicated to Princess Augusta and classifying some 3400 species according to the Linnaean system. Chambers made sure that Kew Gardens attracted attention by publishing *Plans, Elevations, Sections and Perspective Views of the Gardens and Buildings at Kew* (1763).

The person to whom some recognition of his talents were due, but who was entirely ignored by the flurry of royal interest in Kew, was Brown. He had missed the appointment to Royal Gardener at Kensington in 1758. The Duke of Newcastle's dilatoriness ensured that John Greening was able to take over quietly from his father Thomas at both Kensington and Richmond, and John also took on Hampton Court on George Lowe's death in the same year[17]. On the accession of George III, the Kensington appointment was at last apportioned to Hill[18], and when John Greening gave up Richmond in 1762, Bute, who had the patronage as Prime Minister, gave it to a relatively unknown gardener called John Haverfield.

At last, though, Brown's opportunity came. In 1764 Bute had resigned as Prime Minister and his successor was George Grenville, a nephew of Brown's old employer at Stowe. The Greenings had probably not lost royal favour, as they were being paid for gardening works at Windsor up till this date[19], but it appears that Grenville was seeking one of John Greening's posts for Brown. It seemed at one time as if Brown would be given St James's, as Brown drew up a plan of intended improvements, probably in anticipation of this event. However he was soon after offered Hampton Court, which he took.

Royal Gardeners were expected only to maintain the royal gardens, and Brown's salary for this was £2000 per annum, out of which he had to pay the under-gardeners and the costs of gravel and plants. Besides the profit and the status of the Hampton Court post, though, Brown had greater satisfaction in his private business in 1764. Bute asked him to improve his 1200-acre park at Luton Hoo, Bedfordshire. Over the next ten years Brown gave him a 70-acre lake and vast plantations of beech and other species, many of which were supplied by Haverfield from Kew, on the surrounding hills. Also in 1764 the King asked him to alter Richmond Gardens to be suitable as a residence for himself and his new queen. This involved the destruction of most of Queen Caroline's works, including the notorious Merlin's Cave. This commission must have been especially satisfying, for not only did it mark the highest point to which he would aspire in his private business, but he quickly came to be liked and admired by his sovereign.

Lancelot Brown and his Pupils

Brown had won some notable commissions in the mid- and late-1750s, but during the 1760s it seemed as though every nobleman's place in the land must submit to his improving hand. In or about 1760 he started on Chatsworth: Ashridge, Hertfordshire; Alnwick: and Syon, Middlesex. Bowood, Wiltshire, followed in 1761, Gatton Park, Surrey, in 1762, and Navestock, Essex, and Lowther, Westmorland, in 1763. In 1764 there was the triple success of Blenheim, Luton Hoo and Richmond, so that Brown then counted the King, four Dukes and scores of other lords amongst his clients[20].

His commissions varied very much in scale; some like that for the actor David Garrick at Hampton in 1757 was for a mere villa and worth only a few hundred pounds, whilst his improvements to Blenheim between 1764 and 1774 cost George Spencer, fourth Duke of Marlborough, a total of £21,500.

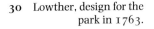

30   Lowther, design for the park in 1763.

This design for Lowther of 1763 was typical of the plans that Lancelot Brown was producing at the height of his career.

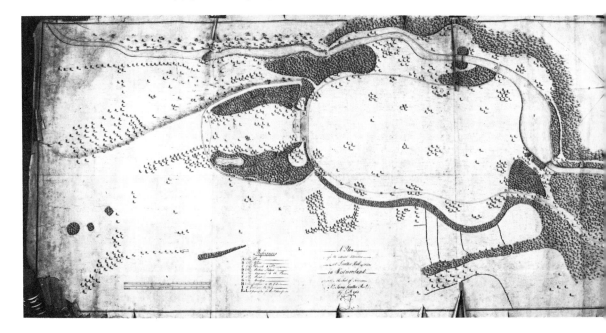

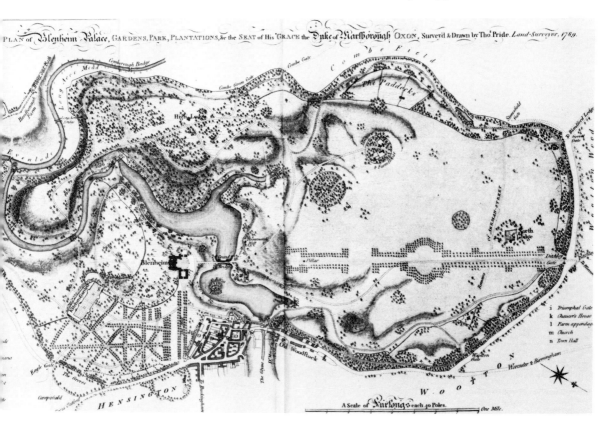

PLAN of Blenheim Palace, GARDENS, PARK, PLANTATIONS, &c the SEAT of His GRACE the Duke of Marlborough OXON, Survey'd & Drawn by Tho. Pride. *Land-Surveyor*, 1789.

Blenheim was a royal hunting park until Queen Anne gave it to the Duke of Marlborough. At 2120 acres, it was one of the largest parks in the country. Only other royal hunting parks, i.e. Windsor (3700 acres) and Richmond New Park (2250), and a handful of others were larger. It dwarfed such early examples of the Natural Style as the gardens of Stowe (250 acres) and Painshill (323 acres). However, Brown was becoming used to designing at such a vast scale through his commissions at Alnwick, Bowood and Luton Hoo. Very large ornamental parks were becoming highly prized, not only because the Natural Style had most scope at this scale and was producing some notable new landscapes, but because such acreages suggested an owner's status in the country. It became common for visitors to be informed how far round a park was, and most were duly impressed.

Although Brown visited numerous places without receiving commissions, he probably improved about 100 places in 35 years of business, and over 20 of these were worth over £3000. The bulk of these commissions, both in terms of the number and their value, were given in the 15 years from 1758 to 1773. Further valuable ones between 1764 and 1773 were Thorndon, Essex, in 1766; Wimpole, Cambridgeshire, in 1767; Ditton Park, Buckinghamshire, and Compton Verney, Warwickshire, in 1768; Fisherwick, Staffordshire, and Claremont, Surrey, in 1770; Combe Abbey, Warwickshire, in 1771; and Harewood, Yorkshire, in 1773.

Apart from the one outstanding case of Highclere, Hampshire, for which Brown supplied the plan but the owner, Henry Herbert, carried out the scheme himself, all Brown's commissions followed the business arrangements which he had established in the 1750s. He would visit a place, charging 10 guineas

31　Blenheim, plan.

The plan was engraved for William Mavor's guide-book of 1789. Lancelot Brown's lake was the object of great admiration.

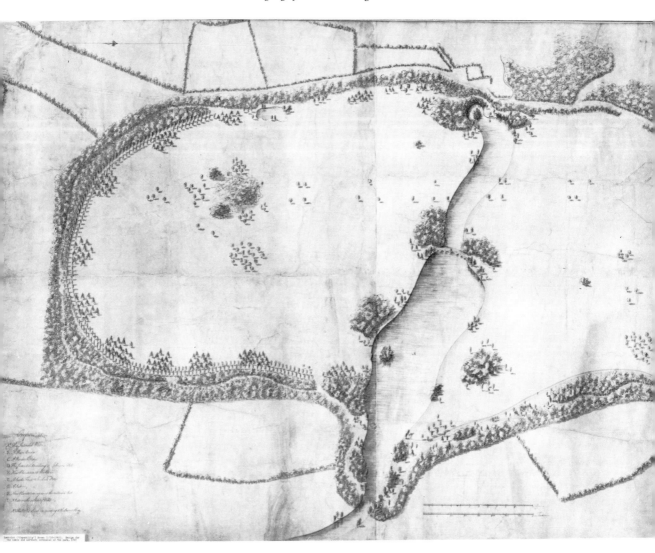

per day, to determine the outlines of his scheme. These brief visits caused his bemused clients to nickname him 'Capability' in about 1760, by way of reference to Brown's frequent and enthusiastic use of the word. Brown required the assistance of a surveyor who would follow him to measure the land, a draughtsman to help him with the drawings, and, if he obtained the commission, a foreman to oversee the work day-to-day.

It is not clear who were Brown's assistants before 1764. All drawings went out signed by 'L.B.', although Brown's strong point was not drawing[21], and he probably did few finished drawings himself. Only one assistant is known about for certain; he was Robert Robinson, who seems to have left Brown in 1760 to go and set up in business as an improver in Edinburgh[22].

Robinson was the third of three brothers. The eldest, William, was in the Board of Works. He was a clerk of works with responsibility for Whitehall and St James's till 1766, and was then Secretary and Clerk Itinerant. In this capacity he reprimanded an indignant Brown in 1770 for the standards of upkeep at Hampton Court[23]. The middle brother, Thomas, succeeded where Brown had failed in obtaining the post of Royal Gardener at Kensington and St

James's in succession to John Greening and John Hill. Robert laid out the grounds of Duddingston House, near Edinburgh, for which William Chambers was the architect, and numerous other places in Scotland from 1761 till eventual bankruptcy in 1782. As might be expected, his styles of design and draughtsmanship proved to be very similar to Brown's, which were not always appropriate in the more rugged Scottish countryside. Nevertheless he was the only improver in the Natural Style working in Scotland at the time, and was also the first of many English improvers to practise on any scale outside England.

In 1764 Brown took on a surveyor and draughtsman called John Spyers and the next year another called Samuel Lapidge, both of whom were frequently to be found travelling from place to place to measure the land. Spyers, at least, seems to have been a competent draughtsman in water colours[24], whilst Lapidge may have been one of the two sons of William Lapidge who was recommended to Sir William Lee for the position of head gardener at Hartwell, Buckinghamshire, in 1759[25]. Brown undertook some architectural work, usually in association with Henry Holland, his close friend and neighbour at Hammersmith, and in 1771 he took on Holland's son, also Henry, as his architectural assistant.

Then there were the numerous foremen. They were the key to Brown's financial success, and he would try to re-employ trusted ones when their work at one place was ended. Hence Benjamin Read, who had been at Croome in the 1750s, was entrusted with Blenheim in 1764. He was still working for Brown in 1772, for in that year Lord Coventry asked for the return of Read so that he could repair a leak in the lake's dam. Another trusted man was William Ireland, who was taken off Burghley in 1767 to work at Luton Hoo and who also worked at Trentham, Staffordshire. Then there was Andrew Gardiner, who worked on Temple Newsam and Sandbeck, both in Yorkshire, in 1764 and 1767 respectively, but who applied in 1770 for the position of head gardener with John Campbell, third Earl of Breadalbane, who was then making extensive plantations at Taymouth in Perthshire[26]. However, Gardiner was back with Brown in 1775 to carry out the improvements at North Stoneham in Hampshire.

Michael Milliken was perhaps unusual in staying on at one place after the works were finished. Brown recruited this young Scot from Chatsworth in 1765 to be foreman of the improvements at Richmond, and Milliken seems thereafter to have entered the King's employ.

Although he maintained a modest lifestyle, Brown was nevertheless quite wealthy. In 1767 he acquired the manor of Fenstanton, Huntingdonshire, for £13,000, and was able to offer half as a down payment. He set the seal on becoming a landed gentleman by becoming the High Sheriff of Huntingdonshire for 1770. He saw to it that his eldest son, also Lancelot, went to Eton and then to Lincoln's Inn to become a barrister.

With all the Greenings but John dead[27], Brown's only serious rival might have been Thomas Wright. However, Wright returned to his childhood home at Byers Green, in County Durham, in 1767[28]. Thereafter he restricted his designing for others to Badminton and Stoke Gifford, also in Gloucestershire, the seat of Lord Botetourt, the Duchess of Beaufort's brother.

There was, though, one other project to which Wright turned his attention: the projected metropolitan palace for George III. In 1766 Wright presented some plans of St James's Park illustrating an extraordinary layout. The gradually tapering space between the Mall and Birdcage Walk was to be planted symmetrically with numerous shrubberies and the canal was to be transformed into an egg-shaped basin. The over-elaborate geometry was such

32 Wimpole, design for the northern park.

The circumferential belt and drive are conspicuous on this design of 1767 by Lancelot Brown. Brown built the mock castle designed by Sanderson Miller years before (see Fig. 16).

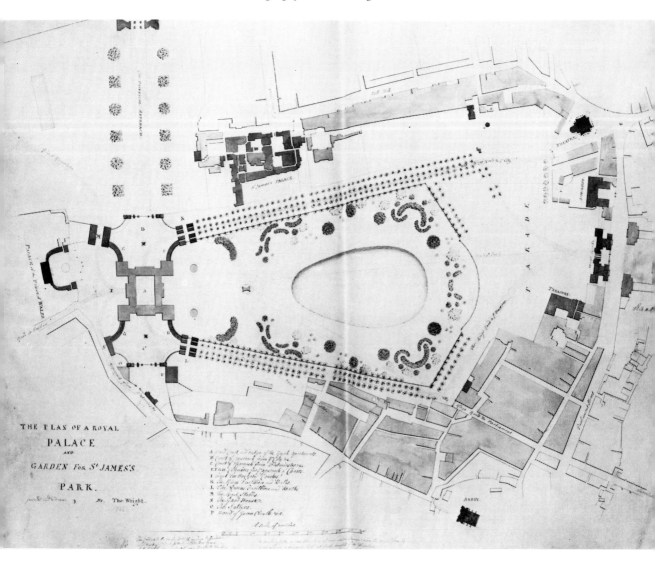

33   St James's Park, design for a palace.

Thomas Wright made this design for gardens to be attached to a new palace in 1766. The symmetry and shaped flower and shrub beds were very idiosyncratic for this date.

a direct contradiction to the prevailing Natural Taste that it can never have been taken seriously.

Wright had a namesake, Stephen Wright, working for Lord Lincoln at Oatlands at this time. Lincoln succeeded as second Duke of Newcastle in 1768 and resolved to build himself a Palladian mansion on his newly acquired estate at Clumber, Nottinghamshire. Stephen Wright started building it in 1770, and set it in a vast grass sward uninterrupted save by the lengthy canal made in 1774 by damming a nearby brook.

If Brown's old rivals had fallen away, there were plenty of new ones eager to share in his prosperity. The first of these was Richard Woods, a nurseryman, who had bought his own nursery at Chertsey in Surrey in 1751[29]. He was, though, already known to Joseph Spence by 1749 when he gave him a design for fencing and a planting plan for a circumferential belt[30]. The latter was extremely similar to Philip Southcote's belt at Woburn, only a few miles away, and Woods's later renown for attractive mixes of species in his plantations makes some connection to the circle of Southcote and Lord Petre probable.

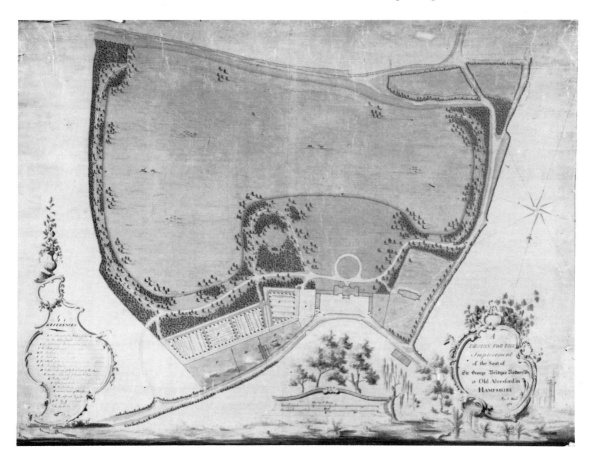

In 1759 Woods was fulfilling a large order to Sir William Lee of Hartwell and the next year supplied a design costing 12 guineas which was for the new garden, greenhouse and pinery. In 1760 Woods was in Yorkshire laying out Cannon Hall Park on behalf of one of Sheffield's leading ironmasters[31]. Planting and three lakes which were very much in Brown's style followed. In 1761 Woods was at Cusworth Hall, also in Yorkshire, to lay out much the same, and in 1764 he was paid for 'setting out grounds' at Harewood in Yorkshire[32].

Woods was finding much work in the south of England. His plan dated 1764 for Old Alresford, Hampshire[33], was accepted by Admiral George Rodney, and the year after he received the commission to lay out the grounds of the Priory at Hatfield Peverall in Essex, the first of numerous commissions in that county[34]. In the late 1760s he rented North Ockenden Hall in Essex, and in 1771 he sold his nursery in Chertsey. He was by now sufficiently renowned for Lancelot Brown to entrust the creation of the Large Pond at Belhus, Essex, to him in 1770[35]. A remote work was at Wardour Castle, Wiltshire. He had designed greenhouses and garden buildings at other places before, but here he turned his hand to more substantial architecture in addition to the plantations. Henry, the eighth Baron Arundell, invited Brown to see his plantations between the castle and the house in 1773, and the following anecdote found its way into a Bath guidebook:

between this edifice and the house, the ground is broken by plantations, suggested by Mr. Wood, of Essex, the judiciousness of which Brown himself had the taste to admire[36].

34 Old Alresford, design for the grounds.

Richard Woods' plan of 1764 shows the influence of Lancelot Brown's system.

Woods' drawings were often notable for their elaborate cartouches.

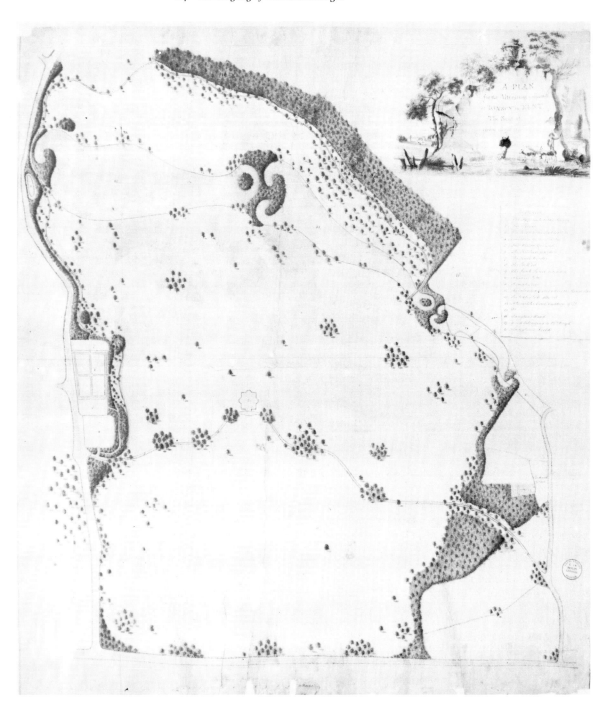

35   Danson, the grounds.

Possibly the design by Mr
Richmond seen by Joseph
Spence in 1763. Taking the
drives through clumps is an
interesting feature.

Some of the new improvers turned to improvement only occasionally and as
a sideline to their main business as surveyors or nurserymen. For example,
James Sanderson, a surveyor and nurseryman of Caversham, laid out the park
in front of Claydon House, Buckinghamshire, for about £3400 between 1763
and 1776[37], but, as far as is known, he did not lay out anywhere else. Three
other improvers, though, had long and successful careers.

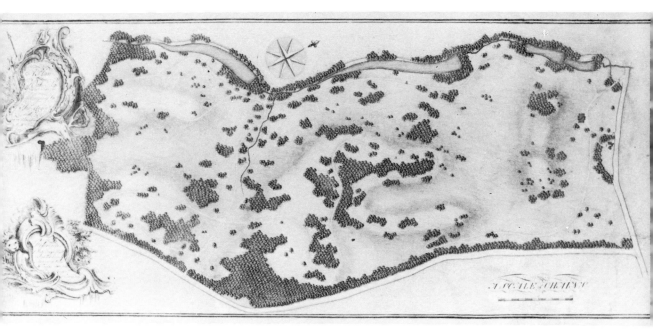

One was a certain Mr Richmond whose plan for Danson park in Kent was put before Joseph Spence in 1763 for comments[38], and who was making the water of 35 acres at Shardloes in Buckinghamshire[39], and working at Stanmer, Sussex[40], a few years later. In 1769 Richmond was improving Saltram, Devon, the seat of John Parker, through a foreman called Henshaw. Evidently he could turn his hand to garden buildings for Parker's sister-in-law remarked in 1772 that her sister

36 Oakedge, design for the park.

The carefully drawn plan by William Emes is dated 1771. It shows very sinuous carriage drives and remarkably natural planting.

is ... fully resolved not to let another year slip but [to plant] the whole top of the Hill immediately without waiting for Mr Richmond who has neglected it these three years. I believe the real reason is because he has not the building of the Castle.

The Castle, an octagonal turret, was being built around that time at the end of a natural terrace overlooking Plymouth Sound. There was disappointment to Richmond over the orangery as well: this was built in wood by a local wood carver and carpenter using one of his designs.

Whereas Richmond's work was all in the south of England, William Emes operated almost entirely in the Midlands and the Welsh borders during his early career. He was appointed the head gardener at Kedleston, Derbyshire[41]. In 1760 Nathaniel Curzon, soon to be created Earl of Scarsdale, began building a new house, which, when it was finished by Robert Adam, was one of the most magnificent in the Midlands. No doubt Emes learnt the business of an improver in creating a setting to complement the house. In 1764 he was invited to Chirk Castle, Denbighshire, to advise on improvement. He undertook a survey in 1767, which resulted in a considerable alteration of highways in the area, and by 1771 the scheme was fully underway and Chirk Castle's magnificent iron gates had been moved from the forecourt[42]. In 1766 Emes started a long association with the alterations of Erddig, Denbighshire, where a substantial section of the older formal gardens was permitted to remain.

At the same time Emes was finding commissions in Staffordshire and Cheshire. Alterations were underway to the parks at Keele in 1767 and Crewe

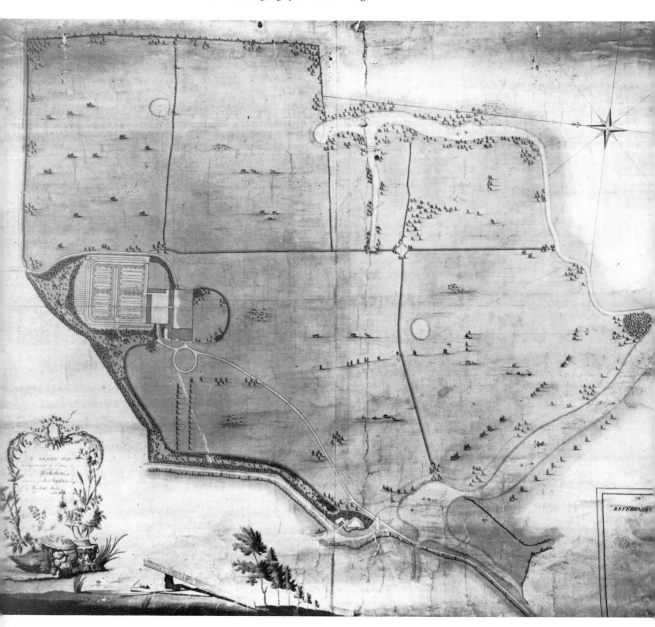

37   Carlton, design by Richard Woods.

This disappointing design kept old field lines and suggested a detached lake with a boat and Chinese bridge. Thomas White's design (Fig. 38) was preferred. North is to the left.

in 1769, and in 1771 he made a survey of Oakedge, adjacent to Shugborough. Oakedge was soon after purchased by Thomas Anson and laid out to a plan of Emes'. His style was very much like Brown's, and it seems from the considerable success that he quickly began to enjoy that he was an acceptable alternative to Brown for landowners in North Wales, Shropshire, Staffordshire, and Derbyshire. Brown may have been reluctant to operate in these parts of the country unless the commission was important. This would explain why, despite the numerous commissions in Staffordshire in the early 1760s, Brown's commissions in these places in the early 1770s were usually for the nobility, as at Trentham and Fisherwick, whilst Emes obtained his commissions mainly from the gentry.

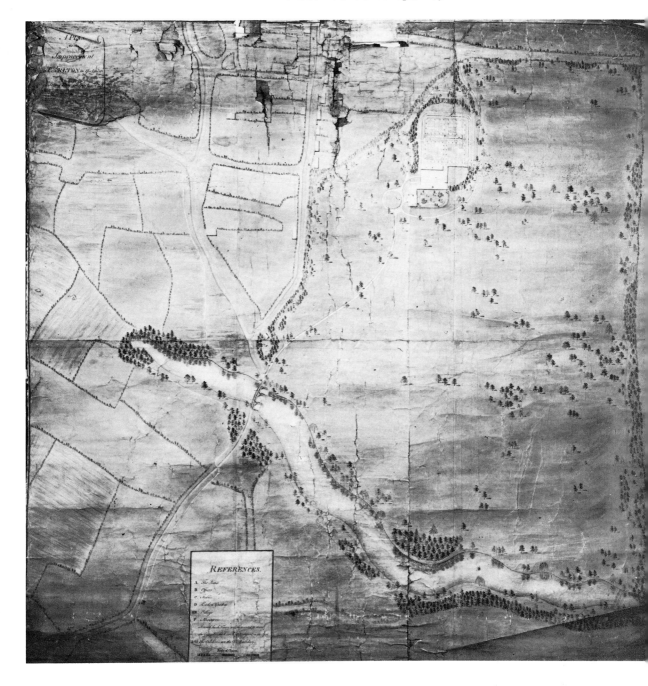

Yorkshire's equivalent to Emes was Thomas White. He was associated with Brown in the early 1760s, but seems to have been far more independent than Brown's other foremen. Brown had been at Harewood in 1758 but seems not to have entered into a contract for its improvement until 1772. In the meantime Woods was there in 1764, but the next year he was replaced by White[43]. Unfortunately White showed a greater enthusiasm for planting than the owner, Edwin Lascelles, could tolerate. White and the foreman, Sparrow, had made extensive plantations around the new Harewood House and

38   Carlton, design by Thomas White.

Though a cruder drawing than Richard Woods' (Fig. 37), White's design of 1765 suggests a more convincing river and more extensive parkland. North is upwards.

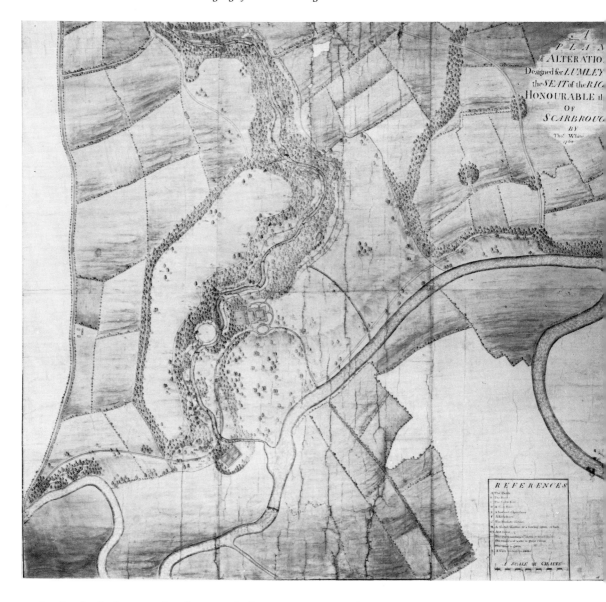

39   Lumley Castle, design
for the grounds.

Thomas White's design is
dated 1768. The gardens,
rides and seats along the
wooded dell behind the
castle would have been
especially attractive.

elsewhere and the nurseryman's bill was £90, for which White was
reprimanded. White's work at Burton Constable in the East Riding from 1768
also followed a visit by Brown some years earlier, and preceded Brown's more
formal involvement in 1773.

White began picking up work that had no connection with Brown. In 1765
both he and Woods submitted plans of improvement in the style of Brown to
Thomas Stapleton for the grounds at Carlton in Yorkshire[44]. Wood's plan was
similar to his plan for Cusworth in that the old avenue and several field
boundaries were kept, but the intended river at Carlton was a most
extraordinary shape. White obtained the commission. There were other
commissions in Yorkshire, Nottinghamshire and County Durham, but White's
largest projects took him far north into Scotland. His penchant for large scale
planting schemes was given full scope by James Duff, second Earl of Fife, and
Francis Stuart, ninth Earl of Moray.

Fife had succeeded to his father's estates in Banffshire, Moray and Aberdeenshire in 1763. He began extensive plantations at his principal residence, Duff House, which was just outside the town of Banff and alongside the River Deveron. White assisted at some stage in laying out these plantations[45], as he did the Earl of Moray's at Darnaway, in Elgin, begun in 1767[46]. The plantations at both places were overwhelmingly Scots pine, though with some oak and beech as well. White's profits from this variety of projects were such that in 1773 he was able to purchase a large block of recently enclosed moorland at Butsfield, in Lanchester parish, County Durham[47], and move home to The Grange at West Retford, Nottinghamshire. He and the other new improvers were indeed sharing some of Brown's prosperity.

Improving One's Own Place

Despite the increasing availability of professional improvers there were still many owners that were dedicated enough to take the trouble and risks in laying out their grounds by themselves. William Shenstone and Charles Hamilton, whose gardens were already famous by George III's reign, continued with their own improvements and were an inspiration to those just starting.

The Leasowes' lasting fame was assured when Robert Dodsley and Joseph Spence stayed for a week in 1758. Shenstone and Spence found they had much in common[48], and the former erected a seat with an inscription on it around an oak tree of Spence's choice to mark the occasion. Spence wrote a description, in which the proliferation of seats, urns and composed 'pictures' is made apparent. However, it was Dodsley who wrote the first printed description. It appeared in the second volume of Shenstone's collected works.

Ironically, though, Shenstone's works appeared after his death in 1763. He had been to see Henry Grey, fourth Earl of Stamford, at nearby Enville, Staffordshire, to see about a government pension such as Samuel Johnson had just acquired from the Bute administration. However he caught a cold on the way back which turned into a fever and soon carried him off. Not all his visits to Enville had been in vain though, for he had helped the Earl with a number of small improvements on the estate. Stamford dedicated one of these, a chapel set in a remote part of the estate, to the unfortunate poet.

Shenstone's ruinous expenditure in improvements unfortunately had a political moral that clouded the judgements of many. Tories such as Samuel Johnson and Oliver Goldsmith had no fundamental objection to Shenstone beautifying The Leasowes; indeed Johnson praised his skill highly, and approved of 'what for several years employed him in a most harmless manner'[49]. However, here was a man with an annual income of barely £300 who spent so much on his cherished earthly plot that his heirs had to sell it to pay the debts. Johnson described Shenstone as 'a lamp that spent its oil in blazing'.

Goldsmith returned there in 1773 and was saddened to see how it had been treated since Shenstone's death. He wrote that the genius of the place had explained:

You see before you, the paternal inheritance of a poet; and to a man content with little, fully sufficient for his subsistence: but a strong imagination and a long acquaintance with the rich are dangerous foes to contentment[50].

He then described how Shenstone's urge for improvement had exceeded good sense, and how 'the first idea of its beauties contributing to the happiness of his life was found unfaithful'.

Goldsmith liked the way that, 'Every urn was marked with the poet's pencil, and every walk awakened genius and meditation'. It was near enough to what he had advocated in describing the imaginary moral garden at Quamsi. However, to those committed to the notion that Nature is a painter, The Leasowes was old-fashioned in that its enjoyment required the association of sentiments with places.

William Gilpin, visiting in 1772, thought that Shenstone had been untrue to Nature in creating too many pools:

In the use of water he has been too profuse. He collects it only from a few springs, which ouze from his swampy grounds. It was a *force therefore on Nature*, to attempt either a *river*, or a *lake* . . . Besides, like the water of all swamps, the water of the Leasowes wants brilliancy . . .[51].

He had 'done *too much* also in adorning his grounds so profusely with urns, statues, and buildings', whereas 'he might have thrown down more of his hedges' and his 'great deficiency lay in not draining, and cleaning his grounds'. On the other hand Shenstone 'has diversified his views very much', and 'it would be invidious not to own, that his cascades, rocks, and streams are all as exact copies of nature, as we anywhere find'—points with which almost every visitor, sympathetic or not, agreed.

London and its Environs (1761) described Painshill as 'but newly laid out', although a few finishing touches were still being added such as the Temple of Bacchus built to house a statue of that god that Hamilton had bought in Italy. Spence recorded about this time that Hamilton

directed and oversaw all the operations, both in the buildings and gardens; would not have the same to go through again for the world[52].

Painshill's most famous embellishment, its grotto, was yet to come, though.

One of Hamilton's nieces had married Alderman William Beckford, whose West Indian sugar plantations gave him one of the largest incomes in the country. This, and a fire that destroyed the old mansion at his Wiltshire estate, Fonthill, in 1755, spurred him into building a vast new Palladian mansion and laying out extensive improvements[53]. These included a lake more than a mile long in full view of the house and encircled by various buildings, gardens and lawns. A later tourist guide described the contribution of

Mr Lane, who exhibited the earliest specimen of his talents in the construction of a grotto, on a very small scale, at Fonthill . . . The structure was formed of *tumblers* found near the spot[54].

This man was Joseph Lane, from Tisbury, two miles away. He was instructed to make alterations as the grotto was too formal, and, along with some planting, it turned out satisfactorily. Extensive plantations of Scots pine on higher land to the west earned the alderman a gold medal from the Society of Arts in 1769. The alderman had no skill in such matters, and it looks as if he was receiving advice from Hamilton.

Whilst this is not certain, Hamilton was certainly impressed with Lane's work, for in about 1761 he was employing him to build a grotto on an island in the lake at Painshill[55]. In 1765 William Gilpin saw the first stage, but described it as

a whimsical little object, procured at a great expense. It is trifling and unnatural on the spot.

One can understand Gilpin saying that it was unnatural: it was built on the outside with tufa, a limestone that was pitted and perforated with irregular holes, and on the inside the plastering battens were formed into numerous spikes to give an extravagant number of stalactites suspended from the roof, covered all over in calcite crystals and other minerals. Although, like Alexander Pope's grotto, the sparkling interior gave a stunning effect, it was quite unlike anything found in Nature. Neither had the tufa exterior any precedent in nature. It was probably Hamilton's version of the Chinese rock compositions that had been illustrated for Western eyes a century before in Nieuhof's *An Embassy to China* (1669).

Bearing in mind Hamilton's strange Gothic temple, the Turkish tent and the diversity of types of planting, one can see that he did not have the same regard for keeping faith with Nature as Gilpin had. Nor would there be anything extraordinary in a Chinese grotto, apart from the circumstance that it was the first ever attempted outside China. As at Kew, the assembling of Painshill's beauties into one huge pleasure ground showed great invention, rather than submission to the genius of the place.

Hamilton's friend, Mary Fox, leased Holland House from 1746, and asked

40 Painshill, plan of the grotto.

The Swedish architect Fredrik Piper made this sketch in 1780. The highly irregular interior and the close connection with the lake can be seen.

for help in laying out its grounds. Between 1750 and 1756, Hamilton planted American trees, various oaks and cedars.

but the greatest proof of his discernment and taste is to be found in a green walk, which, originally an open lane, was at his suggestion turfed, and ornamented ... This verdant glade would have satisfied the fancy of Spenser, when composing his Fairy Queen[56].

Although Hamilton could help others, he was quite unable to save himself financially. He had overstretched himself in building the grotto and a tile-making enterprise failed, and so Painshill was on the market in 1771[57]. By 1773 Hamilton was a resident of Bath. Meanwhile Lane was launched on a career as a grotto builder. He worked on the famous Oatlands grotto with his son Josiah from 1774 to 1778 to embellish it.

Another of the doyens of private improvement had to sell up at the same time as Hamilton; Valentine Morris found himself obliged to return to his estates in Antigua[58], but Piercefield had already spawned other gardens that offered sublime scenery. A rich young Bristol Quaker called Thomas Farr was so impressed that in 1762 he purchased his own gorge, that of the Hazel Brook, at Henbury, nor far outside Bristol[59]. Although not of such overwhelming dimensions as the gorge of the River Wye at Piercefield, Farr's was wooded too, and had several crags, and the confining hills had extensive views. He built a tower, which he called Blaise Castle, on the summit of one of the hills, laid out walks around the woods, built a Root House alongside one of them, and thinned the foliage at points to reveal the most striking points of the view.

At Stowe the Bridgeman layout was continually being softened as the unclipped trees grew. Further buildings and arches, many to the design of William Pitt's young nephew Thomas, were still being added[60]. Pitt himself maintained his interest when he moved to Hayes Place, near Bromley, Kent, soon after 1754. This was despite being Secretary of State and having direction of the Seven Years War. By purchasing adjoining property he built up the grounds to about 100 acres, which he took great interest in improving, even

planting by torchlight, as his peremptory and impatient temper could brook no delay[61].

In 1765 a country gentleman, unknown to Pitt but a great admirer of his, left him his estate at Burton Pynsent in Somerset. Pitt had Brown erect a column to honour his benefactor, and it seemed that he would move there. He sold Hayes Place, but on changing his mind he persuaded the purchaser to sell him back his beloved home.

Walpole's practical interest in laying out grounds during the 1760s concentrated upon the encouragement of his cousin Henry Seymour Conway at Park Place, in Berkshire[62]. Park Place was on a high hill overlooking the constricted Thames Valley and opposite Henley-on-Thames. Not far round the hill there was a combe, across the bottom of which Conway was building a Cyclopean bridge in 1763 so that he could have direct access to the river whilst the public highway passed overhead. At the same time he was fitting up a nearby cottage with a Chinese interior to be a retreat. At the head of the combe James Stuart designed a ruined Greek colonnade, behind which a 170-yard tunnel ran through the hillside to nearer the house. At the house end an extensive grotto was built of flint.

Walpole wrote:

The works at Park Place go on bravely; the cottage will be very pretty, the bridge sublime, composed of loose rocks that appear to have been tumbled together there, the very wreck of a deluge.

A young rector of a nearby parish, Mr Powys, who

> To Nature, in my earliest youth,
> I vow'd my constancy and truth,

wrote a lengthy poem at the cottage in 1766 which appeared in *The Scots Magazine*. Despite Conway's lack of obvious regard for Nature, Powys assumed that he had responded to Nature the painter:

> Whether by contemplation led,
> The rich romantic wild I tread ...
> Or whether, from yon wood-crown'd brow,
> I view the lovely vale below:
> For when, with more than common care,
> Nature had stretch'd the landscape there,
> Her Conway caught the fair design,
> And soften'd ev'ry harsher line;
> In pleasing lights each object plac'd,
> And heighten'd all the piece with taste.

Seven years later Conway found himself flattered for his practical skills in improvement. Richard Weston, an agriculturalist from Leicestershire, dedicated his *Tracts on Practical Agriculture and Gardening* (1773) to him on the following pretext:

Sir, your accurate knowledge of the subjects attempted to be discussed in this work, and that elegant taste, with which you have cultivated one of the most pleasing seats in the kingdom, are more than sufficient to indicate the presumption which induces me to offer you the fruits of my leisure hours.

These *Tracts* had first been issued anonymously in 1769 but now appeared under Weston's name. They are unremarkable except for two matters. First, the 1773 edition included the first attempt at a bibliography of gardening, entitled 'A Chronological List of English Authors on Agriculture, Botany and Gardening'. Second, they strongly advocate planting.

A shipbuilder from Liverpool, Roger Fisher, had urged the same when he published letters from shipbuilders up and down the country in 1763. In 1771 he was called to a House of Commons Committee, and this resulted in an Act to encourage the planting of timber on commons and wastes[63]. As if to remove the last impediments on practical grounds, the Rev. William Hanbury offered the benefit of his wisdom to all in a series of cheap weekly pamphlets running from 1769 till 1773. When bound up they had the title *A Complete Body of Planting and Gardening*.

The Society of Arts continued giving their prestigious medals and premiums for planting, and stimulated the competitive instinct amongst planters[64]. The greatest planter of hardwoods in the 1760s was Edward Turnour, Baron Winterton, of Shillinglee Park, Sussex. In 1761, Winterton received a gold medal for sowing 20 acres with acorns. In 1767 he, as Earl of Winterton, and his son Viscount Turnour received medals for English elm and chestnuts respectively. Robert Fenwick of Leemington, Northumberland, was a keen Scots pine planter. He planted over 100,000 in 1764, and then the same amount in each of the two succeeding years.

Such owners were laying out their grounds on a very broad scale, but a skill in laying out small grounds well was still prized. In particular, it was widely felt that poets should be good gardeners. Even a minor one like the Quaker, John Scott of Amwell, Hertfordshire, laid out a small garden from 1765 for which he sought Johnson's approval[65]. Thomas Gray was keenly interested in the subject but never had his own garden. Gray's friend William Mason was

41   Nuneham Courtenay, the flower garden.

This engraving dated 1777 is by William Watts after a painting by Paul Sandby. It shows the garden laid out by William Mason in a manner that came to be known as 'English' when formal 'Italian' and 'French' flower gardens were later made.

luckier in this respect though. He was given the living of the rectory at Aston, near Sheffield, in 1754, which meant that he could at least lay out the small garden there[66].

However, it was Mason's intimacy with George Harcourt, the heir to the Earl of Harcourt and thus styled Viscount Nuneham, that gave him the most opportunity. They were both extreme Whigs with views opposed to the king's, and Lord Nuneham in particular was famous for his republican leanings. Mason was often at Nuneham Courtenay, near Oxford[67], and would have seen Lord Harcourt's new villa being erected in 1760 and the village being cleared and made into grounds the next year.

Nuneham was a devoted follower of Jean-Jacques Rousseau and his view that man is at his purest and best in a state of Nature. Indeed he supported Rousseau for a short while in 1766 during his self-imposed exile in England. Rousseau was much affected by a published account of George Anson's discovery of two deserted but charming islands, Tinian and Juan-Fernandez, on his voyage round the world[68]. Rousseau believed that Nature had most effect upon the emotions when she was unaltered. He told the Duchess of Portland:

I find that nature, in a garden, is not the same: she has more brilliance, but she does not move me as much. Men say, they make nature more beautiful—but I believe they disfigure her.

Such sentiments led to a fondness for botanizing and the notion of gardens without gardening.

In *La Nouvelle Heloïse* (1761) Rousseau describes how the hero, St Preux, went on Anson's voyage and saw the two islands. On his return he found that his old lover, Julie, had married and had made a garden very much like these islands. Although the area was small it was enclosed by thick shady trees, flowering shrubs and creepers mingled with fruit trees, and the grass was mixed with herbs, flowers and mosses. To St Preux, it seemed as if:

I was looking at the wildest, loneliest spot in the whole of Nature, and I seemed to be the first mortal who had ever penetrated within this wilderness.

It seemed to St Preux as if this beautiful and natural garden was a symbol of Julie's rediscovered virtue.

Mason and Nuneham would have known of this novel, and in 1771 they tried putting the idea into practice at Nuneham Courtenay. Although they included a Temple of Flora and various busts, of which Rousseau would not have approved as showing the hand of man, their flower garden was irregular in outline and layout. There was a honeysuckle bower and trailing plants between trees. The flower beds were irregular in shape and planted promiscuously, as if they were the unaided product of Nature—probably the first time this had been done. The urns and inscriptions were desirable for reinforcing the sentiments of melancholy and love of nature that the garden was supposed to arouse.

The garden's romantic charm was a quite new interpretation of Nature at a time when the great parks were being extended over hill and dale in Her name. As the inscription to Rousseau put it:

Si l'Auteur de la nature est grand dans les grandes choses, il est tres grand dans les petites.

The Picturesque Eye

The 1760s may have been the heyday for park improvements, but they were also remarkable for the establishment of picturesque travel and a vast leap forward in the general quality of English topographical engraving and print-making. During the preceding decades the best print-makers had been Frenchmen working in England such as John Rocque and Jacques Rigaud. English engravers such as Samuel and Nathaniel Buck and Thomas Smith chose interesting subjects, but the standard of the drawings they copied and the quality of the engraving generally fell well short of what was every day achieved in France.

The rise of an English print-making school was marked by the emergence of a native artist of remarkable ability and a print-seller who used his commercial success to exercise considerable and beneficial patronage. William Woollett, the artist, set new standards of copper engraving. Some of his first prints of garden scenes were sets of West Wycombe and Whitton, both made in 1757. Some of the best of those to follow were a scene of Woburn Farm in 1759, Painshill, Hall Barn and other places in 1760, and Kew Gardens in 1763.

The print-seller was John Boydell, whose father was a land surveyor and the agent for Sir John Glynne at Hawarden Castle, Flintshire. Boydell is supposed to have been so impressed by Badeslade's view of Hawarden of 1739 that he abandoned land surveying and walked to London to be apprenticed in 1741 to Badeslade's engraver, W. H. Toms[69]. During the 1750s and 1760s Boydell gradually abandoned engraving for print-selling, and employed English artists and engravers exclusively, including Woollett, Richard Wilson, John Smith, Benjamin West and Joshua Reynolds.

Other artists headed by Thomas Sandby's brother, Paul, quickly rivalled Woollett. Sandby had been a topographical artist in Scotland for the army in the years following the 1745 rebellion, and obtained considerable patronage from Lord Nuneham from the late 1750s. In 1770 he also gained the patronage of Sir Watkin Williams-Wynn of Wynnstay, Denbighshire, who came of age that year. He drew a number of scenes in North Wales which were published as engravings a few years later. Sir Watkin also patronized Richard Wilson, his remote kinsman, whose view of Cader Idris, the mountain in Merionethshire, attracted much attention when exhibited in 1774.

The interest in this work of Sandby's and Wilson's illustrates the new appetite by the public for the wild scenes of Nature, rising alongside picturesque tours. Chief amongst its promoters were Thomas Gray and William Gilpin. As they were concerned to demonstrate that Nature is a painter, their analysis of scenery tended to be in the technical and objective terms of painterly criticism. Gilpin especially laid stress on a scene's qualities as a painting.

This is not to say, though, that all travellers were quickly converted to Gilpin's picturesque appreciation; this was difficult to master, and at first it was confined to a small group comprising Gray, Gilpin, William Mason, Thomas Warton and a few others. The average tourist searched for sublimity rather than picturesque beauty. It was true, though, that other travellers such as Arthur Young and Thomas Pennant used the word 'picturesque'. It was fashionable and so they used it frequently, without perhaps attaching any precise meaning to it.

The continuing interest in the sublime is graphically illustrated by Thomas Smith's engravings of the lakes of Cumberland dated 1761. These emphasize the vastness of the scenery, the jaggedness of the mountains, and the storminess of the weather. They were popular enough to be re-issued by Boydell in 1767.

Gray's *Catalogue of the Antiquities, Houses, Parks, Plantations, and Situations in England and Wales* (1773) was published after his death by Mason, his literary executor. This shows that since he started compiling it in about 1757 Gray had visited every county in the two countries and had noted all the most remarkable places. This is particularly impressive when it is realized that he was a knowledgeable antiquarian and a skilled botanist as well as a connoisseur of scenery. It is known that he visited Hampshire and Wiltshire in 1764, Kent in 1766, Worcestershire and Gloucestershire in 1770 and the River Wye in 1771. However, the only accounts to be published were his letters to his friend, Dr Wharton, about Scotland in 1765, and the Lakes in 1768, published with Mason's *Poems of Mr. Gray* (1775).

Although Gray professed no skill in sketching himself, he warmly advised others with the ability to exercise it on their tours, for:

When we trust to the picture that objects draw of themselves on our mind, we deceive ourselves; without accurate and particular observation, it is but ill-drawn at first, the outlines are soon blurred, the colours everyday grow fainter[70].

For his tour of the Lakes in 1769 he took along a Claude-glass. This is a slightly convex mirror only about four inches in diameter. A view can thus be captured in the palm of one's hand and its composition, colouring and tones analysed as if it were already represented on a surface. The glass was thus of obvious help to landscape painters in assessing whether a scene would make a good subject to a painting, and Gray apparently used it for the same purpose:

I . . . saw in my glass a picture, that if I could transmit to you, and fix it in all the softness of its living colours, would fairly sell for a thousand pounds. This is the sweetest scene I can yet discover in point of pastoral beauty; the rest are in a sublimer style[71].

Whereas Gray seems to have been mainly content to enjoy the scenes of Nature, Gilpin made greater efforts to record his impressions by sketching, and to derive the rules of picturesque beauty. He had no thought of publication at first but simply wanted to improve his own taste for scenery and pass on his observations to his students at his school at Cheam, Surrey[72]. He encouraged them to visualize the scenes in the classics. Just as Pope had done fifty years previously, he called those scenes which would make good history paintings 'picturesque'.

Gilpin's interest in real scenes had started by 1765 when he visited Painshill and made quick sketches of the Temple of Bacchus, the Grotto, the Hermitage and other scenes into a pocket notebook[73]. He criticized the Turkish Tent and a white bridge as 'glaring objects and but spots in the view', although the Temple of Bacchus was 'a noble grand object and nowhere appears as a spot and gives an agreeable variety to the scene by changing it from nature to art'.

At this time he was still attempting to define 'the Principles of Picturesque Beauty', by which he meant the beauty to be found in paintings. The results of

42   Derwentwater from Keswick.

This is one of Thomas Smith's views of 1767. Smith emphasizes the sublimity of the natural scene.

his deliberations were to be found in his *Essay on Prints* (1768). It was not long, though, before he decided to try to apply his principles to the analysis of real landscape. Hence in 1770 he followed the already well-trodden path to Ross-on-Wye, Herefordshire, in order to take a boat down the river to Chepstow. This was to give rise to his first journal entirely devoted to 'examining the face of a country *by the rules of picturesque beauty*'[74].

Several remarks show that Gilpin shared Gray's conception of nature as a goddess and artist:

Nature is always great in design. She is an admirable colourist also, and harmonizes tints with infinite variety and beauty. But she is seldom so correct in composition, as to produce an harmonious whole.

Her defects in composition might be only the result of human limitations, though:

The case is, the immensity of nature is beyond human comprehension. She works on a *vast scale*; and, no doubt, harmoniously, if her schemes could be comprehended. The artist, in the meantime, is confined to a *span*; and lays down his little rules, which he calls the *principles of picturesque beauty*, merely to adapt such diminutive parts of nature's surfaces to his own eye.

Nature's infinite variety meant that, unlike her 'copyists', she was never mannered, so that:

The picturesque eye, in quest of beauty, finds it almost in every incident, and under every appearance of nature. Her works, and all her works, must ever, in some degree, be beautiful.

Gilpin found it helpful to analyse scenes by reference to the materials of nature. The River Wye was especially picturesque because the steep winding banks of the river gave the ground immense variety. However picturesqueness is as much to do with the detail as the composition. Gilpin did not despise the trivia of broken ground, colours of the soil and patches of vegetation, as these provide the foreground to a view. In just the same way he admired the variety that lichens, ferns and mosses gave the surfaces of the remaining stonework at Tintern Abbey.

The other great ornaments to Nature besides ground were wood, rocks and buildings. Rocks were a peculiar case because they had no beauty in themselves, but derive their attraction from their contrasts with intermixed vegetation, water and broken ground, and often from their great majesty. Gilpin was somewhat equivocal about buildings. On the one hand he felt that Nature had no need of embellishments from Art, but on the other hand painted landscapes undoubtedly benefit from the admixture of buildings, as do real scenes to a lesser extent.

He approved of Tintern Abbey as a whole, but, viewing it in the picturesque light, he thought it unfortunate that the gable ends remained in such regular form, and he regretted the Duke of Beaufort's clearance, levelling and grassing of the old interior of the abbey. He was also conscious that there can be too many buildings in a view, particularly when each is of little consequence. Whatever the rights and wrongs of buildings actually existing, 'the moral sense can never make a convert of the picturesque eye'—a sentiment he had expressed over 20 years previously about the garden buildings at Stowe.

His rules of picturesque beauty led Gilpin to some unexpected comments. He liked Piercefield, and considered it 'extremely romantic', but in a picturesque light it had two great defects. One was that the River Wye, being tidal, gave a dirty sluggish appearance, and the other was that all viewpoints were too high. Goodrich Castle, on the other hand, was set amongst trees on a bluff, and when

Gilpin saw it from the river he recognized it as 'correctly picturesque'. He also liked the mile-long approach to Caversham House, Oxfordshire, which had been laid out by Brown along a valley. This was what Nature had dictated. However, Gilpin's painter's eye could not help noticing the many single trees, which he found 'heavy, and offend the eye'. Groups of trees were much more certain to have beauty.

When Gray heard of Gilpin's journal he asked to be allowed to see it[75]. Gray died the month after he had done so, but a mutual friend told Gilpin that Gray had been complimentary. This seems to have encouraged Gilpin to undertake further picturesque tours, for in 1772 he spent June on a more ambitious one to Cumberland[76].

His observations on most of the larger lakes and mountains of Cumberland and Westmorland, and upon 34 country houses that he visited *en route* gave him ample scope for discussing picturesque scenery in much greater depth than he had on the Wye tour. In addition he allowed himself lengthy digressions prompted by the scenery of particular places. Many of his general points repeated observations made on the earlier tour, but those on Burke's theories, on picturesque rules, on architecture and on gardens, were mostly new.

He agreed with Burke that the sublime existed as a category of scenery, but he did not follow him in ascribing the sensation to the arousal of the emotions. Instead he emphasized the wide diversity of scenery and the variety of his reasons for liking it. He was adept at discovering the natural character of a scene, and insisted that this should be respected. English scenery was particularly diverse, he said, because of its quickly changing geology, and yet it differed as a whole from Continental scenery in the appearance conferred by English agricultural systems and by the native oak.

Some scenes are breathtaking in their scale of danger, and these were sublime. However, many more scenes could be described as romantic. Castles, abbeys, and, above all, natural scenery, could impress the imagination with visions of Druids, *banditti*, wolves, medieval knights and so forth. Gilpin also conceded that one might find beauty amongst the lawns, woods and water of an embellished garden. However, neither sublime, nor romantic, nor beautiful scenes were necessarily picturesque; the picturesque was really yet another form of beauty.

Hence, although he was generally polite about Burke's theories, Gilpin had little sympathy with them. According to Burke 'large bodies, adorned with the spoils of beauty, is a tension continually relieved; which approaches to the nature of mediocrity'. However, Gilpin found this to be quite untrue in the case of Ullswater, in which he was '*more pleased* than with any lake I had seen'. Gilpin also took issue with a passage by Burke on 'the reasons why the imagination is often more pleased by a sketch than by a finished painting'. The point of difference was minute, though, and the attention devoted to it suggests that Gilpin was taking pains to discover flaws in Burke's reasoning.

Gilpin was sufficiently sure of himself to propose some rules of picturesque composition in real scenery. His differentiation of moral beauty and pictur-esque beauty proved to be the key to many of them. A well-dressed and hard-working labourer would be preferable to a dishevelled and idle peasant when viewed in a moral light, but in a picturesque light the latter makes the better subject. Similarly the lowly cow is a better subject than a sleek and smooth-coated racehorse, especially in the months of April and May when the cow is shedding its winter coat.

Picturesqueness is also determined by outline and grouping. Gilpin consi-dered that a geometrically shaped hill was unpleasing to behold. He disliked

Thorp Cloud, a steep-sided but flat-topped hill near Ilam, Derbyshire, and was surprised to find that Nature had made Gascadale, a glacial valley near Keswick, completely formal. It had smooth, sloping sides without any adornment from wood, rock or broken ground. A divided summit was another flaw; one peak should be dominant. The same principle extended to buildings. He felt that Appleby Castle, Westmorland, lost much of its picturesqueness by being seen as two very nearly equal parts.

When similar objects were grouped together it was important not to let them dispute for dominance. Hence, for example, when sketching cows for a foreground:

Two will hardly combine. Three make a good group—either united—or when one is a little removed from the other two. If you increase the group beyond three; one, or more, in proportion, must necessarily be a *little detached*. It is the same principle applied to cattle, which we before applied to mountains, and other objects.

Gilpin was well aware of the differences between painting and real landscape. For example a painting can give only a confined view, whilst in real landscape the eye can range around. Also the painter carefully selects a view for its composition, so that it may be from an unusual viewpoint. Nevertheless he thought it fair to criticize buildings and gardens for their general contribution to the real landscape. He must have shocked purists in classical architecture like Chambers when he argued that Vanbrugh's design for Blenheim had been criticized too severely. Although it certainly did not keep to the architectural orders, yet it was a '*magnificent whole*' in keeping with the idea of a palace in extensive parkland. He found Mowbray Castle at Hackfall, on the other hand, to be 'a paltry thing'. The idea of a castle required a closer likeness and more grandeur.

He held ruins in special reverence; examples such as Hackfall showed that no artificial ruin or folly had approached the magnificence of genuine ones. Hence it was with considerable indignation that he viewed another of William Aislabie's works, the clearance of the ground at Fountains Abbey, which he had at last acquired in 1768[77]. A few fragments, Gilpin thought,

are *proper*, and *picturesque*. They are *proper* because they account for what is defaced: and they are *picturesque*, because they unite the principal pile with the ground; on which union the beauty of composition, in a good measure, depends.

Gilpin's early criticisms of Stowe were due to the fact that it was a make-believe world of classical deities and mock heroes, fun for those who joined in the fantasy, but not for those seeking a feast for the eyes. When Gilpin saw The Leasowes, he felt how ridiculous it was to see inscriptions inviting the Naiads to bathe their beauteous limbs in Shenstone's dark and stagnant pools. Likewise he saw the impropriety of some paltry ruins behind the house at Shugborough.

His special admiration was reserved for the scale at which Brown worked, in particular the lake at Blenheim:

Brown himself used to say, 'that the Thames would never forgive him, what he had done at Blenheim'. And every spectator must allow, that, on entering the great gate from Woodstock, the whole of this scenery, (the castle, the lawn, the woods, and the lake) seen together, makes one of the grandest burst, which art perhaps ever displayed.

Formal gardening, both old and new, disgusted him. The flower garden at Blenheim, probably Chambers', 'showed the hand of art to have been straying', whilst the layouts at Corby Castle, Cumberland, and Studley Royal, which dated from the 1710s and 1720s, were severely criticized for their too-numerous buildings, statuary and highly dressed stonework. This showed a lack of respect for their natural character. Cheerful solitude would have been much more appropriate in those secluded valleys.

Observations like these led to suggestions for how places ought to be laid out. At Hackfall, where the situation suggested magnificence, he would have built only two large buildings on the rim of the valley instead of the numerous small ones he found. These would have amply adorned every part of the scenery. Gilpin let his imagination work to the full at the extremely romantic island retreat in Windermere, Holm Island. Since the water was all around the owner 'should not be ostentatious in displaying it', but concentrate upon the inequalities of the small domain. There was really a surplus of water scenes and some areas where the lake was not visible at all would have added to the variety and contrast.

When Gilpin made this and subsequent tours, he was still in a tiny minority of tourists whose primary aim was to inspect the works of Nature. Visiting country houses was very popular, and a large number of private journals were compiled. A few booksellers followed on the example of the Stowe guidebook, and though a number related chiefly to paintings or antiquities, there was usually at least a mention of the gardens. The more complete guides to grounds included Dodsley's on The Leasowes (1764), T. Rodenhurst's on Hawkstone (1766), George Bickham's on Kew Gardens (pre-1771)[78].

The most celebrated tour of all was Samuel Johnson's *Journey to the Western Islands of Scotland* (1773). Johnson had first been interested in the idea ten years before when one had been suggested to him by James Boswell[79], himself a Scot and heir to the Laird of Auchinleck. It was a surprising venture, because Johnson was aged 64 and corpulent, and because he pretended to great prejudice against the Scots. His purpose was to investigate the manners and customs of the Highlanders, which he set out with great understanding, and even a sympathy for their wretchedness.

The only country house of note that he remarked upon was the Duke of Argyll's, at Inverary, Argyllshire, and there were very few comments about the natural scenery. His chief impression of the Scottish landscape seems to have been its extreme paucity of trees. This was the more remarkable to him because he considered it likely that before man took possession of it the world was covered in forests. He found the barrenness of the Highlands repugnant:

An eye accustomed to flowery pastures and waving harvests, is astonished and repelled by this wide extent of hopeless sterility. The appearance is that of matter incapable of form or usefulness, dismissed by nature from her care, and disinherited of her favours, left in its original elemental state.

Gilpin would have shared his distaste, though his reasons would have sounded quite different.

Tan Chet-Qua and the Peasant Slave

The change in gardening style was plain for all to see, but still by the 1760s there was no published manual to tell the aspiring designer how to proceed. It was true that Hogarth, Burke and others had written books on the nature of beauty, but these gave no practical instruction. The first published works to attempt to do so were Lord Kames' *Elements of Criticism* (1762) and Shenstone's 'Unconnected Thoughts on Gardening'.

Kames was a Scottish lawyer whose concern was to show that taste was susceptible to scientific criticism and, therefore, improvement according to rational principles. He had a theory of a hierarchy of the senses with purely intellectual pleasures being on the highest plane and the coarse 'organic' pleasures of touch, smell and taste on the lowest. In between there were the pleasures of the eye and ear which gave refined mental pleasures particularly suited to relaxation and cultivation. He then proceeded,

to examine the sensitive branch of human nature, to trace the objects that are naturally agreeable, as well as those that are naturally disagreeable; and by these means to discover, if we can, what are the genuine principles of the fine arts.

Much of Kames' book was an elaboration upon Burke's discussion of beauty, sublimity, grandeur and novelty, and the emotions aroused. Of Nature, Kames merely stated baldly that:

A taste for natural objects is born with us in perfection; for relishing . . . a rich landscape . . . culture is unnecessary.

In his chapter upon 'Gardening and Architecture' Kames wrote that a garden artist should perceive that 'to humour and adorn nature, is the perfection of his art'. However, this theme, which would have been central to Walpole's or Mason's thinking, was mentioned only in passing. Most of Kames' advice was on how to create a pleasurable sequence of moods, much as Chambers would have done. For him the 'completest plan of a garden' is one that requires 'the several parts to be so arranged as to inspire all the different emotions that can be raised by gardening'.

He also had some comments upon the propriety of regularity. He saw that the garden immediately near the house should 'partake the regularity of the principal object', and that the smaller the garden, the stricter should the regularity be. He disapproved of the 'stars' of walks in woodland, and preferred the progressive revelation of views along walks. He also frowned upon fountains, and especially upon inappropriate statuary such as animals vomiting water. This tone of propriety was carried forward to a preference for Gothic over Greek ruins and numerous other tips that made an odd mix with the lengthy comments on the wonderful gardens of the Chinese.

Although many readers disliked the literary style of the *Elements of Criticism*, it was nevertheless widely admired for its systematic treatment of taste. It also contained a strong commendation of William Kent's gardening and was thus influential in persuading Kames' fellow Scots to convert their gardens to the Natural Style.

Shenstone's approach to the giving of rules for gardening had been quite different to that of Kames. Being a poet, not a lawyer, Shenstone had more highly developed sensibilities to Nature than to logic. It is not to be wondered at, therefore, that his views on laying out grounds were unorganized, fragmentary and generalized. Dodsley was keen to promote Shenstone as a man of taste, and included the 'Unconnected Thoughts on Gardening', written about 1760, in the book *The Works in Verse and Prose, of William Shenstone, Esq.* (1764).

'Unconnected Thoughts' illustrates Shenstone's debt to Addison for his ideas on the pleasures of the imagination and to Pope for his ideas on variety and novelty (or surprise). He had not, though, followed the main streams of thought in England on Taste. He did not follow Gilpin in analysing Nature as if She was a painter. Nor did he wholly embrace Burke's theories on the emotional basis for beauty, although he borrowed from him. Instead, he concurred with the natural philosophy of the Scots, Francis Hutcheson and Alexander Gerard especially, which never relinquished the belief that beauty arises from the mind, rather than the senses or the emotions.

Hutcheson's thoughts on Nature's infinite variety were very congenial to Shenstone, and so was an essay by Gerard which won a prize from the Philosphical Society of Edinburgh in 1756. This essay laid down that pleasurable associations were the fundamental cause of beauty, and that taste consists chiefly 'in the improvement of those principles which are commonly called the powers of the imagination', including novelty, sublimity, beauty and imitation. An illustration of Shenstone's divergent attitude from Gilpin is provided by the pleasures that each derived from ruins. Gilpin had separated picturesque from moral beauties. Shenstone, by contrast, felt that ruins 'afford that pleasing melancholy which proceeds from a reflexion on decayed magnificence'.

Perhaps Shenstone's most original written contribution was a number of forceful phrases or sentences that lodged in people's minds. Most of these were concerned with the role of Art. For example, 'Art should never be allowed to set foot in the province of nature, otherwise than clandestinely and by night'. This did not mean that he abandoned Art in his improvements; just that Art should not be evident where it manipulated Nature. Indeed he was diligent in discovering what aids Art could give Nature, and amongst these the techniques of painting assumed great importance. Hence, 'in pursuance of our present taste in gardening, every good painter of landskip appears to me the most proper designer', and such gardeners would be termed 'landskip gardeners'. These techniques included distancing and 'approximating' (i.e. attracting) and sound like Spence's ideas. He seemed disappointed that no painter had yet turned to gardening.

The anonymous poem *The Rise and Progress of the Present Taste in Planting Parks, Pleasure Grounds, Gardens Etc.* appeared in 1767. The author's bent was clearly towards the enchanted scenes of Nature, much as Thomson would have seen them, and for *fermes ornées*:

> Wooburn for me superior charms can boast,
> Where Nature's still improv'd, but never lost,

But the ostensible purpose of the poem was to celebrate the improvements at Temple Newsam, Yorkshire, by Lancelot Brown for Charles, ninth Viscount Irwin. Great play was made of the analogy of Brown's work and painting:

> At Blenheim, Croome, and Caversham we trace
> Salvator's wildness, Claud's enlivening grace,
> Cascades and Lakes on fire as Risdale drew,
> While Nature's vary'd in each charming view.
> To paint his works would Poussin's Powers require,
> Milton's sublimity, and Dryden's fire:
> For both the Sister Arts in him combin'd,
> Enrich the great ideas of his mind.

Yet this same poem praised Kew, 'where Taste and Chambers's every grace unfold', and contained an extensive passage culled from Chambers' essay on Chinese gardening.

The year after this poem was published a young gentleman from Hertfordshire, George Mason, presented his views to the public in *An Essay on Design in Gardening* (1768). He felt that 'taste is by no means arbitrary', but explained that it was only recently in England that the true model of improvement had been found. He attributed 'our present superiority' to the English love of experiment and observation. It was only with Shenstone's 'Unconnected Thoughts on Gardening' that some of the rules had been put on paper, and he intended his own thoughts to be supplementary to Shenstone's. He had been left the estate of Porters by his father, a maltster from Greenwich, in 1750 when he was only 15[80], and so many of his views could have been derived from personal experience of improvement. Furthermore, his essay showed the signs of wide-ranging tours to Yorkshire, Derbyshire and Wales, as well as the gardens of the Home Counties.

One rule was that 'the *species* of design should generally conform to the nature of the place', a theme that was to figure prominently in discussions of taste for the next 50 years. He remarked that avenues, quincunxes and clumps had all been the preferred forms of planting in the past, but that '*dotting* (as they term it) is the present method'. He disliked the trend towards conifers:

The greatest fault of modern planners is their injudicious application of *fir-trees.*

He considered that 'turning *woods* into *groves* gives an air of freedom ... yet a total destruction of thicket is one of the greatest impediments to design'.

Other remarks were more personal. He though Lord Kames' opinion that 'regularity is required in that part of a garden which joins the dwelling house' was a 'relict of the prejudice of habit'. He condemned 'specimens of *French* and *Italian* gardening' at Painshill as too laboured to be successful as contrasts with the natural gardening there: 'natural negligencies' were much more effective in showing up the beauties of natural gardening.

He was surely aiming at Brown when commiserating with owners who lacked the confidence to carry out a scheme themselves:

The difficulty attending this mechanical part of gardening had induced many proprietors to commit the whole of it to artists by profession, whose contracted geniuses (without the least *capability* of enlargement) have stampt an unmeaning sameness upon half the principal seats in the Kingdom.

No wonder, then, that all his favourite gardens were laid out without the help of a professional improver:

Juster models of artificial disposition are by no means wanting—you will find them within the woods of STOKE (LORD BOTTETOURT's near BRISTOL), at WROXTON, and the *valley* at BADMINTON: OATLANDS, WINDSOR-PARK and WENTWORTH CASTLE will show you, how rivers can be imitated; PERESFIELD may bring to your imagination some romantic paradise of SEMIRAMIS. PAINSHILL has every mark of *creative genius*, and HAGLEY of *correctest fancy*; but the most intimate *alliance with nature* was formed by SHENSTONE.

Mason was not the only young gentleman eager to present his views. Thomas Whately had evidently been undertaking tours as well, and his book *Observations on Modern Gardening* came out in 1770. This was much longer than Mason's, and consisted of very full descriptions of 15 gardens and some natural scenes woven together by a connecting text. Although the descriptions were excellent, it was the connecting text that made the book famous. Instead of a string of unconnected thoughts, it was an organized and lucid account of the theory of English gardening which proved to be required reading by critics of gardening for the next 30 years. A translation into French by François de Paule Latapie appeared in 1771, and it was reprinted in English for the fourth time in 1777.

Whately treated garden design in three ways. First, there were the materials—ground, wood, water, rocks and buildings. Second, there were various aspects of taste—on Art and Nature, on picturesque beauty and on the character of an improvement. Third, there were the different types of improvement—farms, parks, gardens and ridings. By a 'riding' he meant an extended walk or drive through an estate such as the walks at Piercefield, or the circumferential carriage drives found in many of Brown's designs.

Whately's discussion of picturesque beauty shows that, although he did not entirely agree with Gilpin, he was used to envisaging Nature as a painter. He did agree though, over the question of the character of an improvement. He defined three characters—emblematic, imitative and original. The Elysian Fields at Stowe would have been 'emblematical', in that one was expected to recognize the features therein as emblems of an imaginary scene. 'Imitative' gardens were those that sought merely to reproduce scenes elsewhere. Presumably 'Chinese' gardens came in this category. He disliked both these characters, and recommended the third, the 'original'. Gardens of this type were intended to bring out and amplify the particular, or 'original', character of a place.

Gilpin insisted on seeing and appreciating the real landscape. The purpose of 'embellished scenes' was to act as 'a connecting thread between the regularity of the house, and the freedom of the natural scene'[81]. But they would always 'partake of art' and so 'the natural scene will always appear so superior to the embellished artificial one'. Whately was not quite so dismissive of gardens, but he certainly leaned in Gilpin's direction. His discussion of the materials of landscape cited mainly natural scenes, and he preferred The Leasowes to Woburn Farm as it was more frankly a farm.

Just as George Mason had beaten Thomas Whately into print, so Whately had beaten Horace Walpole. Whately's book was one reason why Walpole's own essay was not published until 1780. This was entitled *On Modern Gardening* and it was actually put into its final form only a few months after Whately's book appeared[82]. Although Walpole emphasized that it was a history, and that it was not his intention to lay down rules for improvement, much of his own thinking inevitably showed through. The pre-occupations of the 1750s were still there—viewing scenery and gardens as paintings, warnings that whim and caprice are contrary to propriety, and a reaffirmation that the purpose of Art is to 'chasten and polish' Nature.

He also speculated that the English had once before understood the principle of natural gardening, for the English were known in the Middle Ages for their extensive hunting parks. It was only when Bridgeman invented the ha-ha and he and Kent took 'nature into the plan', that the principle was rediscovered. The main change from 20 years previously, though, was a note of practical experience. The English weather was mentioned several times as a restraint on natural gardening, particularly the modern improver's tendency to surround a house in a sea of grass:

Sheltered and even close walks, in so very uncertain a climate as ours, are comforts ill exchanged for the few picturesque days that we enjoy.

He even recommended that old-fashioned gardens should be held back from improvement if they were sheltered and warm. The frequent clash between beauty and convenience was becoming a topic of increasing practical concern to improvers.

No author until the late 1760s had attempted to express his views on the Natural Style in verse. However, William Mason set himself this task in 1767. Like Shenstone and George Mason, he was concerned with the rules of design, and, also like them, he noted their absence in Pope's *Epistle to Burlington* whilst deferring to that poem's general precepts. Hence Mason's poem was a complement to the *Epistle* in many ways: instructional rather than satirical; specific and not general; and Virgilian in style rather than Horatian. The first part was published in 1772 as *The English Garden*.

Mason of course rejected 'mechanic order' as the deity to whom homage should be given: he named Nature and Variety instead. In an apparent contradiction he dedicated the poem to Simplicity as the 'best arbitress of what is good and fair'. It is probable that Mason, like Joseph Warton, meant straightforwardness or an absence of artifice or affectation. Although advising owners who had some 'lovely unfrequented wild' to keep their property that way, Mason was realist enough to recognize that most were not so fortunate. He assured such persons that 'the desert hills will hear the call of Art; the vallies dark obey her just behests', but warned that:

> Great Nature scorns controul; She will not bear
> One beauty foreign to the spot or soil
> She gives thee to adorn: 'tis thine alone
> To mend, not change her features.

In common with his friends Gray and Walpole, Mason attached great significance to the analogy between painting and gardening. The keynote of his poem was struck in the phrase, 'a Poet's feeling, and a Painter's eye'. He recommended the Grand Tour on which, in Italy:

> . . . your eyes entranc'd
> Shall catch those glowing scenes, that taught a CLAUDE
> To grace his canvass with Hesperian hues:
> And scenes like these, on Memory's tablet drawn,
> Bring back to Britain; there give local form
> To each Idea; and, if Nature lend
> Materials fit of torrent, rock, and shade,
> Produce new TIVOLIS . . .

Composition, colouring, contrast and perspective were all to be the gardener's skills. Mason even believed that prospect was not a proper goal of gardening: he preferred the more secluded and contemplative scenes of Ruisdael. The value of foreground trees was emphasized repeatedly.

Where extensive hill and dale were part of the scene Mason thought that any planting should be ample, uniting hill with hill. He recommended elm, chestnut and oak, but not 'the Scottish fir' which 'lifts its inglorious head' so often. Although he recognized that destroying avenues was a harsh remedy to the works of 'mechanic order' he nevertheless urged that it should be done. Some of the trees might be saved, though, either by transplantation or by breaking up the avenue into clumps with new planting. The artists that he held up worthy of admiration and imitation were Kent, Southcote, Shenstone and Brown. His panegyric of Brown was the more remarkable since Brown was of course still living.

Apart from a few of George Mason's comments, all the literature on the theory of improvement and its practice had remained discreet and gentlemanly in tone. One might have been led to believe that an accommodation had been reached by the protagonists in the most important theoretical argument—whether Dame Nature or the effect of scenes on Man's emotions should have precedence. Authors like Kames and Shenstone had bowed to both philosophies without pointing out that they differed or diverged. However, the identification of each stance with a political viewpoint served to intensify the differences and to transform them into one of the more celebrated controversies of the 1770s.

The controversy was fuelled by two authors who were openly hostile to Brown's mode of improvement. The first was Oliver Goldsmith who had been making numerous excursions all over Britain since the early 1760s[83]. His passion was aroused by the callousness of those great Whig landowners who, in the name of Nature, were prepared to move hundreds of tenants out of their long-established settlements. *The Deserted Village* (1770) was about these park removals, and about one in particular, which he called Auburn. Probably this was Nuneham Courtenay, which Goldsmith saw before it was removed by Lord Harcourt in 1761.

Goldsmith took a sentimental view of the villagers' plight which strengthened his distaste of 'unwieldy wealth and cumbrous pomp':

> Sweet smiling village, loveliest of the lawn,
> Thy sports are fled, and all thy charms withdrawn;
> Amidst thy bowers the tyrant's hand is seen,
> And desolation saddens all thy green:
> One only master grasps the whole domain,
> And half a tillage stints thy smiling plain . . .
> . . . The man of wealth and pride
> Takes up a space that many poor supplied;
> Space for his lake, his park's extended bounds,
> Space for his horses, equipage, and hounds.

The second author was Sir William Chambers, and his criticisms came in 1772 in the form of a greatly expanded version of his essay 'Of the Art of Laying out Gardens among the Chinese', now entitled *A Dissertation on Oriental Gardening*. In the preface he set out his position *vis-à-vis* the professional improvers:

Is it not singular that [this] Art . . . should have no regular professors in our quarter of the world? In this island, it is abandoned to kitchen gardeners, well skilled in the culture of sallads, but little acquainted with the principles of ornamental gardening. It cannot be expected that men uneducated, and doomed by their condition to waste the vigour of life in hard labour, should ever go far in so refined, so difficult a pursuit.

He agreed that the regular style still prevailing on the Continent was 'absurd', but the dangers of unskilled improvers was that English gardens were 'insipid and vulgar'. He objected that:

our gardens differ very little from common fields, so closely is nature copied in most of them; . . . a stranger . . . is treated with the sight of a large green field, scattered over with a few straggling trees, and verged with a confused border of little shrubs and flowers . . .

To Chambers, who believed strongly that the purpose of gardening was to affect the emotions, the answer was obvious: 'a judicious mixture' of Continental artfulness with English naturalism. This led him to propose the Chinese manner as one that had succeeded in this mixture.

Unfortunately for Chambers his *Dissertation* expanded so extravagantly upon the mind-affecting devices of Chinese gardens that he met only with disbelief and ridicule[84]. Although it is very unlikely that he had seen or even heard of concubines, vultures, wolves, tigers, gibbets, volcanoes, electric shocks or artificial rain in Chinese gardens, he described them as if they were common practice. The public's reaction was amazement that a respected architect should have allowed his fantasy to have entered what purported to be a serious work. Horace Walpole knew more of the background to the *Dissertation* and asserted that it was 'more extravagant than the worst Chinese paper, and . . . written in wild revenge against Brown'[85].

Comments by Chambers such as 'peasants emerge from the melon grounds to commence professors' could only be interpreted as spiteful reminders of Brown's humble origins. This thesis was supported by Brown's success in 1769 against Chambers in obtaining the lucrative commission from Robert, Baron Clive, to rebuild the house at Claremont. Brown was the leading improver to be 'polishing and refining' Nature in ways that Walpole and his friend William Mason thought fit. If Chambers could be made ridiculous, then not only would Brown's system be defended, but the artistic credibility of the

Tory court would be undermined. The excesses of the *Dissertation* provided an ideal opportunity, and so, spurred on by Walpole, Mason sat down to write a mock-heroic reply.

An Heroic Epistle to Sir William Chambers, Knight appeared in January 1773 just as London was filling up for the winter season. A short preface reminded readers of the purpose of the *Dissertation*:

It is the author's professed aim in extolling the taste of the Chinese, to condemn that mean and paltry manner that Kent introduced; which Southcote, Hamilton and Brown followed, and which, to our national disgrace, is called the English style of gardening. He proves ... that Nature herself is incapable of pleasing, without the assistance of Art, and that too of the most luxuriant kind.

The poem continued in the same ironic vein. In one passage Chambers was invited to Richmond Gardens where Brown had just finished remodelling Queen Caroline's improvements for George III:

> Come then, prolific Art, and with thee bring
> The charms that rise from thy exhaustless spring;
> To Richmond come, for see, untutor'd Brown
> Destroys those wonders which were once thy own.
> Lo, from his melon-ground the peasant slave
> Has rudely rush'd, and levell'd Merlin's cave;
> Knock'd down the waxen wizard, seiz'd his wand,
> Transformed to lawn what late was fairy land;
> And marr'd, with impious hand, each sweet design
> Of Stephen Duck, and good Queen Caroline.
> Haste, bid yon livelong terrace re-ascend,
> Replace each vista, straighten every bend;
> Shut out the Thames; shall that ignoble thing
> Approach the presence of great Ocean's king?
> No. let barbaric glories feast his eyes,
> August pagodas round his palace rise,
> And finish'd Richmond open to his view,
> 'A work to wonder at, perhaps'—a Kew.

The *Heroic Epistle* was undeniably funny and became one of the century's most popular poems. It was no use Chambers complaining that his views had been distorted or misunderstood, as they had been, but he tried nevertheless. He attached an 'Explanatory Discourse' to a second edition of the *Dissertation* in 1773, and chose to present it as if a Chinaman called Tan Chet-Qua had written it. This lengthy addition attempted to salvage Chambers' central message—that 'your artists and connoisseurs seem to lay too much stress on nature and simplicity', and that 'the appearance of art was admissable, even necessary to the essence of a splendid Garden'.

He attempted to disarm his critics first by stating that his 'free expressions, relative to your Gardeners' were 'by no means levelled at yon stately gentleman in the black periwig' (in other words, Brown). Second, he claimed that he had not intended that the account of Chinese gardens should have been taken too literally, as he had 'cloathed truth in the garb of fiction, to secure it a patient hearing'. Finally, he apologized for his own 'want of perspicuity' in not seeing that the *Dissertation* would cause the widespread 'misapprehensions' that were now so evident to him.

Dr Johnson confessed that the *Heroic Epistle* was very well done[86], but other members of the Literary Club rallied round Chambers. Goldsmith wrote to him that:

Most of the companies that I now go into divide themselves into two parties, the Chambersists and the Brownists, but depend upon it you'll in the end have victory, because you have Truth and Nature on your side. Mr. Burke was advising me about four days ago to draw my pen in a poem in defense of your system, and sincerely, I am very much warm'd in the Cause[87].

However, Chambers dissuaded Goldsmith from this course of action. Chambers's absolute silence in public on gardening matters from this time on leaves the distinct impression that his taste for controversial writing had deserted him entirely.

4

Strictures on Landscape Gardening

The Planting Spirit

Brown's supporters may have won the battle with Chambers, but that alone did not ensure the continuing success of his system. Although landowners were prepared in some instances to take ornamental improvements seriously, in the late 1770s and the 1780s their attention mostly lay elsewhere. This was the age known since as the Industrial Revolution, with large-scale schemes of economic improvement afoot. Canals, turnpikes and stagecoaches vastly improved transport, whilst mine-owners and industrialists could buy Adam Smith's *Wealth of Nations* or purchase a steam engine from Matthew Boulton's manufactory in Soho, near Birmingham, from 1776.

The pervading attitude was a systematic approach to any endeavour, whether in manufacturing, agriculture or planting. This led to great technical achievements, which is as evident in the field of planting as elsewhere.

Planting for oak timber for the Navy continued to be regarded as a matter of national importance. It was both a patriotic and a profitable investment. Montgomeryshire was regarded as the most wooded county in Wales, and reputedly offered the best oak for the Navy. The high prices resulting from the national shortage earned the gratitude of its gentlemen, who in 1781 erected a pillar on Breidden Hill to the honour of Admiral George Rodney[1].

The Society of Arts continued to encourage the planting of oaks and sowing of acorns. In order to be considered for a medal for planting, the planter or his sponsor had to furnish the society with details of species, numbers, areas and fencing arrangements. Certificates from respectable people with first-hand knowledge of the plantations would also be required to attest to the veracity of the planter's claims. Such communications were often substantial articles which came to be published in various unofficial and semi-official accounts of the society's proceedings. Upon the suggestion of Arthur Young, who was chairman of the Agriculture Committee, the first official annual *Transactions* were published in 1783[2]. They contained full accounts of plantations in 1777 and the practice of publishing such communications was continued regularly thereafter.

By far the most impressive plantations in the country as a whole were Scottish. John Murray, fourth Duke of Atholl, and John Campbell, third Earl of Breadalbane, counted their trees, at Dunkeld and Taymouth respectively, in the millions. So did Sir James MacDonald from Skye, whose efforts were, however, ruined by lack of enclosure[3]. So did Francis Stuart, ninth Earl of Moray, George Ross and James Duff, second Earl of Fife, all three of whom had correspondence published in the Society's *Transactions*. Moray had planted nearly eight million Scots pines at Darnaway, Moray, between 1767 and 1781, Ross three million at Cromarty, Ross and Cromarty, up till 1784, and Fife nearly four million at Innes House, Moray, between 1769 and 1787.

Ross was a remarkable man. In 1772 he purchased the Cromarty estate, and set about improvements with the vigour of a young man. He built a new mansion and a new harbour, and made the town one of the few prosperous ones in the generally much impoverished Highlands[4]. Fife was also a hard-headed improver. Referring to his fine park at Duff House, he wrote to the Society of Arts that:

I shall not trouble the society with any account of what I have done for the ornament and decoration of my ground, as that, although it employs many poor labourers, may be considered as foppish dress, and changeable like other fashionable cloathing[5].

Remarkably, the most medals went to Thomas White. He was living at West Retford in Nottinghamshire, and was at the centre of a group of improvers that took planting very seriously. There was William Mellish, Esquire, of Blyth in Nottinghamshire, who received gold medals for 101,600 spruce in 1778 and 47,500 larch in 1780. Nearby there was Joseph Cowlishaw of Hodsock Park, a nurseryman and another advocate of larch, and just over the county boundary in Yorkshire there was Richard Slater Milnes of Fryston, near Ferrybridge, for whom White laid out medal-winning plantations of larch, Scots pine, ash, elm, etc, between 1786 and 1788.

White's experience in advising others at Harewood, Darnaway and Duff House was turned to use in the planting of his own recently acquired estate at Butsfield. He planted 100,000 Scots pine and numbers of other trees on recently enclosed moorland in the spring of 1777. In 1778 the society announced that it was giving him gold medals for Lombardy poplar, larch, Scots pine, occidental plane and silver fir, and a silver medal for spruce. In 1779 he was awarded further gold medals, this time for Norfolk willow and ash. William Mellish acquainted the society in 1780 or 1781 with the 'great credit and applause' which White had gained for 'this spirited undertaking'. The timber would be of great service to the collieries about Newcastle. Further plantations, making 1000 acres in all, were planned, and White had established a nursery within the plantation[6].

White made a further application for medals after a busy spring of 1784. This time he planted 240,523 larch, although it was the 10,000 elms and 37,230 alders that he planted as well that earned him two more gold medals. His eleventh and last medal was a silver for oaks in 1787.

Professional Improvers

Lancelot Brown and other improvers had little comparable with White's achievements in planting. Brown's first client to win a medal was Arthur Chichester fifth Earl of Donegal. Brown made huge plantations of oak with a coniferous nurse crop at Fisherwick, Staffordshire, and this was put to the Society of Arts. Although over 60,000 oaks had been planted Donegal received only a silver medal. One of Brown's old clients, John Fitzpatrick, second Earl of Upper Ossory achieved slightly more success. He was awarded a gold medal for a mixed plantation of Scots pine, oak, beech, chestnuts and other species at Ampthill, Bedfordshire, in 1784.

Brown had more important concerns than his lack of conspicuous success in planting. His business had been on the wane since the early 1770s. He had numerous old clients, it was true, but after he was given Harewood in 1773 he was given only two substantial commissions, Wynnstay in about 1777 and Nuneham the year after.

Sir Watkin Williams-Wynn had already built a seven-mile-long park wall to enclose his 1500-acre park at Wynnstay but he was most remarkable for his

43   Fisherwick, the north front.

John Spyers made this watercolour in 1786. On the right are the mixed plantations admired by William Marshall in *Planting and Ornamental Gardening* (1785).

planting of avenues[7], a practice which most landowners had given up 40 years before. Brown did not interfere with them after putting the pleasure ground in order; his chief concern was to remedy the lack of middle-ground water. To this end he made plans for a series of massive dams and cascades.

However, Brown died in 1783, before his plan could be carried out. Other uncompleted works at his death included Sandleford Priory in Berkshire, the seat of Mrs Elizabeth Montagu, the famous 'blue-stocking'. Such works needed to be brought to some state of completion, and Williams-Wynn set up John Evans of Llwynygroes, Montgomeryshire, a cartographer, as the new director of his improvements. Evans completed the Belan water and its cascade, which was compared by some to the Bowood cascade, and these were opened with great ceremony in 1784. However, Evans' improvements stopped soon after, and he seemed to have returned to his life's work, a map of North Wales.

Brown had willed that any uncompleted contracts were to be carried out by Samuel Lapidge 'who knows my accounts'. Lapidge lived at Hampton Wick, Middlesex, only a mile from Brown's residence at Hampton Court, and did indeed take on the contracts as well as Brown's yards at Hampton Court Green[8]. He thus completed the improvements to Sandleford Priory and Chalfont Park, the residence of Charles Churchill, Walpole's brother-in-law, and where Brown had been working in conjunction with Richmond. He also took on fresh work on his own account. For example, he signed a contract with William Cavendish, fifth Duke of Devonshire, in 1784 for a new carriage drive around the gardens at Chiswick House[9].

Lapidge's task was not always a smooth path. He encountered difficulties with Henry Holland, who as Brown's son-in-law and partner in architectural matters had some claim to Brown's commissions himself. Brown had been to Althorp in Northamptonshire, the seat of John, Earl Spencer, in 1780, and seven years later Holland was making extensive alterations to the house and grounds for George John, the second Earl[10]. Lapidge disputed his right to alter the grounds, but without success. Holland was accepting commissions to amend the layouts at Althorp, Woburn and other places as an extension of his architectural practice, and Lapidge was little hindrance.

Another convert to laying out grounds was the agriculturalist William Marshall. He had a natural flair for agricultural improvements but he had ambitions to be an author. Unfortunately his style was at first a little awkward. He submitted his first book, *Minutes of Agriculture* (1778), to Samuel Johnson, who laughed at it but helped him.

This first performance was important for Marshall, for it took him to Statfold. Samuel Pipe-Wolferstan, one of the gentry of Staffordshire, had come in to possession of Statfold in 1776 and the next year William Emes drew up a plan of improvement[11]. This was not carried out though, and when he read Marshall's little book in 1782 Pipe-Wolferstan was so impressed that he invited Marshall to be his partner in running the estate. Marshall accepted a commission instead, and resided at Statfold from 1784 to 1786[12]. He and Pipe-Wolferstan were as interested in 'rural ornament' as in 'rural economy', and Marshall's *Planting and Ornamental Gardening* (1785) sprang from their endeavours.

Over half the book was taken up by an 'Alphabet of Plants', for which he drew heavily on William Hanbury. There were also sections on timber, hedges and woodlands. Although dismissive of Alexander Hunter's new 1776 edition of John Evelyn's *Sylva*, Marshall reprinted two letters to Hunter. One was from Mr Speechley, gardener to the Duke of Portland at Welbeck, and the other from James Farquharson concerning the Scots fir. Throughout, Marshall displays a sensible attitude, even if expressed somewhat aggressively.

The last 50 pages were devoted to 'Grounds; or Ornamental Plantations'. Marshall showed familiarity with Whately, Gilpin, William Mason and more recent authors such as Daniel Malthus and William Burgh. He emerges as a fervent admirer of William Mason and Horace Walpole, and even reprinted Walpole's *Essay on Modern Gardening* verbatim. He had a few ideas of his own and was not reluctant to give his opinions. He saw the treatment of nature by 'a Dutch gardener in embellishing the environs of a mansion' as the equivalent of South Sea Islanders tattooing their skin or Africans slashing their cheeks. These images may seem strange, but Marshall's views on the imitative purpose of improvement were conventional, and his understanding of Nature as the cultivated countryside, rather than the 'impenetrable roughness of America' or an idealized landscape, was becoming so.

Marshall may have hoped that his book, which appeared so soon after Brown's death, would promote his claims to be a leading improver. However, Brown's death did not immediately leave the way open for him or any other improver. Indeed, Thomas White ceased to work in England at precisely this time[13]; and Marshall built himself a solid reputation as an author of purely agricultural improvement.

Mr Richmond and Richard Woods were approaching the end of their careers in the 1780s. Richmond was still working in 1780 but had died by 1788[14]. He had made a considerable name for himself at Stoke House, Buckinghamshire, and Lee Priory, Kent. Stoke House belonged to Lady Cobham, the widow of Lord Cobham at Stowe, and was one of Brown's early commissions. It was purchased by Thomas Penn and in about 1775 his son John called on Richmond to continue the improvements by forming a serpentine lake and by planting. Penn was later highly complimentary when writing his *Historical and Descriptive Account of Stoke Park* (1813). Lee Priory was the residence of

44   Lee Priory, view from the lawns.

This painting of about 1800 shows the grounds on which Mr Richmond worked 20 years previously.

Thomas Barrett, a quiet picture collector and friend of Horace Walpole. Walpole noted in 1780 that Richmond was making alterations and wrote of the place that, 'There is a small house that is decent, a cheerful vale, an humble stream improved, a few trees of dignity and ground irregular enough for variety'[15]. The most evident signs of Richmond's success at both places are the extremely attractive scenes depicted by a number of artists.

Woods was about Brown's age, and so he too would be likely to take life more easily in the 1780s. He kept working to the end though, for he drew up a plan for some farms at Stanway in Essex in 1792, the year before he died[16]. Once he had settled into Ingrave Hall, in Essex, he took on very few commissions outside that county. Most were small-scale improvements that gave little scope for showing his skills in selecting planting mixtures. Two more prestigious schemes did take him out of the county. He drew up a plan for Hengrave Hall in Suffolk, the seat of Sir Thomas Gage, in 1777. Second, he improved Englefield House in Berkshire, the seat of Nathan Wrighte, from 1781[17].

William Emes was a younger man and at the height of his career. His great success in Staffordshire and the surrounding counties in the late 1760s and early 1770s was followed by a decade of broadening horizons, despite the general low level of interest in improvement. If an unsuccessful foray into

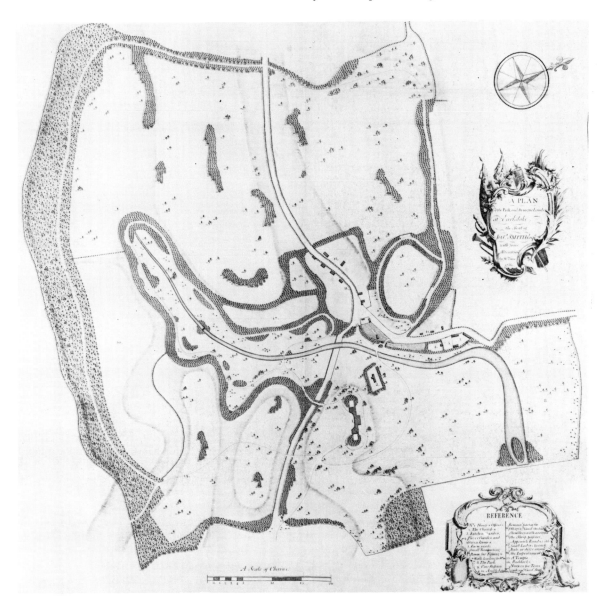

Scotland, at Allanbank, is discounted[18], his work took him as far afield as Anglesey, Wiltshire and Norfolk. The commissions were becoming more prestigious too. For example, from 1777 to 1779 he was improving Viscount Bulkeley's grounds at Baron Hill, Anglesey, embellished by the genuine ruin of Beaumaris Castle[19].

At the same time he was employed by the leading landowner of Glamorgan, the youthful Thomas Mansell Talbot, to lay out grounds around Talbot's romantic new villa at Penrice on the Gower Peninsula[20]. The villa is backed by the ruins of Penrice Castle, and the sea is in view. Emes' lake looked like a creek, and his planting enlivened and directed the view sea-wards. In 1779 Talbot asked Emes to help with Margam, the Mansell's old home made out of an abbey. Talbot wished to demolish the old house but preserve some ruins of the abbey, and the famous collection of orange trees. Emes produced a design for a

45 Earlstoke, design for the park.

One of William Emes' most elaborate designs, it is dated 1786.

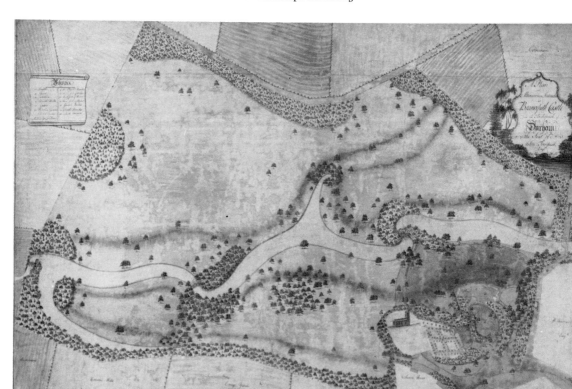

46 Brancepeth Castle, design for the park.

The design is of 1783 and thus one of Adam Mickle's earliest. It is in Lancelot Brown's style, but somewhat crude.

new orangery which was given a final appearance and built by the architect Anthony Keck some years later.

Also in 1779, Emes was at Belton in Lincolnshire, the seat of Lord Belton, and in 1781 he had a small involvement at Bowood[21]. Then in 1784 he was called to Holkham by Thomas Coke to extend the lake[22]. He may well have had a reputation for making lakes because from 1783 to 1787 Emes had men at Hawkstone constructing a mile-long dam to form Hawk Lake[23], and in 1795 he was at Chippenham, Cambridgeshire, and forming a half-mile long lake for the new owner, John Tharp[24]. In all these places the lake ends were similar—tapering down and then a bend into woodland.

By 1783 another improver had set up in business in Thomas White's area, Yorkshire and the North. This was Adam Mickle from Bedale, Yorkshire[25]. He took over The Rand, the house in which the steward to the Squire of Bedale had lived[26]. It is therefore possible that he laid out the grounds at Bedale Hall for the squire, Henry Peirse, who came of age in 1775. In 1783 Mickle made a plan for Brancepeth Castle, County Durham[27]. Four years later he drew up plans for Kippax Park in Yorkshire[28]. He must have been well-respected by this time, for in 1788 he drew up plans for Tredegar House, Monmouthshire, the seat of that county's leading gentleman, John Morgan[29]. His proposals were certainly bold—they involved sweeping away courtyards and stables, breaking avenues, diverting the turnpike road and forming a substantial lake. This would have given a wide expanse of grass between the house and the high ground in the deer park, so that each was reflected in the lake. In the event all this was carried out except the demolition and rebuilding of the stables.

Mickle may have had Thomas White's concentration on Butsfield and Scotland to thank for his commissions. White quickly established himself as

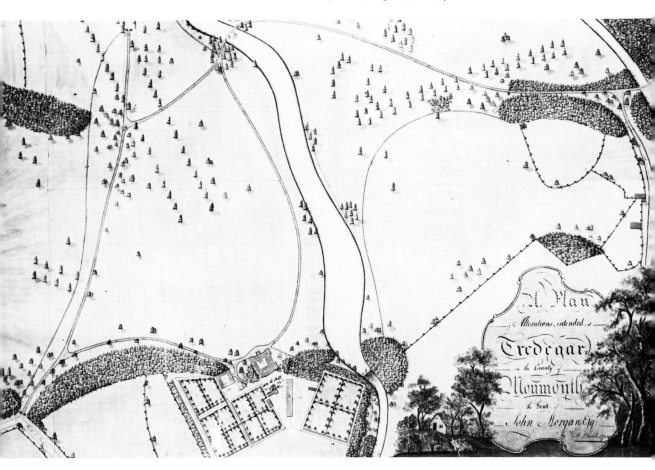

47 Tredegar House, design
for the park.

The southern part of Adam
Mickle's vast plan of
Tredegar. He moved the
turnpike away from the
house and made the lake as
shown in 1790, but the
stables were not resited.

the leading Scottish improver, and no doubt he had Robert Robinson's
bankruptcy in 1782[30] to thank in part for that. Also, though, he already had a
good reputation from his large scale planting schemes, which gave rise to
commissions at Scone Palace, Perthshire, and Donbristle, Fife, both in 1781[31].
The next year he received four more commissions. In one of these, Allanbank,
in Berwickshire, he replaced William Emes.

Apart from a limited number of tree-planting commissions such as at
Fryston, White's last notable works in England were for John Christian
Curwen of Workington Hall, Cumberland[32]. Curwen not only asked him to lay
out the grounds at Workington, but also those on the island of Long-Holme in
Lake Windermere, the island for which Gilpin had suggested a style of
improvement when he saw it in 1772. The owner was a merchant called
Thomas English who had most probably seen the Italian Lakes, and wished
Long-Holme to resemble one of their inhabited islets. Shortly after Gilpin's visit
he embanked the shores and on the highest point built a cylindrical domed
house to the designs of John Plaw. It was said to have been modelled on Villa
Vicenza. English received much criticism for his poor taste and as a result sold
the island in 1781 to Curwen who renamed it Belle Isle, perhaps after his wife
or perhaps after Isola Bella in the Italian Lakes. The next year White laid out a
circumferential walk around to the shore line and planted it uniformly and
thickly[33], both points which Gilpin advised against.

During the 1770s and 1780s the English style of improvement was admired all over Europe. The French architect François-Joseph Belanger came to England in 1778 to make drawings, and was followed by the Swedish architect, Fredrik Piper in 1779. Georges le Rouge published a great mass of engravings and re-engravings, which included numerous details of English gardens, in Paris between 1774 and 1789. The French interpreted the English garden in their own way, and so one could rarely mistake one in France as English. Nevertheless many Frenchmen desired the approbation of an authentic practitioner in the English style, and so it was that Thomas Blaikie, a Scottish plant collector and gardener, came to be involved in some of the great Paris gardening schemes in the late 1770s[34].

Even Russia was not excluded from the English gardening craze. William Gould, from Ormskirk, Lancashire, entered the service of Prince Potemkin in the 1770s. Potemkin was one of Catherine the Great's favourites, and the Crimea was annexed by Russia in 1784 largely through his efforts. It was said that on one of Potemkin's journeys there, Gould laid out an English Garden at every stopping place, even if the stop was only for a day. Gould is also credited with laying out the grounds of Potemkin's Tauridean palace in St Petersburg[35]. Here he invented a system of hot water heating for a conservatory. Gould rose to be the gardener to the Emperor Alexander in the 1800s before returning to Ormskirk in his old age[36]. A Scot, Charles Cameron, laid out the grounds of Pavlovsk, which were begun about 1780.

Private Improvers

Generally speaking, there were few new layouts in the 1770s and 1780s. There was, however, much reshaping of older layouts including those by, or in the styles of, Bridgeman and Kent.

One of the more surprising examples of reshaping was Warwick Castle Park. When George Greville, second Earl of Warwick, began his grandiose scheme of expansion in 1779 it was barely 20 years old. Several streets in the town were demolished in order to widen the narrow gardens, and the roads around the park were completely reorganized to enable its expansion. Both operations took a decade to complete, but by 1791 'Warwick Park', as it was called, amounted to 751 acres and the gardens to another 45. Although the new park was similar in concept to that created by Brown, almost all of Brown's original work had been uprooted or flooded during the expansion.

Most reshapings were still of regular or partly regular layouts, though. The regular grounds of Mount Edgcumbe, on a hill on the Cornish side of Plymouth Sound, were gradually softened from the middle of the century, and the park was laid out with rides and a folly ruin[37]. Dr Johnson, usually reluctant to admire such works, thought the situation the second noblest in Britain when he visited in 1762. Continuous improvements by the first Earl of Mount Edgcumbe himself from the 1760s till his death in 1795 had, by the 1780s, created a much admired landscape in the Natural Style. It was chiefly notable for the contrasts and surprises for which the irregular promontory was so suitable. The huge open vistas over sea and land from the higher points contrasted with the glades and gardens enclosed by landform and wood lower down the slopes; the one was wild and sublime, the others in Italian, French and English styles, highly polished and refined.

The gardens of West Wycombe were converted from an irregularly laid out regular garden in the Batty Langley manner into another fine example of the Natural Style over roughly the same period. From about 1770 Francis Dashwood, Lord le Despencer, employed a land surveyor called Thomas Cook to continue with improvements. Despencer must have been well pleased with

Cook, because he left him an annuity when he died in 1782[38]. During the previous dozen years extensive planting and thinning had irregularized the older layout, the cascade had been modified and many garden buildings added by Nicholas Revett.

Several already well-known gardens saw some attention during the 1780s. Virginia Water at Windsor was one of the best known. A severe flood of 1768 broke down Flitcroft's dam constructed in 1749, and it broke through again in 1782, thereby causing one wit to nickname Thomas Sandby as 'Tommy Sandbank'. Each time Sandby rebuilt, and on the second occasion the new dam was built in a new position and 10 feet higher than the old one. The great increase in size to 130 acres required an Act of Parliament enabling the flooding of waste lands in the Parish of Egham upstream of the park[39]. The new cascade, constructed of massive boulders from Bagshot Heath, excited much admiration for its natural appearance.

Another famous cascade of the same date is that at Bowood. In 1781 William Petty-Fitzmaurice, Marquess of Lansdowne, asked Charles Hamilton, by then an old man living in Bath, to help with a cascade for the lake, made by Brown. Hamilton turned to Josiah Lane, the son of Joseph Lane, to construct

48 West Wycombe house, view from the south.

The view was painted by Thomas Daniell in 1781. Lord Despencer had been softening the earlier regular layout during the previous decade.

the vast and elaborate arrangement of caves and passages[40]. Their combined work was a continuation of the intricate, toy-like grandeur of the Painshill and Oatlands grottoes, and quite different from the massively constructed cascades at Blenheim and Virginia Water. A story that Hamilton was copying the effects seen in a painting by Gaspar Poussin went into circulation[41], and no doubt contributed to the widespread admiration that the cascade enjoyed for 40 years or more.

Hamilton's influence did not continue merely in rockwork. His massed planting of shrubs at Painshill provided a model for the expanding fashion for shrubberies. John Trusler, who lived within a mile of Painshill, was quite likely recalling it to mind when he wrote in *Elements of Modern Gardening* (1784),

An amphitheatre of shrubs rising one above the other, the shortest before, and gradually taller ones behind, as they recede from the eye, so as that the whole may be seen at one view, forms no unpleasing object. In this case, the darker greens should stand behind as a back ground to set off the lighter, and the whole may be enriched with some variegated shrubs or flowers in front, or occasionally intermixed with them. The bloom of shrubs, the hue of their berries, their foliage and their bark, will, if properly mixed, form as pleasing a variety as the bloom of flowers; so will the different tints the leaves assume in autumn ...

Trusler was by profession a miscellaneous writer, and his views were probably received from others. Nevertheless he was one of the few people to be writing about the design of flower borders and flower gardens at the time. The recommended form of flower garden was as at Nuneham Courtenay:

Grass with beautiful clumps of shrubs and flowers scattered with taste, are generally most pleasing, with a hard terrace of gravel for the benefit of walking after a shower of rain, when every thing in bloom gives out its fragrency; or, the form and disposition of the clumps or flower beds, may be very irregular, but not appear broken into too many disjointed patches.

He described how the flowers in a border should be arranged 'according to their heights, their sizes, and their colours, and their times of blowing (sic)'. The whole should form 'one rich variegated mass'. He also described the bedding out of flowers in pots—a subject hardly referred to after the advent of the Natural Style. He gave no examples, but the French gardens at Mount Edgcumbe and Park Place[42], both probably made in the late 1780s, are likely to have had bedding out.

As was the usual practice, these gardens were not in sight from the principal front of the house, but were secluded. They were, however, out of the ordinary at this date for being entirely regular. That at Park Place was at the rear of the house, and enclosed by a wall and trellis-work arcades. The flower borders were arranged around a central basin with goldfish and a fountain[43]. That at Mount Edgcumbe had beds of flowers, a central fountain, high clipped hedges of ilex and bays, and surrounding trellis-work. There was also an Italian garden, with an orangery designed by Lord Camelford. At one end balustraded steps were made to an upper level above a small grotto, as is often to be seen at a larger scale in true Italian gardens[44]. At both places these formal gardens were partly enclosed by, and formed a contrast with, adjacent shrubberies. At Mount Edgcumbe the shrubbery was referred to as 'the English Garden'.

At the broader scale of park improvements, notable examples directed by the owners are noticeably less numerous after 1773 than before. Persons who had made their money rapidly, through trade for example, seemed less susceptible to the slackening of interest in new gardens shown by the rest of land-owning society, perhaps because there was a steady stream of such people wishing to establish themselves as gentry. Admiral Robert Digby was an example. He was

a younger brother of the sixth Baron Digby, but had naval bounty to thank for much of his wealth, particularly from 1779. He bought Minterne, in Dorset, in 1768, and subsequently spent much of his wealth on its embellishment with lakes, a bridge, lawns and lavish planting[45].

Perhaps the outstanding example was Warren Hastings' Daylesford, in Gloucestershire. Hastings' family had owned it till the early eighteenth century and indeed Hastings had known it as a boy before going to India to make his fortune. Regaining it was a lifelong ambition which was satisfied in 1788, the year in which his famous trial for corruption began. During the next six years he lavished £40,000 on his house and grounds, including an extensive lake in a well-wooded landscape, and a grotto[46]. However even Hastings' huge wealth could not withstand the costs of fighting an impeachment, and the improvements to the estate were only ever partly completed.

49 St Anne's Hill, the cottage.

The early-nineteenth-century lithograph shows Charles James Fox's retreat near Chertsey, Surrey, which he improved from about 1786. Grounds like these show that there was no break between the earlier *fermes ornées* and the later *cottages ornées*.

The Picturesque Principle

William Mason's *Heroic Epistle to Sir W. Chambers* may have silenced Brown's antagonists for the time being, but during the succeeding 20 years doubts about the improvers' ruthless reorganization of the countryside for Dame

Nature's sake was expressed by a bewildering number of authors.

Open literary warfare was avoided, however. Mason, for his part pursued his main project, *The English Garden*. Book II appeared in 1777, Book III in 1779 and Book IV in 1782. Books II and III are recitals of his understanding of the practice of improvement, with subjects like paths, fencing, ha-has, and so forth being dully treated in Book II in a ludicrous Classical style, and the disposition of wood, choice of species and the design of lakes following in Book III. Book IV was little more than a tale on the subject of American independence with gardening overtones. The meaning of Mason's poetry was made much clearer when a new edition of all four books came out in 1783 with a copious commentary and notes by William Burgh, a friend of Mason at York.

Brown remained attached by friendship to Mason and his circle and indeed it was Mason who was to write his epitaph in the chancel of Fenstanton church. Lord Nuneham decided soon after he succeeded as Earl Harcourt in 1777 that the park south of the house should be improved by Brown[47]. William Whitehead, Harcourt's old tutor, wrote light-hearted poems to commemorate the improvements:

> Dame Nature, the goddess, one very bright day,
> In strolling through Nuneham, met Brown in her way.
> 'And bless me,' she said, with an insolent sneer,
> 'I wonder that fellow will dare to come here.
> What more than I did has your impudence plann'd;
> The lawn, wood, and water, are all of my hand ...'

Brown's reply to Dame Nature was to point out his improvements:

> 'That ground of your moulding is certainly fine,
> But the swell of that knoll and those openings are mine ...
> The ridges are melted, the boundaries gone:
> Observe all those changes, and candidly own
> I have cloth'd you when naked, and, when overdrest,
> I have stripp'd you again to your boddice and vest;
> Concealed ev'ry blemish, each beauty display'd,
> As Reynolds would picture some exquisite maid ...'

Whitehead's humour perhaps became a little bitter at the end of the poem. Dame Nature had accepted defeat, but then brightened again:

> 'For a lucky conjecture comes into my head,
> That, whate'er he has done, and whate'er he has said,
> The world's little malice will balk his design:
> Each fault they call his, and each excellence mine.'

This last line was becoming increasingly true, as Brown's, and even Mason's, supporters dwindled. The weak poetry of John Scott, the Quaker from Amwell, Hertfordshire, in support of Nature was little consolation. He had made his own little garden with a grotto and a wide variety of shrubs. At length, dissatisfied with his own efforts he exclaimed

> No scene like this (I say) did Nature raise,
> Brown's fancy form, or Walpole's judgement praise;
> No prototype for this did I survey
> In Woollett's landscapes or in Mason's lay[48].

However Scott was not known for his critical faculties, and such subservience could hardly have been valued.

Henry James Pye, another bad poet although Poet Laureate, was complimentary to Mason in *The Progress of Refinement* (1783), a celebration of Britain's artistic prowess. As to garden design,

Secure her fame unhurt by time shall stand
Since Mason's verse records what Brown has plan'd.

The accompanying verse was merely imitative, full of phrases like 'Nature's rural empire', 'her genuine forms', 'to teach the curve in graceful bends to flow', and so forth.

More welcome, perhaps, was a translation by Daniel Malthus of the Marquis René-Louis de Girardin's *De la Composition des Paysages* (1777). Girardin was noted as Rousseau's last patron, and Rousseau was buried in 1778 on an island at Ermenonville, Girardin's country estate near Paris. The translation, *An Essay on Landscape* (1783), was of course useful as a practical guide to those wishing to work to Girardin's precepts, but so was Malthus' general support of Rousseau, Mason and Gray, and his opposition to Chambers, expressed in a preface.

Malthus soon found his translation plagiarized. Readers of *Elements of Modern Gardening* (1784) by Dr John Trusler found themselves advised that

I would recommend either making a draft of the design yourself, or getting some painter to do it, under your supervision.

Girardin's ideas on making mock-ups of buildings using rods, and lakes using sheets, so that the effects of changes could be foreknown, were repeated.

Chambers, Johnson and their circle whilst avoiding a public challenge to Mason, still maintained their conviction that (as Sir Joshua Reynolds put it in 1786).

The great end of all arts is, to make an impression on the imagination and the feeling.... The true test of all the arts ... is to produce a pleasing effect upon the mind[49].

Ostentation continued to displease Johnson. When at Kedleston Hall with Boswell in 1777 Boswell observed:

50 Kedleston, view of bridge and boathouse.

The magnificent house and grounds depicted in this painting of about 1775 did not please Dr Johnson. He said that it excluded only one evil – poverty.

The excellent smooth gravel roads; the large pieces of water formed by his Lordship from some small brooks, with a handsome barge upon it: the venerable Gothic church, now the family chapel, just by the house; in short, the grand group of objects agitated and distended my mind in a most agreeable manner.

'One should think,' said I, 'that the proprietor of all this *must* be happy.'

'Nay, Sir', said Johnson, 'all this excludes but one evil—poverty'[50].

The opposite extreme rather amused Johnson. Lord Kilmorey had no park at Shavington Hall, Shropshire, and Johnson remembered how

he rejoiced in having *no* park. He could not disoblige his neighbours by sending them *no* venison[51].

Many people had wondered why William Mason should have dedicated Book I of his *The English Garden* to Simplicity. Reynolds tackled the question of simplicity in a discourse given to the Royal Academy in 1778, although he was careful not to clash directly with Mason by extending his argument to arts other than painting[52]. He considered simplicity as

implying that exact conduct which proceeds from an intimate knowledge of simple unadulterated nature.

However he could not define it exactly, as it was 'only a negative virtue', in that, whilst it was 'our barrier against that great enemy of truth and nature, Affectation', it did not in itself make any contribution to the creation of works of art. In fact, he warned that 'an ostentatious display of simplicity becomes as disagreeable and nauseous as any other kind of affectation'. This argument, by a master in the art which Mason said gardening was allied to, could have cast a doubt on *The English Garden*'s worth in the mind of anyone who had heard or read the *Discourses* as well.

However rehearsing the old arguments between Mason and Chambers now seemed somewhat sterile, and they were allowed to subside. At the same time Girardin's idea of treating a landscape literally like a painting was being mooted, and the antagonists now found an area of common ground.

Burgh had been thinking along similar lines to Girardin. He was converted to an appreciation of picturesque scenery perhaps more than Mason was. Mason did include a section in Book III on the wild Lake District scenery as if it had been written by Gray, but it was left to Burgh to claim that in Book I 'the picturesque principle was exemplified and applied to the living scenery of nature'[53]. By 'the picturesque principle', Burgh appears to have meant that a garden should be designed to exhibit a series of scenes each of which would look well as a painting. He saw the value of foreground trees in the composition of such scenes, pointing out that 'it would be impossible to retrench even a single bough' from the wooded foregrounds of Claude Lorrain and Gaspar Poussin 'without an injury to the general composition of the scene'.

Burgh recognized the difficulties of his principle:

I seem to hear an objection started to the justice of the doctrine, and to be asked in what manner the practice of the Gardener, who, for the most part, makes excessive neatness an object in his scenes, is to be reconciled with that species of beauty which consists in roughness of surface, and which appears to have been always aimed at by the Painter of Landscape[54].

He gave more of an apology than an answer to this objection. First, the objection could only apply to the foreground, since the distance and the general composition of a scene can both accord with picturesque design. In respect to the foreground, Burgh admitted that 'a rural scene in reality, and a rural scene upon canvas, are not precisely one and the same thing', but felt that the difference between the principle and its application was 'so extremely trivial', that it 'can hardly be admitted as an objection to the introduction of the picturesque principle into the Art of Gardening'.

Daines Barrington, one of Johnson's friends, briefly gave his views on the state of modern gardening at the end of 'On the Progress of Gardening', an historical paper delivered to the Society of Antiquaries in 1782:

Kent hath been succeeded by Brown, who hath undoubtedly great merit in laying out pleasure grounds, but I conceive that in some of his plans I see rather traces of the gardener of Old Stowe, than of Poussin or Claude Lorraine. I could wish therefore that Gainsborough gave the design, and that Brown executed[55].

This mention of Gainsborough was not to be the last. He was increasingly recognized as a great intuitive genius in the portrayal of landscape. He seemed the perfect counterpart on canvas to Gilpin on paper. Although owing no allegiance to the Dutch school of landscape painting, he treated similar subjects in the most picturesque fashion. His great rival in portraiture, Reynolds, who was so different in his rationality, steadfast application and respect for history painting, acknowledged that:

If Gainsborough did not look at nature with a poet's eye, it must be acknowledged that he saw her with the eye of a painter, and gave a faithful, if not a poetical representation of what he had before him[56].

Reynolds' ideas may have been changing. In his Discourse III, delivered in 1770, he had recapitulated the theory of Ideal Beauty, that is the poetical idea of the beauty of nature when the blemishes and defects are corrected. By 1786, he had, with Gilpin and Burgh, deviated from this orthodoxy still being upheld by William Mason, towards an appreciation of picturesque beauty.

All differences between admirers of the picturesque were not yet submerged, though, and Reynolds came out strongly against the Sisterhood of the Arts in a passage that makes an interesting point of divergence from Burgh's ideas. Both acknowledged the differences between the arts, but Reynolds would not allow these to be passed over:

No art can be engrafted with success on another art. ... Each has its own particular modes both of imitating nature, and of deviating from it ... Gardening, as far as Gardening is an Art, entitled to that appellation, is a deviation from nature; for if the true taste consists, as many hold, in banishing every appearance of Art, or any traces of the footsteps of man, then it would then be no longer a Garden. Even though we define it, 'Nature to advantage dress'd' ... it is however, no longer a subject for the pencil of a Landskip-Painter, as all Landskip-Painters know, who love to have recourse to Nature herself, and to dress her according to the principles of their own Art[57].

Sense, Propriety and Congruity

Besides that of Chambers, the other system of improvement often represented as a challenge to Brown's was Shenstone's. It was not founded upon a Classical vision of ideal Nature, but it accepted common nature as found, and sought to strengthen its character and associations through Art. Richard Graves, an old university friend of Shenstone's, continued to advertise Shenstone's precepts in print. In the novel *The Spiritual Quixote* (1772), he introduced The Leasowes, with Shenstone explaining the beauties of the cascades. A gardening theme was employed in another novel, *Columella; or, The Distressed Anchoret* (1779), in which Columella represented Shenstone. He had a small estate, encircled with hills covered with hanging woods, and with a number of ornamental buildings, a stream, a bridge and a view of a church spire. One feature particularly admired by Columella's friends was

a winding walk, which conducted them gently down the hill, where seats of turf or rustic benches were disposed, at proper intervals, and in points of view to catch some striking object or agreeable scene . . .

Graves wished to make the same point about pretentious schemes of improvement as Goldsmith had done. When Columella found an urn to be dislodged and some seats dirtied, he philosophically reflected: 'Why I am afraid, indeed, I myself am to blame in some measure for extending my pleasure-ground beyond its proper limits'. Graves was no supporter of Chambers, as a passage ridiculing the idea of setting up gibbets on a bleak hill showed. Nor was he in sympathy with the classicists; a place in Columella's garden called Tadpole Bottom had been renamed Arno's Vale by one of Columella's more romantically inclined neighbours, and Graves ridiculed such practices—Columella's gardener in his confusion called it 'Aaron's Well'. Also, when Columella visited Stourhead, he found 'the *modern taste* of jumbling together so many buildings of such a different style of architecture, and of ages and nations so remote' to be contradicatory and false.

Graves' last act on behalf of his old friend was to publish *Recollections of Some Particulars in the Life of the Late William Shenstone* (1788).

Younger writers, who had never known the state of gardening before the Natural Style came into fashion, felt little need to justify irregular designs through some theory of beauty. On the other hand, a greater acquaintance with Latin poets had strengthened the respect for general principles such as sense, utility, propriety, congruity, and sympathy. Shenstone's pragmatic but tasteful approach to improvement was thus more congenial than either Brown's or Chambers'.

However, such comments as Walpole's on preserving old-fashioned gardens if they were comfortable were agreeably pragmatic too. George Mason's *Essay on Design in Gardening* (1768) was strongly inclined towards a reliance on proper attitudes for determining taste, and notable for the absence of any theory of beauty. Perhaps, though, the clearest expression of the new emphasis on the exercise of judgement, as opposed to the imagination or the emotions, was Joseph Cradock's *Village Memoirs* (1774).

Cradock compiled some 'Strictures on Landscape Gardening' which he represented in his book as 'Mr. Arlington's'. His breadth of reading of the Classics was indicated by a review of their references to gardens or natural beauty. He thought he had discovered the 'dawn of taste to rise with the old Bard [i.e. Homer] in his description of Calypso's bower'. As to modern gardens, the difference between the contrived landscape of Stowe, for example, and 'that genuine taste which *Shenstone* and nature have brought us acquainted with' was 'immense'.

He noted that 'to remedy the ill effects of a straight line, an uniform curve is now adopted', and commented that such 'alteration is not always improvement'. This hinted that he held no abhorrence of straight lines, and indeed he objected to the prevailing practice of felling avenues without a thought as to whether they were appropriate. His view was that they could be kept, but

They must be long and wide, and should properly lead to a Gothic castle, tower, or any other large and ancient building.

Such ideas were quite contrary to William Mason's advice, and, as might be expected, Cradock was critical of Brown.

Cradock invented a character, Mr Layout, who was a megalomaniac improver such as Cradock imagined Brown to be. One passage in *Village Memoirs* ran:

Dear Charles,

The alterations already made at Marleston are so great, that I hardly know my own village—Mr Massem every day makes purchases of ground, no matter at what expence, that Mr. Layout may at least acknowledge he has scope enough for his invention. I hear of nothing but Obelisks, Statues, Gazebos, Terminations, and a Laurel-belt—they talk of taste as if it was to be brought down in a broad-wheeled waggon, and they had nothing to do but to scatter it at random—Mr. Layout thinks there should be a clump, and there is one; the squire thinks it would look pretty to cut a vista through it, and it is cut; . . . the grove on the right hand . . . condemned to be cut down as well as the large one, which Mr. Arlington had used to call Shenstone's Grove, for the urn to his memory was prettily executed . . . where expence is only considered, or mistaken as another name for taste, I feel so much disgust, that I turn away my eyes from false ornament, to contemplate nature herself in a simple form, unbroke-in upon by a Mr Layout.

Cradock could speak from a small degree of personal experience of improvement. He had laid out both his mother-in-law's garden at Merivale Hall, Warwickshire, and his own at Gumley, Leicestershire from the late 1760s. William Hanbury planted 20 acres at the latter. The walks through some plantations were thrown open to the public, and became a fashionable resort in the area[58]. He must have been flattered when one visitor in 1781 left a poem on one of the seats.

The death of Thomas Lyttelton, the second Lord Lyttelton, under curious circumstances in 1779 gave rise to wild speculation, including ghost stories. A book of letters, purporting to be his, was published the next year. However, it later transpired that the author was actually William Combe, a journalist. One of the letters made stringent comments upon improvement. Echoing Graves, one letter[59] ran

The system of modern gardening, in spite of fashion and Mr. *Brown*, is a very foolish one. The huddling together every species of building into a park or garden, is ridiculous.

It continued in a vein of sense and propriety with which Cradock would have agreed:

The verdure of British swells was not made for Grecian temples: a flock of sheep and a shepherd's hut are better adapted to it.

At Hagley there were many classical buildings:

This was an evident preference of strange gods, and, in my opinion, a very blasphemous improvement.

The letter approved that

The environs of a magnificent house should partake, in some degree, of the necessary formality of the building they surround. This was *Kent's* opinion, and, where his designs have escaped the destruction of modern refinement, there is an easy grandeur which is at once striking and delightful.

As to the wider scene:

Where Nature is grand, improve her grandeur, not by adding extraneous decorations, but by removing obstructions.

These points would indeed have been remarkable if from the hand of the first Lord Lyttelton's son, and no doubt this is what induced the *Westminster Magazine* to reprint the letter[60].

The theme of what style was appropriate in a particular situation was further developed by William Falconer, a physician of Bath, in a paper read to the Literary and Philosophical Society of Manchester in October 1782[61]. This was a review of taste in ancient and modern gardening, from what Falconer thought of as a 'rational viewpoint', that is in relation to climate and politics. For example the gardens of Babylon seem in many respects to have been laid out with good taste. Their elevation, not only produced a variety and extent of view, but was, also, useful in moderating the heat.

Although disappointed by the topiary at Pliny's gardens, Falconer warned against censure because shearing trees could thicken the shade, and fountains cool the gardens, which 'may still be in perfectly good taste in Italy'. Regular design in Pliny's gardens was, he thought, a reflection of the rigid and despotic government of his times, and the same was true of English regular gardens.

As to contemporary design, Falconer considered that

The general method of laying out grounds, in this country, seems at present to be very rational. Natural beauties, or resemblances thereof, are chiefly attempted; which are the more proper, as being conformable to the climate and situation of the people ...

Groves, grass and natural streams were more 'rational' than alleys, gravel walks and fountains, and the greater extent of English gardens over the Italian ones was a rational consequence of the pleasures of exercise in the one and indolence in the other. Furthermore, England was particularly suited by its verdure and lushness and variety of foliage to designs after Nature.

This is not to say that Falconer necessarily objected to beauties of the artificial kind:

After all, it is possible to err in too closely following Nature, as it is in neglecting her. There are beauties of the artificial kind, as well as natural, which are proper ...

He was a friend of Erasmus Darwin, Anthony Fothergill, John Coakley Lettsom and other botanically-minded physicians, and so perhaps it is not surprising that he should attempt a defence of the flower *parterre* 'so rarely seen at present':

A square, or an oblong border, has nothing obviously absurd or disgusting in its appearance; and as to its being artificial, it may be said in defence of it, that it is not an imitation of anything in nature, nor meant to be so, but solely calculated for utility, as an instrument necessary to the production of beauty; and, considered in this view, we might, with equal reason, object against a house, as an unnatural, and therefore, an improper object, as against the divisions of a flower parterre.

No author or practitioner likes to think of his own works as devoid of sense, propriety or congruity, and even authors who slavishly followed William Mason readily adopted these standards. Inconsistencies were then almost bound to appear. The prime example was William Marshall, who elaborated on the different species of improvement appropriate to different types of property in *Planting and Ornamental Gardening* (1785). This was a theme first raised by George Mason. William Mason in his writings, and Brown in his practice, had considered it very little, as their conceptions of ideal Nature allowed for little departure from it.

Marshall's eminently rational starting point was that

the house must ever be allowed to be a principal in the composition. It ought to be considered as the center of the system, and the rays of art, like those of the sun, should grow fainter as they recede from the center.

The types of house that he examined were the hunting-box, the ornamented cottage, the villa and the principal residence. The grounds of the first should take on a 'masculine' style, with little obvious art and the hardier sorts of shrubs. In those of the ornamented cottage

ostentation and show should be cautiously avoided; even elegance should not be attempted.

By contrast, the villa's grounds should be elegant, rich and grand. With the principal residence, there was the additional object of displaying as much of the estate as possible from the house and drives. The gardens should unite the house with the adjacent country through shrubberies and other planting. The house should not appear 'desolate and inhospitable', nor the country 'naked or flareing'. Marshall then criticized Brown's designs for their bare foregrounds and for their sameness, and he regretted that such a style had been copied by 'the inferior artists'. Such comments were partly promoted by Marshall's combative style towards rivals, but once he gave himself over to considering the matter rationally the divergence from Mason's ideals was probably inevitable.

Yet another form of attack on Brown's system of improvement was William Cowper's refined and spiritual advocacy of humility towards Nature. It persuaded much of the poetry-reading public that aggressive schemes of improvement could not be right. This poetry appealed to sentiment rather than intellect, and it is perhaps only a slight exaggeration to say that the daughters of every country parson in the land must have read it. Cowper was no follower of Shenstone, but a devout Christian with a naturalist's eye and feeling towards the countryside, developed during many years of long walks in the vicinity of Olney, in Buckinghamshire. A first collection of poems was published in 1782, and a second, including the famous 'The Task' in 1785.

Some idea of Cowper's attitude to Nature can be discerned from his poem 'Hope':

> Banks clothed with flowers, groves fill'd with sprightly sounds
> The yellow tilth, green meads, rocks, rising grounds,
> Streams edged with osiers, fattening every field,
> Where'er they flow, now seen and now conceal'd;
> From the blue rim, where skies and mountains meet
> Down to the very turf beneath thy feet,
> Ten thousand charms, that only fools despise,
> Or pride can look at with indifferent eyes.

To Cowper Nature was the countryside as he found it. He was so enraptured by its detail and incident, and so oblivious to the working farmers who had made it that he stated:

> God made the country and man made the town.

He had no theory of why the countryside was beautiful except that

> 'Tis born with all: the love of Nature's works
> Is an ingredient in the compound, man,
> Infused at the creation of the kind.

The love of the country was to be felt, not understood. Fashions in improvement meant nothing to Cowper. In fact he was grateful to John Courtenay Throckmorton of Weston-Underwood, Bedfordshire, for permission to wander through his decayed and unfashionable formal landscape:

> Thanks to Benevolus—he spares me yet
> These chestnuts ranged in corresponding lines,
> And, though himself so polish'd, still reprieves
> The obsolete prolixity of shade.

Cowper also enjoyed Throckmorton's wilderness and the grove, in the same way that he enjoyed the sights and sounds of the surrounding farmland.

Cowper expressed his horror of the unfeeling changes exerted by nobility and gentry of position and fashion. Such persons used their country estates merely

> To exchange the centre of a thousand trades,
> For clumps, and lawns, and temples, and cascades.

Indeed he devoted a whole poem, 'Retirement', to them:

> The statesman, lawyer, merchant, man of trade,
> Pants for the refuge of some rural shade . . .

Such a person wished to

> Improve the remnant of his wasted span,
> And, having lived a trifler, die a man.

Cowper's advice was:

> Happy if full of days—but happier far,
> If ere we yet discuss life's evening star, . . .
> We can escape from custom's idiot sway,
> To serve the sovereign we were born to obey.
> Then sweet to muse upon his skill display'd
> (Infinite skill) in all that he has made.
> To trace in Nature's most minute design
> The signature and stamp of power divine.

The wholesale alterations of Brown filled him with revulsion:

> Improvement, the idol of the age,
> Is fed with many a victim. Lo! he comes,—
> The omnipotent magician, Brown, appears. . .
> He speaks. The lake in front becomes a lawn,
> Woods vanish, hills subside, and vallies rise,
> And streams, as if created for his use,
> Pursue the track of his directing wand . . .

In this, in his sentimental love of the rural poor and in his distaste of Whig principles generally, he had much in common with Oliver Goldsmith.

Tourism

John Brown's letter to Lord Lyttelton gained wide circulation in the late 1760s through publication as a note to John Dalton's *Descriptive Poem Addressed to Two Ladies at Their Return From Viewing the Mines Near Whitehaven* which appeared in George Pearch's *Collection of Poems* of 1768–70. Arthur Young's various *Tours* from 1768 contained much of interest to the tourist though they were essentially agricultural surveys. Gray's accounts of his visits to Scotland in 1765, and Cumberland and Westmorland in 1769, were published when William Mason edited his letters and *Poems* in 1775. Thereafter tourism became popular whilst the ever-improving turnpikes made it easier. Printers responded by publishing guide books at bewildering speed.

At first the usual form of the guide books was a narrative journal enriched with historical, topographical and scenic information. An account of the Lakes of Cumberland and Westmorland, *Excursion to the Lakes* (1774), was written by William Hutchinson, an antiquary. He used the same language of Nature as a painter as had John Brown. Four years later a rival description, *A Guide to the Lakes* (1778), appeared by Thomas West, a Jesuit with keen interest both in medieval monastic architecture and in the landscape.

West noted that the roads had improved even since Gray's visit, and that 'all ranks have caught the spirit of visiting'[62]. In the Lakes they would find:

Alpine scenery, finished in nature's highest tints, what refined art labours to imitate; the pastoral and rural landscape, varied in all the stiles, the soft, the rude, the romantic, the sublime.

He promised that,

whoever takes a walk into these scenes, will return penetrated with a sense of the creator's power and unsearchable wisdom, in heaping mountains on mountains, and enthroning rocks on rocks.

He suggested a number of stations for views. However, West relied largely on previous published descriptions of the scenery, and even these were disappointingly short compared to the space allowed for antiquarian information and local knowledge.

The Wye, the lakes of Cumberland and Westmorland, and Scotland had hitherto received most attention. Wales was as yet little prepared for tourists. Nevertheless, Samuel Johnson made a visit to Denbighshire and Caernarvonshire in 1774 in the company of the Thrales who had family connections there. Johnson experienced the sublime at Hawkstone and on the new turnpike built in 1772 on the side of Penmaenmawr Mountain. He noted that, at one of Mrs Thrale's relatives' houses, 'there was an avenue of oaks, which in a foolish compliance with the present mode, has been cut down'.

Henry Penruddocke Wyndham, who was also in North Wales in 1774, regretted this neglect of Wales:

the Welsh tour has been hitherto strangely neglected ... the author did not meet with a single party, during his six weeks' journey through Wales[63].

He saw Tintern, Piercefield and Margam before turning northwards to reach Cader Idris via the Cardigan Bay coast. In leaving North Wales he visited Chirk and Powis Castles. His guide, *A Gentleman's Tour Through Monmouthshire and Wales* (1775), was one of the first on Wales, and was instrumental in promoting it to the public.

Joseph Cradock had long been interested in Wales, as he fancied that his surname was of ancient and princely Welsh origin. His tour of 1774 was published as *An Account of Some of the Most Romantic Parts of North Wales* (1777). He had ascended both Snowdon and Cader Idris. Although he remarked of such views,

who could behold so bountiful a Display of Nature without Wonder and Ecstasy?[64]

the passages on scenery were generally perfunctory compared to his detailed observations on Welsh history, language and customs. A third bookseller offered a tour of Wales in 1778 when Thomas Pennant's tour in 1773 was published as *A Tour of Wales*. North Wales had then established itself as a rival to the Wye and Scotland in the space of a very few years.

Hitherto William Gilpin's journals of his tours had remained private manuscripts, circulated only to friends amongst that small group of devotees of 'Nature as a painter'. The tour of the lakes of Cumberland and Westmorland was mentioned with praise by William Mason in his compilation of Gray's *Poems* (1775). Margaret, the Dowager Duchess of Portland, had also seen the manuscript, and she in turn had shown it to Queen Charlotte. The Duchess urged Gilpin to publish it, even offering to start a subscription[65]. Mason advised against a subscription, and the Duchess died anyway in 1782, but by that time Gilpin had decided that he would test the public's reaction by publishing the journal of his tour of the Wye. This was a smaller work, and therefore less of a financial risk.

Gilpin need not have worried. His *Observations on the River Wye, and Several Parts of South Wales, etc. Relative Chiefly to Picturesque Beauty* (1782) was well received. Although it has much topographical, historical and other forms of information, its principal use was to improve tourists' critical judgement of scenery, and this was a marked improvement over formerly published journals. The journal of his tour to the lakes of Cumberland and Westmorland was published four years later, with a dedication to the Queen.

Guide books on country houses continued to be offered in various forms, the Stowe guides remaining the pre-eminent examples. Most famous places were still shown by their gardeners but some owners wished descriptions of their gardens to be committed to writing, usually as part of a description of the house. Horace Walpole's *Description of the Villa ... at Strawberry Hill* (1784) and William Mavor's *Blenheim Guide* (1787) were amongst the better cases, both having accompanying prints.

A hack journalist, Joseph Heely, wrote a guide to the three Midlands gardens, Hagley, Enville and The Leasowes, published in 1777. Separate guides to Hagley and The Leasowes were also available in the same year. Purchasers of William Marshall's *Planting and Ornamental Gardening* (1785) would find his descriptions of Piercefield, Stowe, Fisherwick, The Leasowes, Hagley and Enville. Whately's *Observations on Modern Gardening*, meanwhile, remained in print.

Another form of country house publication took on a new lease of life from the 1770s. This was the collection of prints, usually with a short accompanying text. This was a formula already established for *Vitruvius Britannicus*, which had reached a fourth volume in 1767 and a fifth in 1771. Then in 1779 William Watts commenced *The Seats of The Nobility and Gentry*, which by 1786 amounted to 84 copper plates after drawings by Michael Rooker, Sandby and other excellent artists. The series was continued by William Angus from 1787. However, the most prolific artist of quality in the 1780s was Paul Sandby, whose *Collection of 150 Select Views* was published by Boydell in 1782 and 1783.

The horrid or curious scenes of industry were sought after by tourists and engraved by artists. For example Matthew Boulton's Soho manufactory near Birmingham was commonly visited, more as a place of wonder than of aesthetic delight. Ironbridge in Shropshire, though, was both. When built in 1779 by the Coalbrookdale iron-founder, Abraham Darby, it was the world's first iron bridge. It formed a good composition in its setting in the Severn gorge, and was itself an object of grace and beauty. Darby paid Rooker to paint it in 1780, and the result was engraved the next year for the tourists who flocked to wonder at it and enjoy its picturesque qualities[66].

5

Repton and the Picturesque

Humphry Repton, Landscape Gardener

It was perhaps inevitable that attempts would be made to put William Burgh's 'picturesque principle' into practice sooner or later. They differ from the use of painting techniques, such as perspective and shading, and from the conventional belief in the Sisterhood of the Arts, by which the mood and content of a natural or improved scene were analysed in the same way that a connoisseur would analyse a Claude, a Poussin or a Salvator Rosa. The 'picturesque principle' was to improve a real landscape purely for picturesque effect. The emphasis on appearance rather than content forced attention onto the difficult practical question of a suitable foreground.

Writers like Cradock and Falconer were less inclined to condemn the regular gardens of previous ages, and those who had seen the terraced gardens of Italy now began to appreciate that they had been rendered wonderfully picturesque through time and accidental decay. An early instance of this observation being turned to advantage in practical improvement was the saving of the terraces at Powis Castle, in Montgomeryshire. William Emes had proposals in the mid-1770s for blowing up the early-eighteenth-century terraces with gunpowder. When Richard Payne Knight, the young squire of Downton, Herefordshire, who had recently made a tour of Italy, heard of these proposals he spoke to George Herbert, fifth Earl of Powis, about them. He argued that a smooth green slope was a poor substitute for the terraces, with their massive balustrades, overgrown yews, and rampant ivy, as a foreground to the distant views of mountains. The terraces were then preserved[1].

At the same time Knight had some original ideas for building his own castle at Downton. He enjoyed the mixture of classical and Italian medieval architecture to be seen in Claude's paintings, and he thought that medieval castles in Britain shared a common Roman ancestry with the Italian. He designed an outwardly austere castle as if it were in the same tradition[2]. He shared Robert Adam's appreciation that such castles were more picturesque than Palladian buildings, but went further in this respect by building on an asymmetric plan. When it was built, from 1774 onwards, Knight's castle was an unprecedented venture in country house design.

The position of Downton Castle was on a flat-topped hill above the wooded gorge of the River Teme. The gorge recalled, though less dramatically, the sublime landscapes at Hackfall and Hawkstone. Knight's improvements to these grounds were a break from tradition as well. Walks were taken along by the river's side, and kept at an intimate scale, almost as if they were the marks of trespass. Knight was glad to keep an old packhorse bridge, and at another place he set up some felled trees as an 'Alpine bridge', such as he may have seen formed by accident in the Alps themselves. Everywhere, then, there was a rough foreground, and the stems and branches of trees framed views of the castle above, the river below (in some places still, deep pools, and in others running over shallows), and some exposed rock faces of the gorge. These wild and picturesque pleasure grounds were completed prior to 1784, when they were drawn by Thomas Hearne.

In June 1788 Humphry Repton, whose wish to remain one of the gentry of Norfolk was then close to frustration, launched out as a professional improver. He had much the same intention as Knight—to abide by the picturesque principle. Repton's qualifications for his suddenly adopted profession rested merely on his abilities as a watercolourist and his by no means exceptional knowledge of botany, agricultural improvement and taste in garden design. However he reasoned that ornamental improvement had lacked direction and leadership since the deaths of Brown and Richmond, and he intended to use his slender social connections to the full. He also set about acquiring in a determined manner what practical skills he lacked[3].

Repton's reading on the theory of improvement was Burgh's edition of *The English Garden*, Gilpin's tours of the Wye and the lakes of Cumberland and Westmorland, Whately's *Observations on Modern Gardening* and Malthus' translation, *An Essay on Landscape*. The first two would have encouraged him to view improvement in picturesque terms, whilst the last advised that 'no scene in nature should be attempted till it has first been painted', that proposals for water should be tested by laying out sheets, and that the outline of

51   Downton Castle, gorge of the River Teme.

Richard Payne Knight opened up a network of paths running through the gorge in the 1770s, and this and other views were made by Thomas Hearne in 1785.

plantations or the line of paths should be represented by 'little rods stuck in' to the ground. Whilst Repton thought that some of Girardin's ideas were a little unrealistic, he was thoroughly converted to the principle that the improver should 'form a just idea of effects before they are carried into execution'. This faculty of 'foreknowing effects' was the landscape painter's contribution, with which he would combine 'the gardener's practical knowledge in planting, digging, and moving earth'. The title he took for himself, 'landscape gardener', was to reflect this.

Recognizing the strides that he would have to make on the practical side, Repton absorbed all he could from Dr James Edward Smith, a boyhood friend and by 1788 already an eminent botanist, and the elderly Robert Marsham of Stratton Strawless, Norfolk, an experienced planter. In August 1788 Repton was ready to announce his intentions. He had a trade card printed, and circulated letters to friends. One of them was to the Reverend Norton Nicholls, who had been Thomas Gray's companion on his tours. Nicholls had seen himself as an authority on taste in gardens, and had laid out his own grounds at Blundeston, Norfolk, and those of Sir William Jerningham at Costessey, Norfolk. Repton no doubt wished to dissuade Nicholls from any attempt to compete for the ears of potential clients. Repton would also have told William Windham, of Felbrigg, Norfolk, a former neighbour, a friend and a powerful help through his political connections.

Repton's first client was Jeremiah Ives, the mayor of Norwich and a political associate of Windham's. Ives wanted Repton to lay out the grounds around his new villa, Catton Hall, just outside Norwich. In September 1788 they walked over the grounds together, and then Repton had them surveyed. A month later Repton was back, marking out the improvements, much as *An Essay on Landscape* had suggested, making adjustments to the map, and making working drawings. This commission and its immediate successor were fairly slight, but in early 1789 Repton was given one with substantial earth-moving and drainage works. This was Brondesbury Park, in Willesden, Middlesex. For this place Repton prepared a book of proposals, dated March 1789 and containing watercolours of various designs and a discussion in copper-plate handwriting. This was the first of Repton's famous 'red books', named after their binding in red Morocco leather.

Not long afterwards Repton was consulted over Ferney Hall, Shropshire, which was not far from Downton. Richard Payne Knight had a dread of improvers like Brown and Emes, and so he was at first apprehensive about Repton[4]. However,

when I found that improver to be a man of liberal education, ... skilled in the art of design, which he executed with equal taste and facility, my fears were suddenly changed into the most pleasing expectations, which were still heightened and confirmed when I heard him launch out in praise of picturesque scenery, and declare that he had sought the principles of his art, not in the works of Kent or Brown, but in those of the great landscape painters; whose different styles he professed to have studied with care and attention, in order to employ them as occasion required, and thus to merit the new title which he had assumed, of *Landscape Gardener*.

Repton produced the Ferney Hall red book in October 1789. He was still feeling his way in business, and was keen to accept advice, especially over a place like Ferney, which, with its rocky dell near the house, was unlike any of his previous commissions. He had a liking for forest scenery, and admired Knight's improvements at Downton, so he asked him for his comments. Knight was the sort of person who made his points forcefully, and he criticized Repton's proposals severely on the basis that they did not match the fine words that he had heard before. Thus humbled, Repton asked Knight for practical

52   Bulstrode, plan.

The plan shows Bulstrode
after Humphry Repton had
worked on it for a decade. It
was printed in Repton's
Observations (1803).

advice, and a meeting at Ferney. This was agreed, and prevented only by the owner's death.

Few of Repton's other commissions were so fraught, and his facility for impressing through words and watercolours enabled him to concentrate upon building up patronage. Another of Windham's political associates was Thomas Coke, and Repton made his red book of October 1789 for Holkham *gratis* as one of a series of acts to ingratiate himself with this powerful Whig[5]. At length Repton saw that he was gaining little advantage from Coke, but then found that another of Windham's political allies, William Bentinck, third Duke of Portland, was becoming a highly satisfactory patron at Welbeck Abbey, Nottinghamshire, and Bulstrode, Buckinghamshire. Mainly through the duke Repton found himself employed by many famous names—Lord Sheffield at Sheffield Park, Sussex, Lord Darnley at Cobham Hall, Kent, Lord Loughborough at Rudding Park, Yorkshire, and Earl Fitzwilliam at Wentworth Woodhouse, Yorkshire. In 1791 William Pitt the Younger became a client at Holwood, Kent. These persons brought a host of other patrons in their trains, so that by the end of 1793 Repton had been consulted at about 100 places up and down England.

This rapid acquisition of patrons is astonishing, but did not amount to a wholesale transformation of country estates like that which Brown had directed. Repton's red books were intended, and were treated, as advice between one cultivated gentleman and another, and there was no obligation on the part of the patron to act upon the advice. Repton made daily charges—5 guineas when visiting, and 2 guineas when back at home preparing the red book. He would supervise the ground workers if requested, when he would charge on a percentage basis as architects did, but such fees were not his bread and butter. Probably the number of schemes carried out exactly as Repton had advised was only a small proportion of his commissions, although most patrons acted on some of his advice, or on modifications to it.

Although Repton became a national figure through this style of working he had largely foregone that intimate association with particular places that Brown's office and the lesser improvers had gained through their contractual work. Although it would be unfair to accuse him of making superficial judgements on the places he advised upon, he was inclined to be less interested in them than in their owners. The danger of this was that he could identify himself too closely with each and every patron's wishes, and that any sense of a system of improvement was lost in successive adjustments of viewpoint.

It does not seem that Repton ever held a vision of an ideal Nature upon which he could found a system. He mentioned Her frequently, it is true, but only whimsically. He defended Brown not because he followed Brown's system, but on account of the profession as a whole. In fact Repton was an admirer of Burke's theory of the sublime and the beautiful—the theory that had sustained Brown's great antagonist, William Chambers. The difference was that whereas Chambers recommended the improver to appeal to the emotions, Repton was a man of taste appealing to the understanding:

True taste in *landscape gardening*, as well as in all other polite arts, is not an accidental effect, operating on the outward senses, but an appeal to the understanding, which is able to compare, to separate, and to combine the various sources of pleasure derived from external objects, and to trace them to some pre-existing causes in the structure of the human mind[6].

As a man of Taste Repton shared Cradock's and Knight's preoccupation with abstract qualities. Although he had emphasized Picturesque Effect to Knight, his close identification with his patron's requirements led him to

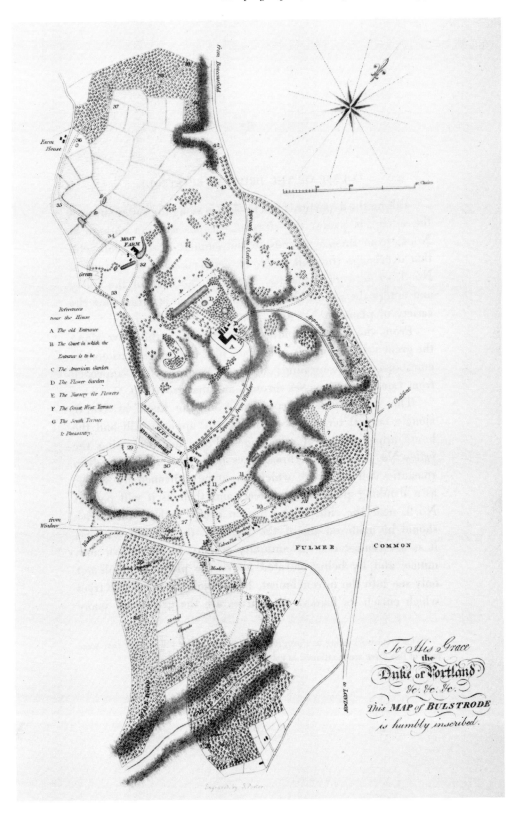

References
near the House

A The old Entrance
B The Court in which the
    Entrance is to be
C The American Garden
D The Flower Garden
E The Nursery for Flowers
F The Great West Terrace
G The South Terrace
    & Pheasantry

FULMER   COMMON

To His Grace
the
Duke of Portland
&c. &c. &c.
This MAP of BULSTRODE
is humbly inscribed.

consider that Character and Convenience overrode even this. The first of these leading objects arises because,

we expect to see a marked difference in the stile, the equipage, and the mansions of wealthy individuals; and this difference must also be extended to the grounds in the neighbourhood of their mansions, since congruity of stile and unity of Character are the first principles of good Taste[7].

In consequence Repton paid much attention to lodges. They are a hint of the architectural style and grandeur of the mansion, and could, by their evident distance from it, 'mark a command of geography'. In order for the greatness of Character of parks to be apparent they had to be clearly set aside for ornamental purposes, and distinguished from agricultural land. Repton disliked *fermes ornées* because they blurred this distinction.

The principle of Convenience was firmly impressed upon Repton by Reginald Pole Carew, who commissioned a red book for Antony House, Cornwall, in 1792. Repton and Carew had a difference of opinion over the importance of Convenience relative to Repton's other objects of Taste. The question was left open in the red book:

I deem that to be false taste, which in all cases recommends the sacrifice of convenience to picturesque effect. Where the two objects are at variance, ... it becomes the duty of the Landscape Gardener to state fairly how much must be sacrificed of the one to obtain the other, and the proprieter must alone decide on their equivalent merits.

53   Antony House, design for the park.

The plan from the Antony red book dated 1792. Repton relied upon his watercolours to put his ideas to a client, and his plans looked sketchy and unfinished.

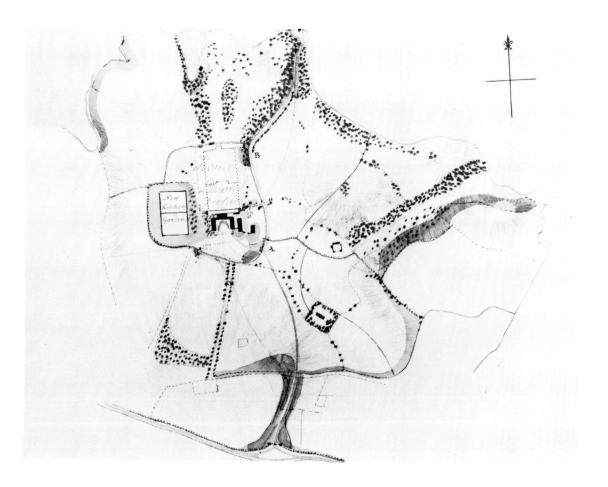

Carew did indeed decide—in favour of the convenience of keeping the seventeenth-century square forecourt, and against Repton's advice.

Repton felt it his duty to comment on architectural matters, as congruity of style is a powerful aid in establishing a consistent character to the whole. Hence parapets, the roof outline, outbuildings and even the colour of the house paint came under his scrutiny, and in recommending lodges, seats, and garden buildings he tried to make them match. He was not committed to any one style, and since each place had a different Character he dabbled in a wide range of them.

He was frequently discussing Situation in relation to Character. His appreciation of a place's Situation was Repton's equivalent to consulting the Genius of the Place, or pronouncing on its 'capability'. He realized that the situation of the house, whether on a hill, or rising ground on the side of a valley, or on a plain, was an important matter in deciding its Character and the general form of the improvements. If, as at Stanmore House, Middlesex, the house was on rising ground in a valley, then the traditional formula of water in the valley bottom, and planting on the hills to exclude the surrounding agricultural landscape, was suitable[8]. If, as at Brondesbury, the house was on a hill then the surrounding landscape should perhaps be opened out to view, and the desired privacy could be obtained if

a sufficient quantity of land round the house be inclosed, to shelter and screen the barns, stables, kitchen garden, offices, and other useful, but unpleasing objects; and within this inclosure, though not containing more than ten or twelve acres, I propose to conduct walks through shrubberies, plantations, and small sequestered lawns, sometimes winding into rich internal scenery, and sometimes breaking out upon the most pleasing points for commanding distant prospects.

This treatment was more suited to a villa than a mansion.

A mansion on a flat plain had always been difficult to treat satisfactorily, but Repton was adept at making necessities into virtues. He wrote in connection with Milton Park, Cambridgeshire:

There is always great cheerfulness in a view on a flat lawn well stocked with cattle if it be properly bounded by a wood at a distance, neither too far off to lessen its importance, nor too near to act as a confinement to the scene ... Uneven ground may be more striking as a picture, and more interesting to the stranger's eye, it may be more bold, or magnificent, or romantic, but the *character of cheerfulness* is peculiar to the plain[9].

Great judgement is required when working within a system of Taste as mutable as Repton's, and fortunately he was able to display his good taste on numerous occasions. Some of his comments may have seemed unimportant or too concerned with detail, but it takes perception to realize which details or commonplace effects are crucial in establishing a place's character. He also had a fine sense of composition. He was painter enough to appreciate the shape of the ground. He even suggested running fencing up hills at some places because it would show off the swell of the ground. He disliked individual round clumps and flat belts enclosing one man's property, preferring his planting to sit well in the landscape.

Partly for antiquarian reasons, and partly because he felt that formality could be convenient and appropriate next to a mansion, Repton often advised the retention or creation of terrace walls. A further and increasingly important reason seems to have been for the picturesque effect of balustrades and flower pots. This occasional preference for formality in the more private parts of the garden extended to the design of flower gardens[10]. One he had designed to go within a shrubbery at Courteenhall, Northamptonshire, had an oval pool from which the beds radiated within a larger oval[11].

After five years of highly successful practice, in which he had clearly emerged at the head of his profession, Repton decided to publish a selection of his comments from red books. His primary source was the Welbeck red book, but 56 other places were mentioned in his text. The red book for one of these, Warley, in Worcestershire, was quoted[12] in order to give Repton's opinion, as it was in 1794, of the causes of 'that pleasure which the mind receives from landscape gardening'. He listed: Congruity; Utility; Order; Symmetry; Picturesque Effect; Intricacy; Simplicity; Variety; Novelty; Contrast; Continuity; Association; Grandeur; Appropriation; Animation; and the seasons. This list is a perfect demonstration of his diffused and sometimes self-contradictory attitudes to the principles of improvement.

The Tasteless Band of Followers

Repton does not seem to have supervised alterations to many places himself, but left this to experienced contractors. In other ways, though, he was the successor to Brown in more than one sense. Not only had Brown's son given him his father's plans, but Repton frequently devolved the improvements themselves to Samuel Lapidge, who was carrying on Brown's contracting business from Brown's private yards at Hampton Court. Lapidge worked on Bulstrode, and by 1799 he was working on the nearby Chalfont House, the seat of Thomas Hibbert, and where Repton had designed improvements to 150 acres of enclosure land[13]. At both these places Lapidge's foreman was William Ireland, who had formerly been one of Brown's.

Not all Lapidge's work came from Repton, though. For example he was altering Llanarth House, Monmouthshire, in 1792, and he followed Emes to Chippenham Park in the late 1790s[14]. The half-mile-long lake and a million trees were amongst the expensive improvements there designed to alleviate the dullness of this flat, open, landscape. One of Lapidge's last contracts before his retirement was carrying out some minor changes to Brighton Pavilion, probably Holland's scheme of 1795, for which he was paid off in 1802[15].

Holland felt that other designers of grounds were unnecessary when he could do the work himself. He justified his work on the gardens at Woburn Abbey to Francis Russell, fifth Duke of Bedford, by saying that if he had not made the designs himself,

Some such person as Repton or Eames or Haverfield or Malcolm must have been employ'd[16].

Although Brown's son-in-law, he was remarkably uninterested in the wider landscape, and it is clear from his designs that he was really concerned only with the approaches and immediate surroundings of his architectural commissions. Even more surprising, his designs for Althorp, Northamptonshire, in 1790, and for the Brighton Pavilion in 1795 included regular private gardens based on circles.

Holland's work at Woburn included a Chinese dairy and a classical greenhouse in 1789, and a grand new principal entrance to the park in 1790. The Chinese dairy was really part of the pleasure grounds, and was placed behind a pool. It was also the termination of a lengthy covered walkway, by which one could reach the greenhouse from the house, and then continue round the back of the stable block and offices to give access to the pleasure grounds. In his plans for Althorp of 1790 he suggested that the system of avenues in the parkland be kept, and once again his ideas centred around the approach to the house, the connection to the stables and the private pleasure grounds next to the house. One of his last schemes for grounds was that for

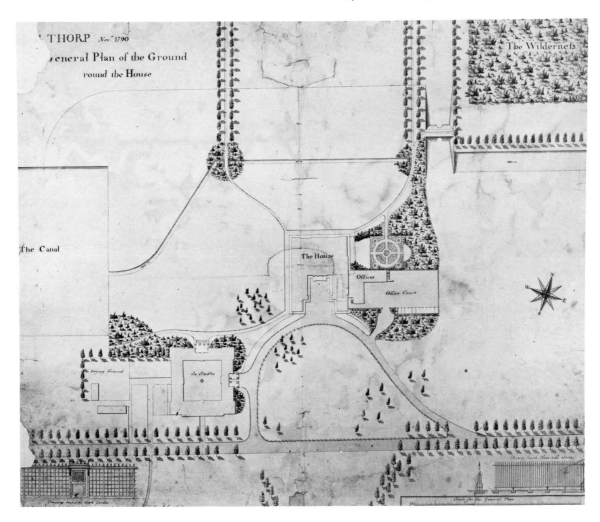

THORP *Nov. 1790*

eneral Plan of the Ground
round the House

The Wildernefs

The Canal

The House

Offices

Office Court

Southill, Bedfordshire, the seat of George Byng, fourth Viscount Torrington. The plan of 1800 for this place shows the same concerns.

'Malcolm', to whom Holland referred in his letter quoted above, could have been William Malcolm, a nurseryman of Stockwell, Surrey, or perhaps his son James.[17] Like Stephen Switzer and Richard Woods before him, he was one of a number of nurserymen offering designs.

John Haverfield Junior, mentioned alongside Malcolm, was following the tradition of royal gardeners in doing the same. This was mainly because Richmond Gardens were increasingly seen as an adjunct to Kew by George III. When his mother, Princess Augusta, died in 1772 he moved into Kew Palace and demolished Richmond Lodge. Joseph Banks, a wealthy gentleman keenly interested in botany, became George's adviser on botanical matters in 1772, and under his directorship the botanical collection at Kew expanded rapidly. William Aiton's position rose accordingly. His appointment to be the Royal Gardener of the whole of Kew Gardens was well overdue when John Haverfield Senior died in 1784, and in 1795 John Haverfield Junior felt it wise to quit Richmond in favour of Aiton's son, William Townsend Aiton. In 1802 the lane between the two gardens was closed and their physical assimilation completed.

54 Althorp, design for the ground round the house.

Henry Holland made a number of alternative designs dated 1790. It is remarkable that Lancelot Brown's former partner would let the avenues remain, and even proposed a regular flower garden.

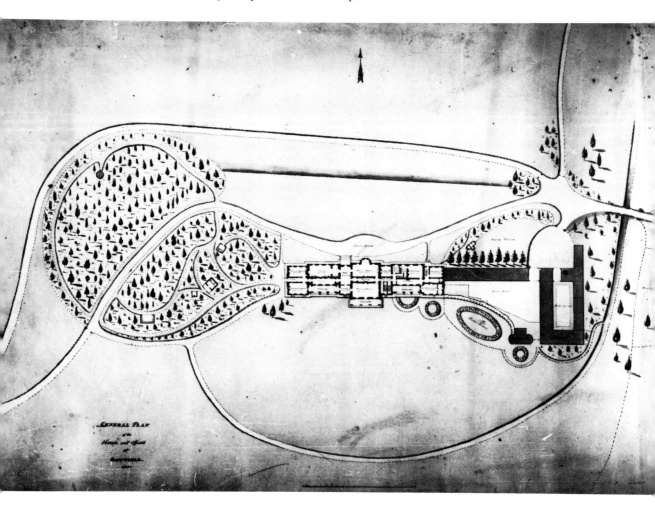

55   Southill, plan of the gardens.

The plan is dated 1800, and shows that Henry Holland did not just complete Brown's schemes, but turned improver himself. However this one is dull and constricted in scale.

This meant in effect that Haverfield and W. T. Aiton had exchanged roles, for the latter had been making designs for villa gardens in the late 1790s till he succeeded his father at Kew in 1793[18]. An example was the grounds of Heathfield House, at Turnham Green, Middlesex, laid out in 1789–90 for George Augustus Eliott, Baron Heathfield, the defender of Gibraltar[19].

Haverfield's career as a designer extended at least till 1812, for he was altering the grounds at Walsingham Abbey, Norfolk, from 1804 till 1812[20]. The owner started proceedings to move a number of roads away from the east front in 1804, and this permitted the river nearby to be enlarged into a lake, a road in the view to be sunk out of view, and a new approach over this road and lake to be laid out. Meanwhile features of antiquarian interest, a medieval gate and a packhorse bridge, were renovated. The great east window of the abbey then formed a highly picturesque focal point in the new lawns and shrubbery that replaced the remaining formal gardens.

The two remaining provincial improvers, Emes and Mickle, were, like Lapidge and Holland, becoming aged by the 1790s. Emes was relatively wealthy and in about 1790 he took a 21-year lease on Elvetham, Hampshire, in order to enjoy a partial retirement[21]. He did not cease working altogether, though. He is thought to have laid out a number of properties in the area, including Cuffnells in Hampshire and Chute Lodge just within Wiltshire. He drew up and coloured an impressive plan of Wimpole, Cambridgeshire, in 1790[22]. Nevertheless, from 1792 at the latest he devolved much of his work in the Midlands to his pupil, then partner, John Webb. For example in 1792 he visited Locko Park, Derbyshire, and was followed by Webb who staked out the position of the intended lake. The contract was signed by both, but Emes seems merely to have supplied the design, and Webb carried out the works. The same arrangement was made for Dodington Park, Gloucestershire, where in the following year they modified Brown's improvements of the 1760s[23].

One of Webb's first commissions without Emes was for improvements to Shugborough, following disastrous floods of 1795 which seem to have swept away the pagoda[24]. The loss of this and other whimsical features of the *ferme ornée* was not regretted, and the new improvements of 1798 diverted the River Sow away from the house, filled in part of the channel surrounding the Chinese House, and laid the remains of the hamlet of Shugborough into the park. Subsequent improvements were the diversion of the Stafford-to-Rugeley turnpike in 1804, the conversion of the old road into a lengthy drive, a massive scheme of planting on enclosed land and Cannock Chase, and the construction of a model farm[25]. Much of Webb's other work of this period was inherited from Emes. For example he was at Holkham in 1801–3[26], and then at Oulton Park and Crewe Hall in Cheshire and Sandon in Staffordshire[27].

Adam Mickle appears to have become quite well-respected in the 1790s. He drew a plan for the grounds north-east of Harewood House in 1790[28], and in about 1795 he laid out a new approach to Piercefield from a new lodge[29]. Swinton, Yorkshire, appears to have occupied much of his time from 1796[30]. He was employed on a salaried basis to direct the estate's head gardener and the foreman in their alterations to the 1760s layout, with pools made by a Mr Jones. These pools were to be given a more varied outline, and huge stones were brought down from the nearby moor and placed at the water's edge. Other stones were assembled as a large 'Druid's Temple' on the edge of the moor. These works were accompanied by much planting of larch and pine.

One large-scale improvement that seems to have escaped the attentions of a professional improver was at Arundel Castle, Sussex. The scenery enclosed for the new deer park was very susceptible to picturesque improvement. Charles Howard, eleventh Duke of Norfolk, acquired the extensive area of downland north of the castle and overlooked from the Hiorne Tower in 1797. Road diversions were facilitated by an Act of Parliament in 1803, whilst a mill pond formed the basis of Swanbourne Lake, a huge ornamental pool. By 1810 the park wall enclosing 1100 acres was complete, new plantations were thriving and the park had been stocked with 1000 deer[31]. Arundel Park was one of the last great parks to be made from new.

Whilst agricultural improvement continually reached new heights, one of its practitioners, William Marshall, continued to be engaged on ornamental improvements intermittently. In 1791 he visited Buckland Abbey, the seat of Sir Francis Henry Drake[32]. Groves planted in the early eighteenth century had become very overgrown. The abbey sits in a narrow valley, and Marshall felt that the groves made the air around it unwholesome. So he proposed to cut the trees back in order to help ventilate the place. This would be done so as to show the undulations of the ground and leave well-formed masses of wood. Marshall gave similar advice to the Earl of Breadalbane—to clear away trees from near the house at Taymouth in 1792.

These forays into 'Rural Ornament' were far less important to Marshall than his busier career in 'Rural Economy', which had taken him to both these places. Interest in agricultural improvement was running very high from 1790 till 1810. Marshall and Arthur Young found their services much in demand, and so did Nathaniel Kent, an estate agent operating in Norfolk for William Windham[33] and other landowners. George III was becoming more interested in Windsor Great Park in the late 1780s, and his Surveyor General of Woods and Forests, John Robinson, entered into disputes with Thomas Sandy, the deputy ranger. These were resolved when the Duke of Cumberland, the ranger, died in 1790, and George III took the rangership into his own hands. Kent was soon after appointed his bailiff.

Kent was well known to the Society of Arts. He had produced a paper on the use of chestnut in 1792, and in 1798 he contributed an account of his improvements to Windsor[34]. He made the 'Norfolk Farm' of 1000 acres on light soil and the 'Flemish Farm' of 400 acres on good loamy soil, both farms being named after systems of husbandry. In his view his improvements had improved the appearance of the park since the clearance of trees and undergrowth from the valleys gave a bolder effect to the woody scenes on higher ground. The woody scenes remained the predominant part of the Great Park, and here Robinson had the responsibility for a vast scheme of afforestation. He sowed 11,225,000 acorns in and about the Great Park between 1788 and 1801[35]. If 'Farmer George' displayed little enthusiasm for building and ornamental gardening, he was at least keen on his botanical gardens at Kew, the improvements at Windsor and those at Richmond Park.

Improvements in technical competence and achievement in planting continued unabated throughout the 1790s and into the 1800s. In Westmorland, for example, Richard Watson, Bishop of Llandaff, commenced great plantations of larch and ash at Calgarth, near Ambleside, in the 1780s, and received gold medals for them from the Society of Arts in 1788 and 1789. He in turn encouraged John Christian Curwen to sow acorns on the mountain above Belle Isle, just across Lake Windermere, for which he received a gold medal in 1799. Great numbers of larch were later planted round about, and Curwen received further golds in 1801 and 1803.

The leading medal-winner in the south of England was Lewis Majendie of Hedingham Castle, Essex. He won golds for oak in 1791, chestnut and ash in 1793, and ash again in 1796. Henry Nevill, second Earl of Abergavenny, was another prodigious planter on his Eridge estate in Sussex from 1788. No doubt he was advised by his father-in-law, John Robinson.

Beauty, Sublimity and Picturesqueness

William Gilpin sent his account of his Scottish tour of 1776 to be published in 1789, and it was as much of a success as his former ones. In it he digresses into speculation upon the improvement of the lakes of Cumberland and Westmorland. This tendency increased in his *Remarks on Forest Scenery* (1791). Although the second volume of this latter work described tours in the New Forest as the earlier tours had, the first volume was a highly analytical account of trees' contributions to picturesque beauty. One long chapter is an enumeration of the picturesque qualities of all the common forest trees, whilst other chapters consider trees collectively as clumps, copses and forests, and in different weather and seasons.

Some comments amounted to rules for improvement. For example

the use of clumps is to lighten the heaviness of a continued distant wood; and connect it gently with the plain

and 'no regular form is pleasing'. He had observed that 'Nature ... seldom passes abruptly from one mode of scenery to another', and this suggested that

I Claremont, view of the bason.

William Kent's revision of the bason in the mid-1730s included extending the water around the island, the temple, the cascade, the ha-ha and thinning the grove into small clumps.

II Wentworth Castle, view from the east front.

The painting by Thomas Bardwell, dated 1752, shows the natural-looking lakes recently made by Tivoli Temple.

III Woodside, the orangery.

Probably from the 1750s, the painting by Thomas Robins shows great attention to the flowers of the garden and is typical of his style.

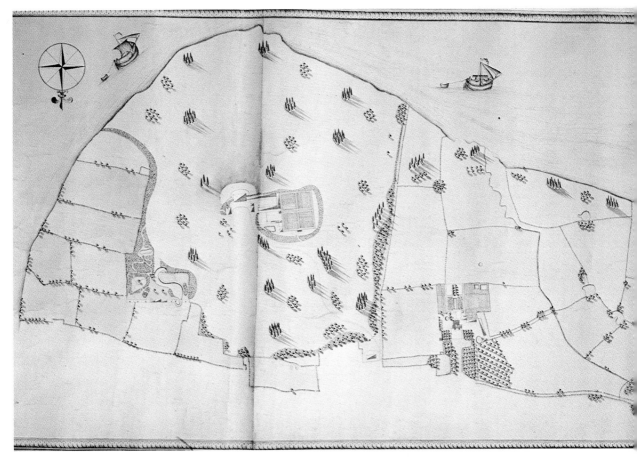

IV Hale, plan of proposed improvements.

This plan dated 1758 is by Francis Richardson, one of the first designers after Kent and Brown to think on the scale of a park.

V Painshill, view from the Turkish Tent.

Attributed to George Barret the elder, the painting dates from about 1770, by which time the Gothic Temple, the bridge and the elaborate grotto had been built.

VI Bowood, the cascade.

The cascade was built under the supervision of Charles Hamilton in the mid-1780s, supposedly in imitation of a Gaspar Poussin painting.

Opposite
VII Wimpole, plan with some alterations.

This plan of 1790 was one of William Emes's most magnificent and colourful.

VIII Stoke Park, plan for improvements.

Humphry Repton's plans were generally rather sketchy, and this one of 1797 can be considered one of the more carefully drawn.

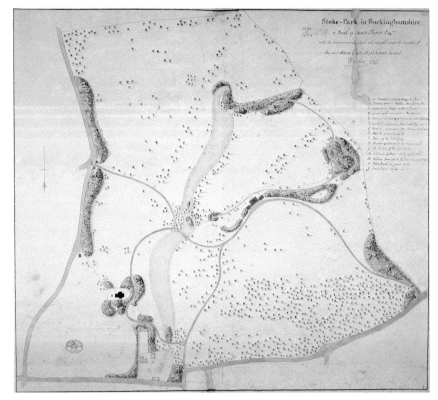

IX Harewood House, view from the south-east.

One of a series by J. M. W. Turner dating from 1798, the view shows the park laid out by Brown in the 1770s.

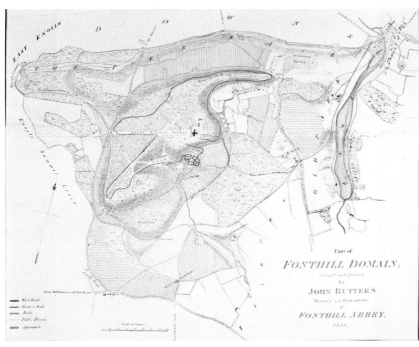

X Fonthill Abbey, plan of the grounds.

The plan is from John Rutter's *Delineations of Fonthill*, 1823, by which date William Beckford's planting of the 1790s was showing its intended effects.

XI Bolton Priory, view from the north.

Painted by J. M. W. Turner in 1809, this scene shows the valley of the Wharfe along which walks were being laid out by the vicar of the church at the priory.

XII Deepdene, steps to the south wing.

Thomas Hope's exotic taste in combining architecture with gardening is shown by the China barrell, the aloe and the peacock in this watercolour made by W. H. Bartlett in 1825.

as the park is an appendage of the house, it follows, that it should participate of its neatness, and elegance

and that

as the garden, or *pleasure-ground*, . . . approaches nearer to the house, than the park, it takes of course a higher polish.

His taste for Nature and simplicity remained, though, particularly in his liking for natural glens and streams.

His comments on Brown were generous. After asserting that every form of scenery is capable of being brought 'to serve the purpose of beauty', he added:

The many improvements of the ingenious Mr Brown, in various parts of England, bear. witness to the truth of these observations.

He also praised Brown's facility in the management of water, bridges and planting so that drives should wind for seemingly good reasons. However,

Mr Brown, I think, has failed more in river-making than in any of his attempts.

Furthermore Gilpin disapproved of temples, Chinese bridges and artificial ruins in parks, and remarked that Brown's lake and Chinese bridge at Paulton's, Hampshire, had offended him.

Gilpin was sensitive to the criticism that he thought nothing pleasurable to the eye unless it was picturesque. He acknowledged that most people preferred scenes of plenty, and disliked scenes of wildness and horror. However he was concerned with that particular form of beauty which looked well in a painting. He returned to this theme in *On Picturesque Beauty* which was one of three essays he had published in 1792. He explained in the dedication that,

We picturesque people . . . make a distinction between scenes, that are *beautiful*, and *amusing*; and scenes that are *picturesque*. We examine, and admire both.

The essay's main theme therefore was to establish a 'distinction . . . between such objects as are *beautiful* and such as are *picturesque*'.

Gilpin considered that beauty was related to smoothness, and, with some reservations, cited Burke in support. Indeed qualities of smoothness, 'instead of being picturesque, in fact disqualify the object from any pretensions to *picturesque beauty*'. William Burgh had already identified roughness with picturesqueness, and Gilpin did not hesitate to do the same:

We do not scruple to assent, that *roughness* forms the most essential point of difference between the *beautiful* and the *picturesque*.

The axiom that Nature is a painter still underlay Gilpin's thoughts, and it suggested affinities between the works of God and picturesqueness, and the works of Man and beauty. As a result:

From the scenes indeed of the *picturesque kind* we exclude . . . in general the works of men.

Although he had identified roughness and smoothness as the characteristics of the two types of beauty, Gilpin could give no explanation of why this was so. The most obvious explanation would rest on the connection between the works of God (i.e. Nature) and picturesqueness, and on the common observation that objects in Nature are naturally rough. It would then follow logically that the picturesque eye delighted in roughness. However, this was not sufficient since,

The picturesque eye, it is true, finds its *chief* objects in nature; but it delights also in the images of art, if they are marked with the characteristics which it requires.

An obvious example would be the ruins of a castle, which no painter would exclude because they are artificial.

It happened that a Herefordshire landowner, Uvedale Price, of Foxley, was thinking hard about picturesque beauty at the time when Gilpin was publishing these more analytical works. Price had cleared away the old-fashioned terraces around Foxley, probably during the 1770s, and had come to regret having done so[36]. He took a great deal of interest in the writings of Burke, Mason, Gilpin and Reynolds, and his ideas on the use of the hints that natural scenes afforded for improvement were similar to Burgh's 'picturesque principle'.

He shared this interest with Richard Payne Knight, who introduced him to Repton during the Ferney Hall episode in 1789[37]. He and Repton were together in a party on the River Wye in 1790 or 1791. By then, Repton had found that the affinity between painting and gardening was not as great as his enthusiasm for the picturesque had originally led him to believe[38], and Price found his ideas being treated lightly.

At about this time Price began to write *An Essay on the Picturesque*. Its whole purpose was to apply the principles of painting to improvement, but it was conceived from a highly theoretical standpoint. Nobody had attempted to reconcile Gilpin's theories on the picturesque to Burke's on the sublime and the beautiful. Possibly this was because Burke's distinction between the sublime and the beautiful was in some degree analogous to Gilpin's between the picturesque and the beautiful. Admittedly, their approaches to the causes of beauty differed, but this had not provoked much debate. Price, though, was not content with this, and a unified theory was to be the first object of his essay.

Price chose Burke's theory to be the basis of his new one, but acknowledged that it did not adequately incorporate the picturesque. He felt that the emotion of curiosity is distinct from the love or complacency that gives rise to beauty, and astonishment to sublimity. He thought that curiosity gives rise to 'picturesqueness', and 'corrects the languor of beauty, or the tension· of sublimity'. Not confined merely to the sense of sight, like sublimity and beauty, it is a general character that is applicable to the senses of the touch and the hearing.

Whereas the most powerful causes of sublimity are greatness of dimension, terror, uniformity and infinity, and those of beauty are smoothness and gradual variation,

I am therefore persuaded that the two opposite qualities of roughness, and of sudden variation, joined to that of irregularity, are the most efficient causes of the picturesque.

Price also identified freshness and decay as causes of the beautiful and the picturesque respectively.

When he saw Gilpin's essay *On Picturesque Beauty*, Price at first thought that the distinction it made between beauty and picturesque beauty on the grounds of roughness anticipated his own work, but then he realized that there were important differences. Gilpin's definition of the picturesque as the quality of looking well in a picture was too confined for him. For example a lake, despite being smooth, was considered by Gilpin to be picturesque. Price's criterion was roughness, and so he considered a smooth lake to be beautiful, and not picturesque. Also, whereas Gilpin refused to assign a cause to the sensation of picturesque beauty, Price thought that he had found it in the emotion of curiosity.

His new theory gave Price the justification he wanted for criticizing the prevailing style of improvement and putting forward his own ideas on the subject. His criticisms stemmed from a belief that the principles of painting, such as composition, harmony of tints, unity of character and the effects of light and shade,

are in reality the general principles on which the effect of all visible objects must depend, and to which it must be referred.

A modern improver ignored the principles of painting, but considered 'the eternal smoothness and sameness of a finished place ... as the most perfect embellishments'. Price believed that

it is from attempting to make objects beautiful by dint of smoothness and flowing lines, that so much insipidity has arisen.

Much of the criticism was directed at Brown in person, and much of it was virulently hostile. A milder observation was that

Mr Brown was bred a gardener, and having nothing of the mind, or the eye of a painter, he formed his style upon the model of a parterre; and transferred its minute beauties ... to the great scale of nature.

Price was particularly scathing of Brown's smooth-banked lakes and rivers, and ridiculed the sameness and predictability of his designs. Some more respectful criticism was directed at Repton. Price declared that Repton would 'correct the errors of his predecessors' if he were to add 'an attentive study of what the higher artists have done' to his other skills as an improver.

In Price's view, the great merit of roughness is that it conveys the ideas of

56 William Gilpin's idea of a picturesque scene.

The aquatint was printed in Gilpin's *Three Essays* (1792). It illustrates Gilpin's emphasis on landform (*cf* Fig. 57).

'animation, spirit and variety', and so it is 'the source of our most active and lively pleasures'. He came to many of the same conclusions as Gilpin: he liked unimproved streams, and broken ground, for example. He was fond of intricate landform such as could be found in his native Herefordshire:

What most delights us in the intricacy of varied ground, of swelling knolls, and of vallies between them, retiring from the sight in various directions amidst the trees or thickets, is, that . . . it leads the eye on a kind of wanton chace . . .

He hated Brown's belts which ran up hill and down dale along a park's boundaries, and which so effectually checked these pleasures. He particularly cited Painshill and Mount Edgcumbe as places that he admired.

Price shared Joseph Cradock's views on avenues and regularity:

Now everything is in segments of circles, and ellipses: the formality remains.

As to avenues:

The destruction of so many of these venerable approaches, is a fatal consequence of the present excessive horror of strait lines.

However, he went further than Cradock in believing that

whatever is connected with the mansion, should display a degree of art and of ornament . . . all roads, walks and communications immediately connected with the house, should be completely regular and uniform.

How he must have regretted the loss of the terraces at Foxley!

Richard Payne Knight knew of Price's intentions to publish the *Essay on the Picturesque*, and decided that a poem of his own composition, dedicated to Price, should accompany its publication[39]. Though he agreed absolutely with Price's proposed system of picturesque improvement, Knight had arrived at the same conclusions from a different starting point. He had not, for example, read Mason's *English Garden*, nor does he seem to have agreed that beauty or picturesque beauty were best explained by an analysis of the emotions. Instead his extensive readings of the Classics had led him to connect beauty with ideas of fitness for purpose, freedom of expression by educated minds and harmony in design. In this, his ideas showed much affinity with Joseph Cradock's.

If this meant that Knight relied on intellectual judgement, rather than emotion, this did not mean that his enthusiasm for landscape painting was less than Price's. Great painters like Claude and Hobbema had shown on canvas what the qualities of visual beauty are. The painters' three distances, trees in the foreground acting as frames, and rich near-ground detail were all advised to improvers by Knight. In fact so disgusted was he by the flat insipidity of improvers' near-grounds that when he saw them he prayed:

> Again the moss-grown terraces to raise,
> And spread the labyrinth's perplexing maze;
> Replace in even lines the ductile yew,
> And plant again the ancient avenue.

The formal scenes that he had particularly in mind were the Italian gardens such as those so often depicted in paintings.

Knight rather despised the rising vogue for mountains:

> 'Tis form, not magnitude, adorns the scene;—
> A hillock may be grand, and the vast Andes mean.

His disgust that 'Keswick's favour'd pool is made the theme of every wondering fool' seemed almost like a deliberate slight to Gilpin. To Knight, Nature's perfect expression was unkempt forest that 'rose in savage pride', and of which painters had traditionally been fond. Windsor Forest and the woodlands of the

Welsh Marches that he knew so well were particularly beautiful. A great part of his poem was an attempt to explain that Nature should be allowed a much freer rein that was the current practice. This meant in effect far more woodland, and a tolerance of broken ground and ancient trees.

Where an obviously man-made object such as a drive was to be made, it was the turn of the designer's mind to be free. Knight hated the 'acquired restraints or affected habits' of 'mechanics', but laid great faith in the apparent carelessness and unmannered style of masterly skill. Common sense would prevail with such liberal minds:

> For, as the principle of taste is sense,
> Whate'er is void of meaning gives offence.

He disliked needlessly serpenting paths. Indeed, avenues would be appropriate if the obvious route to take was a straight line. However:

> ... When you traverse rough, uneven ground
> Consult your ease, and you will oft go round.

The same principles led to an abhorrence of paltry follies with no purpose:

> No decoration should we introduce
> that has not first been naturalised by use.

57   Richard Payne Knight's idea of a picturesque scene.

This engraving by Thomas Hearne was printed in Knight's *The Landscape* (1794). Knight liked forest scenery and broken ground (*cf* Fig. 56).

By this Knight meant that he found mills and other useful buildings of the agricultural scene to be far more appropriate as built features. As to the landscape itself, he was not averse to hedges and arable fields; indeed he much admired Philip Southcote's *ferme ornée* at Woburn Farm.

Knight cursed the prevailing neatness of shrubberies. His taste was for controlled wilderness, giving way to terraces next to the house. In the grounds he liked quarries, boulders, clapper bridges, bridges made by fallen trees and seats made of stumps. The owners with a real abbey, castle or cottage was considered fortunate. Knight would even accept a classical ruin, provided that it was well mouldered, covered in ivy, honeysuckle, woodbine, moss and weeds, and set amongst thorns and tufted trees. He advised the use of native species of trees, and gave advice on their selection for different situations based on a generally sound scientific understanding. The 'nice embellishments of art' should be confined to terraces next to the house, as should any planting of exotic species.

He chose one particular instance to contrast his approach with that of professional improvers. In visiting his bookseller in 1793 he happened to observe some extracts of Repton's red book for Tatton that were on display in the shop as an example of what was to be published in *Sketches and Hints on Landscape Gardening*, and for inviting subscriptions. Repton proposed in the red book that the arms of the squire concerned would be displayed on the inn, any public buildings or even milestones, which would suggest the extent of his client's property and influence. Knight seized on this as an example of a mechanic's preoccupation with boundaries and the display of wealth, rather than with the beauties of the landscape. Always the lover of controversy, he aired this matter too in *The Landscape*.

The Picturesque Debate

Knight's poem was published several months before Price's *Essay* appeared in May 1794. The poem drew an immediate response from Repton who complained in a letter to *The Times* that the Tatton red book had been quoted unfairly[40]. An article in *The Monthly Review* critized Knight for quoting the red book as it was a private manuscript, and for burlesquing Repton's unpublished drawings with the engravings by Hearne. A bad poem, *A Sketch From the Landscape* (1794), also appeared. Its author was Dr John Matthews, for whom Repton had just laid out Belmont, in Herefordshire[41]. Matthews saw Brown as 'the great destroyer of an unnatural and absurd system', and he mocked the discomfort and unpolished form of Knight's ideal landscape. The poem contained much good-natured sarcasm, such as:

> Shave, then, no more, good friends, but friz
> The lovely locks round Nature's phiz.

Repton was handed an early copy of Price's *Essay* and a journey to Matlock and other parts of Derbyshire gave him the opportunity to read it[42]. Aware that 'many pages are directly pointed at my opinions', he wrote comments on certain passages intending a reply. William Combe made stylistic improvements, and it was then published. Repton's main point was that although he agreed with Price over the theory of the picturesque in relation to painting, he could not allow that picturesqueness was the overriding consideration in the practice of landscape gardening. He had, though, always considered the study of pictures 'to be not less essential to my profession than hydraulics or surveying'. He admitted that he had at first thought that the attainment of picturesque effects was of the greatest importance, but he had come to the view that 'propriety and convenience are not less objects of good taste, than picturesque effect'.

Repton looked to Gilpin as the authority on the subject, and noted that 'one of the keenest observers of picturesque scenery (Mr Gilpin)' had often regretted that few natural scenes were capable of being represented in a painting. He had also found that objects suitable as the subjects of painting, such as the ragged gypsy, the wild ass and the shaggy goat were certainly not more suitable in a gentleman's park than the sleek-coated horse or the dappled deer. Since Price had made a distinction between these animals as picturesque in the first case, and beautiful in the second, Repton made the observation that

beauty, and not 'picturesqueness', is the chief object of modern improvement.

He thought that Knight and Price may have been led to their advocacy of the picturesque in gardening because

you are in the habits of admiring fine pictures, and both live amidst bold and picturesque scenery: ... your palate certainly requires a degree of 'irritation', rarely to be expected in garden scenery; and, I trust, the good sense and good taste of this country will never be led to despise the comfort of a gravel walk, the delicious fragrance of a shrubbery, the soul expanding delight of a wide extended prospect, or a view down a steep hill, because they are all subjects incapable of being painted.

Repton had been provoked by the severity of Knight's and Price's criticisms of Brown and his 'tasteless band of followers' into a defence of English gardening as 'the happy medium betwixt the wildness of nature and the stiffness of art'. He drew an analogy with the British constitution and its happy medium between 'the liberty of savages, and the restraint of despotic government'.

He also pointed out that those much-despised features of Brown's style— clumping and belting—had their purposes. The fenced clump with a nurse of fir was an expediency for the establishment of more natural-looking groups of trees in parkland. If the firs and fences remained this was only because of the neglect or bad taste of his employers. Clumps of firs only were a total misconception for which Brown himself could not be blamed. Repton's defence of the belt was that it provided the enclosure that proprietors wished for. If it was in places too narrow, this was because of the parsimony of his employers. Repton did, though, confess that many a belt was 'tiresome in itself, and highly injurious to the general scenery'.

Improvement was something that every gentleman knew something about, and Price's theory of the picturesque was within the intellectual reach of most. It appears that the controversy between Price and Knight on the one hand and Repton on the other quickly became a popular topic. It even reached George III who, in preferring Repton's slim booklet, exclaimed somewhat flippantly that 'the truth lies in a small compass'[43]. Repton received a great many other expressions of support. One of the first was from William Windham, who reminded Repton that 'you know of old that I am quite on your side in the question between you'[44]. Windham, a keen agricultural improver, naturally felt that:

Places are not laid out with a view to their appearance in a picture, but to their uses, and the enjoyment of them in real life; and their conformity to those purposes is that which constitutes their beauty.

Knight's system in effect meant that we should live in caves and encourage *banditti* if we wish to live in a Salvator Rosa landscape. This was 'absurd' and 'unphilosophical'.

Also in 1795 Repton received a letter from Daniel Malthus[45]. Malthus remained convinced of the importance of painting principles in improvement, but he disliked Knight's and Price's presumption in writing as connoisseurs, and deplored their personal attacks on the departed Brown. He was therefore 'very much pleased' with Repton's letter, 'which is so easy, friendly and gentleman-like, that it defeats at once the pertness of your antagonists ... at the same time ... you have put your finger on the very pith and marrow of the question'.

Repton received another sort of letter—from Price[46]. It was a reply to 'the short note of your's, which has occasioned so large a comment', and was of such a length that if arguments could have been won by weight of paper alone, Repton would surely have been crushed. Repton's defence of Brown had perhaps been unwise, for it gave Price the opportunity to imply that Repton's arguments were entirely 'against my principles of improvements, and in favour of Mr Brown's practice', when this was not Repton's case at all.

Repton had, however, identified Price's system with a seeking for picturesqueness, and the object of professional improvers as beauty. Price clearly thought on reflection that this was not an acceptable division, and set out to correct any impression that only Gainsborough and the Dutch landscape painters could be followed in his system:

I will beg you to reflect on what some of the higher artists have done both in their pictures and drawings, and on the character of their productions; you must be sensible that the mixture of gay and highly cultivated nature, with the most splendid and finished works of art in Claude Lorrain—the studied uniform grandeur of the landscapes of N. Poussin, the style of his compositions, sometimes approaching to formality, but from that very circumstance deriving a solemn dignity,—are both of them ... as distinct from the wildness of mere forest scenery as they are from the tameness of Mr Brown's performances.

The beautiful scenes of Claude and Poussin were, then, perfectly suitable as models for improvement.

The delight of a scene does not depend merely upon its ingredients, for 'broken rocks, and rugged old trees with a stony torrent dashing among them ... may be so unhappily mixed together, as to produce little or no effect'. Instead it depends upon 'the qualities of union, harmony, connection, etc.'. Price did not object to Brown's improvements because they were beautiful, but because they were formal and insipid, and lacked union, harmony and connection. In order to show what he meant by a beautiful scene formed according to these qualities, Price gave a description of an imaginary one in

a glade, or a small valley of the softest turf and finest verdure; the ground on each side swelling gently into knolls, with other glades and recesses stealing in between them; the whole adorned with trees of the smoothest and tenderest bark, and most elegant forms, mixed with tufts of various evergreens and flowering shrubs: all these growing as luxuriantly as in garden mould, yet disposed in as loose and artless groups as in forests; whilst a natural pathway led the eye amist these intricacies, and towards the other glades and recesses. Suppose a clear and gentle stream to flow through this retirement, on a bed of the purest gravel or pebbles; its bank sometimes smooth and level ... but all rudeness concealed by tufts of flowers, trailing plants, and others of low growth, hanging over the clear water ...

Unfortunately very little of Price's letter was as soothing as this. The bulk of it was taken up by fine points of criticism interspersed with refined abuse. His criticism of Repton's principles of Convenience and Propriety provides an example. These, said Price, were 'objects of good sense, and good judgement, rather than of ... taste'. Further, 'the strictest observance of them will give a man but little reputation for taste'.

Repton's woes were increased shortly after by the second edition of Knight's *The Landscape*, which appeared in early 1795. In the 'advertisement' prefixing it, Knight returned to the question of milestones at Tatton, and made Repton's complaints on this head seem very ridiculous. He was even more merciless in his ridicule of poor Matthews' 'doggerel ode', which, he said, was 'blundering dullness vainly attempting wit, and producing nonsense'.

The unity which Price and Knight expressed as to their practical prescriptions for improvement was unexpectedly brought under strain by Price's letter and some notes that Knight added to his poem. Knight had never firmly believed in Burke's theory of the emotions, nor with Price's differentiation of picturesqueness from beauty and sublimity. He looked to the intellectual perceptions of fitness and harmony for our sense of beauty, but he had nevertheless not explained before the evident differences between the most admired paintings and the most admired real scenes. Now he thought that he had the answer. Each of our five senses has a different set of laws governing its satisfaction. He saw, then, that

the picturesque is merely that kind of beauty which belongs exclusively to the sense of vision.

Further, since 'smoothness and harmony of surface is to the touch what harmony of colour is to the eye',

our landscape gardeners seem to work for the touch rather than the sight.

This being the case, Knight had no reason to depart from his preference for forest scenes (although he certainly did not despise the accidental characters that cultivated countrysides acquired from their husbandry, building and planting). However, Price's explicit acceptance in his letter of smooth, or beautiful, scenes meant that he was making the same mistake of working for the touch that the inferior improvers had always made. Repton had written in his letter that he hoped that gravel walks, the fragrance of shrubberies and wide prospects would not be despised because they were not subjects capable of being painted; Knight agreed to this with some irony, but hoped that an improver who provided these pleasures would call himself a '*walk maker, shrub planter, turf cleaner, or rural perfumer*', and not 'a landscape gardener'.

Meanwhile Repton's printer had at last produced the *Sketches and Hints on Landscape Gardening*. The long delay had given Repton the opportunity to insert some comments on the first edition of Knight's poem and Price's *Essay*. As might have been expected, there was one complaining of Knight 'indulging his spleen' on the subject of milestones. Repton also added extracts from red books in which he had already discussed the picturesque principle. By doing this he was able to show that 'although the inquiry was originally suggested by conversations I have occasionally had, both with Mr. Knight and Mr. Price, at their respective seats in the county of Hereford', his conclusions were the result of mature deliberation.

In the Holwood red book of 1791 Repton had observed that William Mason, in discussing the use of the painter's three distances in improvement, 'supposes an affinity between painting and gardening, which will be found, on a more minute examination, not strictly to exist'[47]. If an improver did acknowledge three distances,

the first includes that part of the scene which it is in his power to improve; the second, that which it is not in his power to prevent being injured; and the third, that which it is not in the power of himself, or any other, either to injure or improve.

His red book of 1792 for Stoke Park decried Girardin's idea that a scene should not be improved till it had been painted[48], and in 1793 his red book for Holme Park set out five reasons for the 'great difference betwixt a scene in nature, and a picture on canvass'[49]. He continued the debate for the benefit of his patrons in a number of red books made after 1795. Indeed that for Attingham in 1798 contained quite a furious denunciation of Price's ideas[50].

Price and Knight had incurred the displeasure of many other writers besides Repton. There was an immediate response to Knight's second edition by Matthews, defending himself as best he could. In an advertisement he proclaimed himself proud to be 'one of the *Little admirers* of *Browns*'s memory', and invoked Walpole and Mason in their praises of Brown.

Walpole himself certainly objected to Price and Knight, and urged Mason to write another Heroic Epistle to the two 'infidels' who would destroy the English garden[51]. Mason did nothing but write to Gilpin about these two 'coxcombs' who had presumed to supplant Gilpin as the leading theorist of picturesque taste. Walpole, Mason and Gilpin were by now all aged, and in the event none of them responded publicly.

Nevertheless Mason had the satisfaction of seeing others join battle, and giving Knight and Price some lengthy and abusive criticism in return. He was delighted by William Marshall's *Review of the Landscape, a Didactic Poem: Also of an Essay on the Picturesque* (1795). Marshall ridiculed Knight's views on forest scenery, as 'the Poet takes it for granted that *every place* to be improved abounds with natural wood,—like his own'. Landscapes take a century to perfect, and Marshall thought that Knight had forgotten this in desiring forest scenes instantly. He attacked Knight's dislike of the larch, 'the most valuable exotic, of the ligneous tribe, this Island has ever imported'. As to Knight's proposals to 'plant again the avenue', 'this we pass, as being intitled only to pity, or ridicule'. Other remarks describe Knight as 'absurd', 'frivolous', 'a silly fool' and 'trite'.

Marshall's attack on Price commenced by complaining justly of the *Essay*'s length in relation to its message. Clearly he detested picturesqueness, and he even invented the word 'picturable' so that he could avoid using the term. Marshall was firmly in favour of working for beauty, and averred that 'picturesqueness is the child of deformity'. Further, 'it appears as a vicious habit—depravity—similar to that of eating devils, drinking drams, and smoking affafoetida'. Woe betide the patron who submitted his grounds to picturesque gardening:

Having made the entire environs as ugly—pshaw!—deformed—as may be—why what then?—Why so let them remain, until it shall please the Genius of Picturesqness to do away the deformity. If this should not happen during the lifetime of the deformer—pooh!—the improver,—his son, or his grandson, may be able to look out of his window without d——g the Picturesker.

Joseph Cradock was considering enlarging the small essay on gardening that he had inserted into *Village Memoirs*, but conceived it to be superseded by the new edition in 1795 of George Mason's *Essay on Design in Gardening*[52]. This essay was greatly enlarged by reviews of the work of improvers and of writings on taste in gardening since the first edition of 1768. Whereas Whately and other writers received unfavourable notices, Mason was generally favourable to Cradock. He used Cradock's books and his own to show that Price's *Essay* and Repton's *Letter* had been preceded in many points.

Mason added little that was new to the picturesque debate, but added his weight to Repton's main arguments, whilst he advised him 'not to take such a mill-stone about his own neck, as a vindication of Brown's clumps'. He added that most thinking people were unconvinced by Burke's theory that the sublime springs from terror. He resented the intrusion into gardening of the 'picture-bigots' whose use of Nature for painting was highly selective:

It would be strange indeed, if the *general* arrangement of rural-scenery could *only* be known by studying particular parts of it, and that too merely for the purpose of imitating them by a particular art.

Many criticisms of Price's *Essay* did not emerge till later. Thomas Mathias' second dialogue of the *Pursuits of Literature* (1796) mocked the system that 'grounds by neglect improve'. As late as 1820 Price's *Essay* was mentioned unfavourably by Dugald Stewart, the Scottish philosopher, in his *Philosophical Essay*, and Thomas Green the younger in his *Diary of a Lover of Literature*.

Price, it seems, could not be stopped writing. A second edition of the *Essay* appeared in 1796 with responses to various points by George Mason. Price still felt the need to explain his practical ideas more fully, and in 1798 three more essays appeared. The *Essay on Artificial Water* described how Price would have achieved his aim of forming picturesque lakes by using common labourers. The *Essay on the Decorations near the House* examined the character of the old Italian gardens, and the principles on which their excellence is founded. The conclusion of this essay was that the most picturesque effects are obtainable by a mixture of the rich decoration of terraces and garden architecture with the fresh tints and pliant forms of vegetation. The *Essay on Architecture and Buildings, as Connected with Scenery* sought to derive some rules for the siting and general design of country houses and cottages from the paintings of the great masters.

At this point, the only author still willing to combat him was George Mason, who added appendices to his book[53]. He had found the *Essay on Artificial Water* to contain 'no positive direction: something like principles, ... but by no means of a general nature'. Otherwise his points were minutiae. Price was not yet exhausted though: he turned to Knight's contention that the distinction between beauty and picturesqueness is imaginary. However he was quite unable to show in the lengthy *Dialogue on the Distinct Characters of the Picturesque and the Beautiful* (1801) that Knight was wrong. All he could show were apparent contradictions. A scene that Price would class as beautiful could be classed as ugly to the sense of vision by Knight. Buildings become more picturesque when ruined: Price would have said that the building lost beauty whilst gaining in picturesqueness, but Knight would have said that it gained in beauty too.

These lengthy writings on small or unresolvable differences were quite indigestible for most readers, and more simple and traditional points of view again appeared. A contributor to *Walker's Hibernian Magazine* published in Dublin in 1797 gave two anecdotes that illustrated 'the plainness and integrity' of Brown's mind[54]. In the same year William Mavor brought out a fourth edition of his *New Description of Blenheim*, to which he prefixed a 'Preliminary Essay on Landscape Gardening'.

Mavor noted that Brown, 'this mighty master of picturesque embellishment', had been 'severely censured by some of his own countrymen, who, indulging too much in the visions of theory, have derived him the merit of practical excellence'. Mavor claimed that,

Brown possessed an originality of conception, a poet's eye, and an instinctive taste for rural embellishment ... he viewed nature with the enthusiasm of a lover.

Blenheim was Brown's *chef d'oeuvre*, and very instructive:

to the picturesque landscape which pleases the sight, it adds the moral landscape that delights the mind.

To Mavor, the foundation of design was 'natural taste', which was defined as

that quick perception of the beauties and deformities of nature which enables a person at once to decide. No faculty is more rare. It requires the union of a poetic imagination with a correct judgement.

These were sentiments that Lord Cobham could have expressed 60 years before. If Mavor spoke for the average country-house tourist, Price evidently had not yet succeeded in converting his generation to his views.

Sequestered Glades

The rage for 'Gothic' novels was at its height in the 1790s. Although most were set in medieval times, their essential characteristic was their appeal to the emotions, for which the mysterious and romantic Gothic backgrounds were appropriate. A taste for the sequestered glade set amidst the primaeval forest was the approximate counterpart in rural improvement. The glade was usually envisaged as highly cultivated, as a contrast to the forest, and a liking for exotic trees and shrubs, especially American ones, accompanied that for ancient native ones.

This taste was Richard Payne Knight's, and indeed it was closely associated with picturesque sensibilities. However Knight was not the only wealthy and romantically inclined landowner. There were others who independently but simultaneously believed in the power of the landscape to impart emotional or even spiritual values. They included William Beckford, Thomas Johnes and of course Uvedale Price. Each had his own reasons for liking forest scenery, and despite Price's efforts there was no concerted drive to establish a new system of improvement.

Indeed attempts at picturesque gardening were few and diffuse. The new approach to Warwick Castle in 1796 was a winding cut through solid rock, festooned with ivy and other creepers[55]. Perhaps it was one such attempt. Another, rather later, example would be the quarry garden created by Sir Charles Monck when he began his work of building a new house for himself at Belsay, Northumberland, from 1807[56].

The best known examples, though, were by Price himself and his brother William. Price's unremitting alterations to the densely wooded Foxley estate were frequently admired, whilst friends like Sir George Beaumont of Coleorton Hall, Leicestershire, welcomed his advice[57]. Major William Price was an equerry to the king, and thereby Queen Charlotte obtained at Frogmore, near Windsor, one of the first gardens avowedly designed on picturesque principles. The ground was unpromisingly flat, but Major Price contrived to give the impression of a sweetly sequestered spot amidst the ancient forest[58]. It was described in the *Beauties of England and Wales* (1801):

An area of thirteen acres is laid out in a beautiful pleasure garden, diversified with a canal winding in different directions ... The devious path, the umbrageous thicket, the dilapidated ruin, and secluded temple, all conspire to render it peculiarly interesting ... The Ruin was erected from a design by Mr. Wyatt; and being seated on the water's edge, partly immersed in woods, and diversified with the creeping ivy and fractured wall, it constitutes a truly picturesque ornament ... The surrounding scenery is judiciously contrived to assimilate with the character of the place, the view of every distant object being excluded by trees and underwood.

Frogmore was a relatively paltry scheme beside the two greatest romantic schemes of the day—Beckford's Fonthill and Johnes' Hafod. It is no exaggeration to say that these two wealthy persons created the landscapes of their imagination.

Beckford stepped up the planting at Fonthill from 1789 with great numbers of larch, spruce and fir. He later estimated that in 1796 alone he planted a million trees[59]. This was no exercise in rural economy; Beckford was creating ornamental grounds on a fabulous scale. He had been captivated by Alpine monasteries such as that in the Grande Chartreuse, set in sequestered paradises and amongst wild forests and mountains. He was attempting to evoke on his own land the feelings that he had experienced at these places. This required an entirely new face for his bleak chalk hills in Wiltshire. It was a feat of the imagination which only wealth as fabulous as his could contemplate. He fully intended that overwhelmed visitors would view the exotic scene in disbelief.

In 1790 he was planning some ruins which were not undertaken, but in 1793 he started another building project. This was 'The Barrier', a seven-mile wall surrounding 519 acres at the core of his domain. He had been deeply wounded by his rejection by society resulting from an accusation of homosexuality. The Barrier was a revenge against society; within it he could choose his own company. It was also a protection for wild animals, for which he felt tenderly. Hares would eat out of his hand, and a visitor in 1799 noted 30 tame swans on Bitham Lake.

After some delays Beckford met the architect, James Wyatt, in 1794. They set about building a triangular 'chapel' at the highest point of the grounds, from which Alfred's Tower at Stourhead was visible. This chapel was raised to a height of nine or ten feet, and then abandoned in favour of an 'abbey' on a lower hill overlooking Bitham Lake. The abbey rose to a completed state between 1796 and 1799. It had a ground plan that was far more irregular than any genuine Gothic abbey; and it was highly picturesque, with a short buttressed spire on a central tower, and pinnacles and castellation elsewhere. As soon as the abbey was finished, though, Beckford commissioned Wyatt to rebuild the tower to be monstrously high. Its 276 feet added to its position on a hill made it one of the few more recent landmarks to equal those of the Middle Ages.

58 Fonthill, the American Garden.

William Beckford's lavish planting from 1789 transformed this bleak hill into his version of an earthly paradise.

Meanwhile the abbey's setting was being created. Beckford declined Repton's offer of professional assistance, and undertook the planning of the improvements himself. The main object of his planting was to give an air of cultivation amidst a wild and natural, though Alpine, forest. He also laid out avenues; the Great Western Avenue, which led to the great west door of the abbey, was well over half-a-mile long. Instead of planting rows of the same species, though, he planted a variety of trees and shrubs irregularly and promiscuously so as to form a broad vista between impervious thickets on each side, looking as if it had been cut through virgin forest.

Other notable improvements within The Barrier were: Bitham Lake, which he had invested with the character of 'the crater of an ancient volcano', perhaps with Lake Nemi, near Rome, in mind; the American Plantation, where a large collection of American plants including magnolias, azaleas, rhododendrons and robinias were set amongst firs overlooking the lake; the 'Forest Lawn', abounding in American and other exotic oaks; and a 'Clerk's Walk', bordered by the scarlet thorn, variegated hollies and other shrubs[60].

Thomas Johnes' alterations to Hafod, Cardiganshire, had a similar reputation as a mysterious paradise, although in Hafod's case this arose from its real isolation in the mountain fastnesses of central Wales. Johnes was an enthusiastic planter who also altered the entire scene. Between October 1795 and April 1801 he planted 1,200,000 larches and numbers of other species to reach a total of 2,065,000 trees[61]. In the process he gained three gold medals

59   Hafod, the Cavern Cascade.

Thomas Johnes had the cavern excavated so that the cascade could be seen to best advantage. This aquatint is from James Edward Smith's *Tour to Hafod* (1810).

from the Society of Arts; and three more golds were to come for subsequent planting.

Like Price and Beckford, Johnes was a keen horticulturalist. He had John Nash build an extensive conservatory in 1793 as part of the rebuilding of the house in a Gothic style. Further up the valley he had a walled flower garden of irregular outline[62] constructed for his daughter Mariamne, and the walk between it and the gardener's cottage was planted with American shrubs[63].

Despite the apparent similarities of Hafod to Fonthill, though, Johnes' ideals were quite different from Beckford's. Johnes had a vision of a smiling peasantry in a smiling country, each drawing strength from the other. Investment was required to raise each to the blissful state, and ultimately the scheme foundered on the tenantry's failure to respond. However the country showed no unwillingness to be improved, and this was his lasting achievement.

The house was situated on rising ground in the valley of the River Ystwyth, where lush pastures were surrounded by mountains. In his love and respect for natural wildness Johnes shared many of the principles of his cousin, Richard Payne Knight. By 1796 Johnes had laid out an extensive system of rides and walks to take advantage of the cascades on the mountain streams. One cascade

is placed by the hand of Nature in so deep a hollow, and encompassed with precipices so steep, that none but the adventurous mountain shepherd had probably beheld it, till Mr. Johnes conceived the happy idea of piercing the hill by an artificial cavern ... we enter it, and after walking a few paces in the dark, a sudden turn displays the cataract at once to our view[64].

One walk laid out after 1796 ran up the Ystwyth, giving constant views of its 'truly Alpine bed', and of the whole valley below.

Though neither Knight, nor Beckford, nor Johnes, would have greeted happily the suggestion that their work shared much with Lancelot Brown's, it happened that Fonthill and Hafod were amongst the last places to be modelled after an ideal landscape. Their romantic idealism was at variance with the general drift of improvement towards the refinement and embellishment of the prevailing and well-established style. However not all romantic improvements were inspired by idealism. Price had no idealism—just a theory of perception.

The walks in the valley of the Wharfe between Bolton Priory and Barden Tower in Yorkshire are a case in point. The land was the Duke of Devonshire's, but the improvements were by the minister of the church in the nave of the priory, William Carr. He took up his position in 1789 after leaving the University of Oxford, and pursued literary and antiquarian interests. Local history and folklore had preserved incidents relating to the White Doe of Rylstone, and the Boy of Egremond. The latter is supposed to have perished when he fell into The Strid, a turbulent passage of the river where it is forced through a deep cleft in the rock.

This kind of local history made its way into the *History and Antiquities of the Deanery of Craven* (1805). Its author, Thomas Whitaker, wrote of his indebtedness to Carr, and, in respect of Bolton:

This sequestered scene was almost inaccessible till of late, that ridings have been cut on both sides of the river, and the most interesting points laid open, by judicious thinnings in the woods.

The meadows of the valley floor needed no clearance, but its steep sides were densely wooded. Stepping stones near the priory led to a ride that rose high above the river, giving fine views of the priory. Further north the ride passed by cascades where becks from the high fells descended the sides of the valley. After three miles the ride reached Barden Tower. This was once the residence of

Henry de Clifford, fourteenth Baron Clifford, who earned the epithet 'The Shepherd Lord' by adopting this guise whilst in concealment during the Wars of the Roses. The picturesque setting complemented the romantic local history. Whitaker was so affected by it that he felt that, for picturesque effect, Bolton Priory had no equal amongst the northern houses. As to Barden Tower:

The shattered remains of Barden Tower stand shrouded in ancient woods, and backed by the purple distances of the highest fells. An antiquarian eye rests with pleasure on a scene of thatched houses and barns, which in the last two centuries have undergone as little change as the simple and pastoral manners of the inhabitants.

In his almost total reliance upon the rugged and interesting forms of nature, Carr was improving in the tradition of the sublime landscapes of Piercefield and Hawkestone, although perhaps 'picturesque' would have been a more appropriate epithet in his day. The earlier 'sublime' layouts came to be appreciated for their picturesque qualities, and one of them, Blaise, received substantial additions between 1796 and 1799[65]. Blaise had been purchased by another Quaker, John Scandrett Harford, who made purchases of the heavily wooded ground beyond the Hazel Brook. A drive through the woodland, and across the gorge of the brook, would obviate the need to approach the house through Henbury village. In 1796 Harford called in Repton. Repton found a route to cross the gorge, and suggested a 'woodman's cottage' which would give an appropriately sequestered atmosphere to its section of the grounds. He also, in his usual manner, suggested a lodge, which was built with minor modifications in the 'Tudor' style in 1801.

Theory and Practice

Repton's busiest years were already over by 1794. The rate of commissions received halved from over 20 per annum (1790–1793) to under 10 per annum (1794–1802). It is probably no coincidence that 1793 was the date at which Great Britain found herself at war with revolutionary France. The other explanation—that the disputes with Uvedale Price and Richard Payne Knight damaged Repton's reputation in the eyes of his clients—is difficult to judge because from the mid-1790s the clients were by and large a different sort of person from the country squire with whom he was familiar. Many of Repton's new clients had made their money in banking or one of the professions, and now wanted villas or small country houses, often where no previous residence existed.

These 'creations', as Repton referred to them, clearly required the assistance of a competent architect. Repton had met John Nash and now preferred him to William Wilkins, whom he had used previously. Nash was perhaps a strange choice, as he was at this time close to Uvedale Price[66]. He had probably met Price when he was working at Hafod, during which time Price visited Aberystwyth and Devil's Bridge. In about 1795 Price asked Nash to design a house for him at the edge of the cliff near the castle at Aberystwyth. Price told Sir George Beaumont in 1798 how this came to be Nash's introduction to picturesque principles in architecture:

I told him that I must have, not only some of the windows but some of the *rooms* turned to particular points, & that he must arrange it in his best manner; I explained to him the reasons why I built it so close to the rock, showed him the effect of the broken foreground & its varied line, & how by that means the foreground was connected to the rocks in the second ground, all of which would be lost by placing the house further back. He was excessively struck with these reasons, which he said he had never thought of before in the most distant degree . . .

Nash's buildings thereafter tended to asymmetry and irregular outlines, whether they were in castellated or Italianate style. Nash joined Repton at Corsham, Wiltshire, as architect to Paul Cobb Methuen[67]. He placed an octagonal drawing room in an early Tudor style on the north front. Repton then asked Nash to work with him on Point Pleasant, a new villa near the river at Kingston-on-Thames, Surrey. The lessons learnt at the Castle House, Aberystwyth, were put to use. The villa was set at 45 degrees to the river, so that two fronts had good views of it. Repton's improvements on such a small and flat site were fairly mundane—consisting of drives and peripheral belts giving a feeling of as much spaciousness as possible.

In 1797 Nash and Repton co-operated on two more villas near London—Sundridge, in Kent, and Southgate Grove, Middlesex—and in 1799 they co-operated on a villa at Luscombe, Devon. Shortly thereafter the partnership broke up over differences between their understanding of each other's obligations. Repton had gained little from his association with Nash, but Nash reaped plentiful benefits in terms of commissions and introductions. Some introductions served him well years later. For example, he was not required by Lord Berwick when Repton went to Attingham in 1797, but in 1802 Nash designed a villa for the estate, and in 1807 a picture gallery for the house.

These were the years of some of Repton's more notable red books. As before, his suggestions ranged from minor alterations, perhaps the felling of a few trees, to major 'creations' from agricultural fields. His restraint was often admirable. At Attingham he advised against the extension of the park eastwards[68], whereas many improvers would have done the reverse. At West Wycombe his suggestions amounted to the removal of some mature trees and the diversion of the drive[69].

At the other end of the scale he made designs for a new mansion at Bayham Abbey, Kent, in 1800. He deliberated carefully on the style of architecture, and the most appropriate form of landscape gardening. Since the house was to be 'the established mansion of an English nobleman's family' (in fact that of John Jeffreys Pratt, second Earl Camden), he described its desirable character as one of 'greatness and durability'[70]. The architectural style would reflect this, and its siting would take account both of its intended character and the character of the scenery. The ancient Bayham Abbey was on the estate, and the valley was well wooded. Everything pointed to a Gothic building, and an eminence was found above the floor of the valley where a castle might suitably rest. Repton's son, John Adey, drew up elaborate plans, whilst Repton applied himself to the setting. The valley was flooded, giving a long, broad lake, and various areas were either cleared of trees or planted with them. Repton delighted in this opportunity to form a unity of character embracing the house and the landscape, but unhappily Camden did not proceed with the castle.

One heartening aspect of the Attingham and Bayham work, for Repton, was that there was still, clearly, a number of the nobility desiring improvements, and that not all his work needed to be for the new professional classes. In 1798 he was called to Plas Newydd, Anglesey, one of the seats of Henry Paget, Earl of Uxbridge, where he suggested a Gothic pavilion modelled on the idea of a chapter house[71]. In 1799 he was consulted by the fifth Earl Cowper on a new house at Panshanger, Hertfordshire[72]. Repton's recommended site for the house was later adopted, and the lake was formed straight away.

Next year Repton was at Harewood, where he advised on the approaches[73]. A magnificent gateway was later built, but not facing directly onto the village street as Repton had suggested. In 1801 he was at Wimpole and Cassiobury. At both places he advised judicious removals of timber. In 1803 he reached a new peak with patronage from the Prince of Wales, although the actual alterations to the gardens of Carlton House were quite minor. A more substantial commission that year was the Longleat red book, leading to siting new stables, alterations to Brown's 'river', thinnings to open views and further planting.

1803 also saw the publication of Repton's *Observations on the Theory and Practice of Landscape Gardening*, dedicated to George III. This is a sizeable book, with hand-coloured reproductions of a number of watercolours from the red books and some engravings mainly of architectural drawings.

Repton made no secret that his profession had its detractors, and his professed intention was to 'establish fixed principles' in landscape gardening. The leading feature of the taste of his times was, he thought, 'the just sense of *general utility*'. He did not defend Brown's idealistic view of Nature, nor much of Brown's practice. Indeed Repton took pains to point out features of modern gardening which were absurd by the standard of 'general utility'. These included nakedness of the ground around the house, devious approaches, pairs of lodges, belts with ridings around the verges of parks, water on eminences and sham bridges.

Other 'fixed principles' were practical. The laws of optics, colour and proportion were afforded much space. These were important in order to manipulate the apparent size or distance of objects. He cited his advice to the owner of Hurlingham House, Middlesex, to stock his lawns with Alderney cows, which, because of their diminutive size, would increase the apparent distance between the house and the Thames. Similarly he advised a three-arched bridge over the artificial river at Stoke Park in order to give the river more importance. The management of viewpoints can affect the apparent form of the ground, and Repton explained how this occurs.

The connection between the artificial house and the natural landscape was

60   Stoke Park, view from the east.

The view, painted by Joseph Farington in 1801, shows it after Humphry Repton's improvements. Repton advised the three-arched bridge to give the river more consequence.

a question that Repton returned to frequently. He admitted that Brown's solution of bringing the natural scenery apparently up to the door was mistaken, and several remarks show that he shared Cradock's and Knight's views that frankly artificial gardens immediately surrounding the house were desirable. In 1795 he recommended that the series of small terraces behind the house at Burley-on-the-Hill, Rutland, should be replaced by one grand terrace wall in keeping with the magnificence of the house:

I therefore make a compromise between ancient and modern gardening, between art and nature, and by increasing the height, or rather the depth, from the upper terrace to the lower level of the ground, I make *that* the line of demarkation between the dressed ground and the park[74].

Repton was still very far from a whole-hearted conversion to regular gardens on a grand scale, as shown by his clearance in 1800 of the gardens laid out by George London at Dyrham, Gloucestershire. However he was showing an increasing interest in Tudor and Jacobean gardens as part of a more general concern for the more private pleasure grounds around the house. Repton admired Mason's flower garden at Nuneham, where seats, temples, statues and bases harmonize with the profusion of flowers and curious plants, but he did not want to be tied exclusively to this form of the modern English garden. By 1802 Bulstrode, where he had been working for over a decade, boasted an 'ancient garden', an 'American garden', 'modern terrace walks', and a flower garden, all in the gardens originally laid out by London a century before.

Repton was given a further chance to develop an assemblage of gardens when he obtained the commission for Woburn Abbey from John Russell, sixth Duke of Bedford, in 1804. Up till then Henry Holland had assiduously kept all landscape gardeners at bay. Repton clearly felt that this was one of the most important red books that he was destined to compile. He therefore produced his most magnificent ever, with 47 plans and sketches at double the normal size[75].

His feelings about his predecessor's work led him to 'condemn what Mr. Holland has done at Woburn as a landscape gardener'. Nevertheless he happily incorporated Holland's covered walk to the Chinese dairy. He made the pool next to it more Chinese by the addition of water lilies and other Chinese plants. East of this he planned an 'Arboretum and American Garden', laid out informally with American trees and shrubs disposed along circumferential paths around a central lawn. On a descending slope south of this he planned a huge walled botanical garden with a conservatory at the top and descending by levels towards an open area for keeping ornamental birds. The old conservatory, by now the sculpture gallery, was the centrepiece of a dressed lawn, or 'rosary', to its south. Connecting all these gardens to each other and the covered walk was an 'English garden, or shrubbery walk'.

Holland had left the wider landscape almost untouched. The park, at about 2800 acres, was one of England's largest, and there was an extensive tenanted estate besides. One of Repton's proposals was for a new drive from the London road to the west front. The old approach was another relic from George London's time—a drive down an avenue, and around a large circular bason. Repton did not want to destroy the bason, but proposed that it should be irregularized and given islands[76]. The drive would be diverted away from the central line, and go round the base of a knoll to be built of spoil from elsewhere. He reckoned that this would provide a better view from the house, and the visitor's first sight from nearly in front and from below would be more imposing.

The duke had remarked that he had never seen a Gothic estate cottage that

61   Woburn, gamekeeper's lodge at Apsley Wood.

This plate from the Woburn red book was published in Repton's *Fragments* (1816). It shows an early attempt by Repton at the reconstruction of a Tudor garden. More elaborate designs were made for Ashridge and Beaudesert in the 1810s.

did not betray its modern character, and so the Reptons agreed to design a timbered gamekeeper's cottage in the style 'prevalent from the reign of Henry VI to Henry VIII' for Apsley Wood, on the Woburn estate. John Adey's antiquarian tastes were given free rein, and he pieced together the architectural design, whilst his father scoured the picture gallery at the abbey for hints on old gardens. He made planting lists of the flowers that he could identify—columbine, clove-pinks, marigold, double-daisy, a white rose, yellow lilies and so forth. The hints must have been more appropriate for palaces, and so it is not surprising that the garden was far too elaborate to suit a gamekeeper's cottage. Nevertheless the whole was made as designed in 1810[77].

Repton was also asked by the duke to lay out Russell Square in Bloomsbury, then on the periphery of London. Clipped hornbeam and privet formed the perimeter screen. Inside was a broad gravel walk encircling a grass lawn, at the centre of which was a flower garden. He laid out Cadogan Square in Chelsea for Charles Sloane Cadogan, Earl Cadogan, at about the same time[78].

Picturesque Improvement

Although the early 1800s were satisfactory to Repton in many respects, they brought a fresh antagonist in the picturesque debate. This was a young Scot from Edinburgh called John Claudius Loudon. His early training was under John Mawer, a Scottish garden planner. During that time he must have absorbed the picturesque principles of Uvedale Price. Loudon arrived in London in 1803 announcing himself as Price's 'profound admirer and disciple', and as Repton's opponent. He was planning a book, to be called *Observations on Architecture, Landscape Gardening, Improving, &c.*, in which he was to claim:

I believe that I am the first who has set out as a landscape gardener, professing to follow Mr. Price's principles.

In fact *Observations* was not quite Loudon's first work in print: there were some 'Hints respecting the manner of laying out the grounds of the Public Squares in London to the utmost picturesque advantage' which he sent to *The Literary Journal* on the last day of 1803. These hints did not amount to much, and pointed towards what Repton actually did to the Russell and Cadogan Squares in 1805. Perhaps the most useful hint concerned the choice and disposition of plants. He recommended that they be selected for fragrance and for attractive foliage and flowers in the winter months. He also wanted to see the choice of species vary between different sections of the surrounding tree and shrub screen.

Observations, when it came out in 1804, had the more cumbrous title of *Observations on the Formation and Management of Useful and Ornamental Plantations; on the Theory and Practice of Landscape Gardening; and on Gaining and Embanking Land from Rivers or the Sea*. In his introduction to the second of these three subjects he roundly condemned Kent and Brown, and praised Price and Knight. He seems to have paraphrased parts of George Mason's *Essay on Design* and Whately's *Observations*. In discussing flower gardens he differed from Repton only in his greater inventiveness in naming different forms. He listed the following: the general flower garden, gardens for winter, spring and autumn, the garden of bulbous roots, the botanic garden, and modern British, Chinese, Grecian, Roman, Italian, Dutch and French gardens. A number of these together would form an agreeable contrast with each other, Loudon thought.

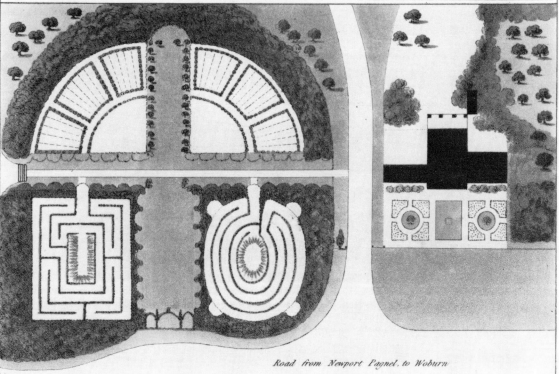

Road from Newport Pagnel. to Woburn

62   Design for a square.

John Claudius Loudon's model for London squares published in his *Hints ... on Pleasure Grounds* (1812). Repton's actual layouts of the 1800s were not dissimilar.

Hence little of what he wrote justified his pretensions. He even shared the principles of Convenience and Utility with Repton:

A knowledge of *utility* is ... necessary for the landscape gardener or layer out of grounds, who, in all his operations, must unite *convenience* with *beauty*.

Observations was clearly an immature work. In his *Treatise on Country Residences* (1806) he was better able to explain his theoretical standpoint, point out the practical differences between his and Brown's styles, and drive home some apt criticisms of Repton's work and writings. Brown's and William Mason's idealization of nature was quite foreign to Loudon's conception of taste. He inherited the Scottish tradition in natural philosophy, and his debt to Lord Kames was especially marked. Kames had borrowed from Burke, and shared his analytical approach and a belief in more elevated forms of the senses with Burke's other disciple, Uvedale Price. George Mason was to Loudon's liking too, perhaps because he had written that 'taste is by no means arbitrary'.

Loudon wanted to show that he was able 'to lay down rational principles of action', whereas Repton had not. Unfortunately for his readers, Loudon had a compiler's mind, and his discussion of taste was a mass of half-digested excerpts from these authors together with discursive observations of his own, and was not well-argued nor concise.

Nevertheless he followed Kames in his belief that 'taste is inherent in the human mind, though in degrees varying perhaps according to the education, habits, and moral sentiments of men'. The purpose of criticism was to give men a sound judgement, and he emphasized the connection with morality, as had Kames. By 'education' and 'habits' Loudon meant that 'taste ... is improved by exercise', and that a state of higher sensibility, or 'secondary perception', can be reached. For example,

we are at first most pleased with simple soft colours, as green, blue, violet, and gentle gradations of shade, as in round bodies; afterwards we acquire a relish for strong contrasts and harmonies, and dark shadows abruptly mixed with lights.

Differences in taste, Loudon thought, arise partly because the 'secondary sensations are not always present or perfect in each individual'.

In considering the objects of taste Loudon listed the various agreeable qualities they might have. They were remarkably close to Repton's long list published in *Hints* (1795). Utility, Symmetry, Order, Contrast, Variety, and Intricacy were in both. Loudon also listed Nature, Fitness, Uniformity, Unity and Harmony, and these had parallels in Repton's list. Loudon felt that these qualities, when found in combination in real scenes, produced their different characters, listed as Sublimity, Beauty, Deformity, Picturesque Beauty, Sculpturesque Beauty, Wildness, Age and Ruin, Novelty, and so forth.

George Mason was one of the first to state that the style of design should conform to the character of the place—a theme picked up by William Marshall. It became one of Loudon's primary rules of improvement. Indeed, in comparing his style to 'the affectedly graceful, or modern style' of Brown, White and Emes, he called his own 'the characteristic or natural style'. As he explained.

I call it *characteristic*, because its leading principle is to create or heighten natural character. The other styles ... produce a monotony of artificial character.

Both George Mason and Price had written about picturesque gardening (although the term may not have meant quite the same to both), and this became the other main feature of Loudon's proposed style. He preferred to call his work 'picturesque improvement', rather than 'landscape gardening', and he repeatedly insisted that good taste derived from natural scenery. He may have identified himself so closely with Price because Price had been quite specific on the practicalities of improvement. Loudon even went to Foxley to speak with Price about it. However he didn't follow him so slavishly that he couldn't recognize merit elsewhere. He could

express my general approbation of the mode of planting at Fonthill ... It is impossible for me not to feel a high degree of interest in the success of that place, which, when finished, will probably contribute more to the establishment of my ideas of Picturesque Improvement, than any thing that I can write.

63 Farnley Hall, the Woodwalk.

John Claudius Loudon worked at Farnley from 1804. This painting by J. M. W. Turner of about 1818 shows that Loudon's style of 'picturesque improvement' had been followed.

He had himself improved only a small number of usually second-rate country houses or villas. The most prestigous had been Scone Palace, Perthshire, for which he had made a series of plans in 1803 and his 'Treatise on Scone' in 1804[79]. His only work in England in 1803 besides hothouses appears to have been Brunswick Lodge in Blackheath and an ornamental farm at Kingswood Lodge, Surrey. He tried for a commission at Harewood by making elaborate plans for recasting Brown's lake with highly indented margins and scattered planting in Price's picturesque style. This came to nothing, but in 1804 he did persuade Walter Fawkes of Farnley Hall, not far from Harewood, to dismiss a landscape gardener and go for his style of picturesque planting. In 1805 John Jones of Llanarth altered his rather tame river and park, made only in 1792 by Lapidge, according to Loudon's plans. Also in 1805 Loudon gave plans for the improvement of Hopton Court, Shropshire, as an ornamental farm which the owner was to carry out[80].

This did not amount to very much, and it was of course all of recent standing. Nevertheless Loudon was convinced that he had struck out a new system. He saw the main advantages of his style over Brown's as: harmonizing the residence with the landscape rather than separating it; merging the planting into the surrounding field hedgerows rather than enclosing the park with a belt; producing a natural-looking lake instead of an unnaturally still river; and giving a wild forest character to parks rather than a smooth and shaven surface.

He saw himself as the champion of a new and rational system which must vanquish Repton, who kept alive his old system by deception and shallow principles. In his enthusiasm to pull down Repton and the worth of Repton's *Observations* (1803) Loudon charged:

1st, That the author has no general or fixed principles upon which he proceeds.
2d, That his precepts, reasoning, and practice, are in direct violation of natural taste; and,
3d, As a consequence, that there is no absurdity in regard to effect which he may not produce, and no limits, or certain data, in regard to the expense, in which those who follow his directions may not be plunged[81].

Whilst such a spirited condemnation is best treated as hyperbole, Loudon had made some points which lent it some weight. Undoubtedly Repton's treatment of water was open to criticism, and his knowledge of the practical aspects of planting was all too clearly weak. He had proposed to naturalize the cascade at Thoresby, Nottinghamshire, by arranging massive rocks from the Creswell Crags to give the impression of a waterfall over a natural stratum of rock. Repton had hoped that 'the violence done to nature' was 'the more allowable, since it is within a *short distance* of Derbyshire'[82]. Loudon reckoned that the 'short distance' to the rock scenery mentioned was nearly 30 miles[83]! This clearly was a violence to Nature, as was the other alteration by Repton that Loudon specifically criticized—the flower garden at Valleyfield, Perthshire[84]. This was laid out as a rectangular canal in a rectangular enclosure to be hidden in a natural dell.

Loudon also criticized Repton's use of the folding flaps, or 'slides', attached to his red book watercolours. With some justice he pointed out that the 'after' scene was always made to look better, and the 'before' scene worse. Furthermore the before scenes were prejudiced by the presence of the flap which could not be ignored[85]. In fact Loudon produced reports akin to Repton's red books, though he generally called them 'Treatises' or 'Notitiae'. His views did not have slides, and the emphasis was on giving instructions on the alterations, but overall they owed much to Repton's ideas.

6

Regency Gardens

Landscape Gardeners and Their Clients

Humphry Repton's clients during the early part of his career were rich and, on the whole, cultured. When Loudon moved to London in 1803 he was entering a very different world of patronage. His skills as a designer and writer were required mainly by the new urban classes risen with the Industrial Revolution. By and large they had little taste and no vast acreages. Loudon's incessant and self-appointed task was to guide and correct their taste; he must often have despaired.

Even when the New Rich were establishing their positions in society through the traditional means of purchasing estates, this was no encouragement to landscape gardening. Repton remarked, towards the end of his career, in his *Fragments on the Theory and Practice of Landscape Gardening* (1816) that,

The sudden acquirement of riches, by individuals, has diverted *wealth* into new channels; men are solicitous to *increase* property rather than to *enjoy* it; they endeavour to improve the *value*, rather than the *beauty*, of their newly purchased estates[1].

Repton also remarked upon the rate at which these people were replacing the established landed classes, a process that was equally obvious to a very different observer of the rural scene, William Cobbett. Whilst upon one of his *Rural Rides* in Sussex, Cobbett wrote in his usual hard-hitting fashion:

If I had time, I would make an actual survey of one whole county, and find out how many of the old gentry have lost their estates, and have been supplanted by the Jews, since PITT began his reign. I am sure I should prove that, in number, they are one-half extinguished[2].

However this turnover had not been brought about just by the 'Jews' (Cobbett's name for bankers, manufacturers, traders and sinecure holders) infiltrating landed society; the strength of the gentry had been sapped by income tax, inflation, excessive expenditure upon politics and, not infrequently, improvement. By and large it was only the more innovative (amongst whom much of the aristocracy could be found), who continued to flourish. Those who had entered into agricultural improvement with a zest, who had exploited the mineral rights held as lords of the manor, and who had made investments in canals and the new industries, survived the bad times.

The number of traditional clients was thus on the decline anyway, but in late 1803 the Napoleonic War restarted with threats by the Emperor to invade Britain. Naturally, the attention of all landowners was turned to the defence of the realm. Even after the Battle of Trafalgar in 1805 the fear of invasion persisted, leaving as a permanent memorial a host of follies of a new kind—the Martello towers along the south coast. Repton considered that the war had seriously depressed his business, and indeed his practice boasted very few large parks after 1804[3]. He remarked on this in his *Fragments*:

In the last ten years, the art of landscape gardening, in common with all other arts which depend on peace and patronage, has felt the influence of war, and war taxes, which operate both on the means and the inclination to cultivate the arts of peace[4].

The war affected other landscape gardeners in different ways. Old Adam Mickle found himself appointed ensign of his local militia, the Bedale Volunteers, in 1804[5]. John Webb's practice actually seemed to thrive, with commissions in Cheshire, Staffordshire and Hertfordshire. By 1810 he was also practising as an architect in Ireland, specializing in the Gothic style[6]. Meanwhile Loudon turned to farming and made a small fortune.

Loudon's conversion to farming happened almost by accident. Late in 1806 he was at Tremadoc, Caernarvonshire, where he was advising W. A. Madocks on the reclamation of the 7000-acre Traeth Mawr from the estuary of the Afon Glaslyn. He returned to London on the outside of the coach in the pouring rain. Rheumatic fever set in, and left him with a stiff knee. He leased a farmhouse at Pinner, Middlesex, for his convalescence. Here he developed an intense interest in farming, and became convinced that improved farming methods could solve the problem of the wheat shortages brought about by the wartime interruption of imports. So he persuaded his father to leave his farm near Edinburgh, and to take out the lease of the farm where he was convalescing[7].

Loudon set out his ideas on farming in a pamphlet in 1808[8] which, being highly topical, attracted some attention. Colonel Stratton, the proprietor of Tew Park, a 1500-acre estate in Oxfordshire, was one of those interested by Loudon's proposals. Stratton offered him the management of Tew Park in exchange for a lease of part of it at a nominal rent. Loudon accepted, and left his father to carry on alone at Pinner. Whilst at Tew, Loudon ran a course for the sons of the landed gentry and aspiring land-stewards, which was remarkable for being the first instance of a formal training in agriculture. His father died in December 1809, and in February 1811 Loudon withdrew from Tew in order to concentrate once again upon picturesque improvement. If he had failed in freeing the country from wheat shortages, at least he and his father had benefited from the consequent high prices. He now had a fortune of £15,000. The war seemed to be nearly over, and so from March 1813 he took an 18-month tour of Scandinavia, Russia and Germany.

At this date Repton had almost retired from practice. This was mainly because of the angina he suffered as an outcome of a carriage accident in 1811, and his subsequent convalescence[9]. Thereafter he limited his commissions, and most were favours to family, friends or valued past clients. For example he wrote to his son Edward, who had gone into the church, concerning gardens that would be appropriate to almshouses at Crayford, Kent[10]. When he visited places he had to be carried around for much of the time, but he would submit to this in order to further the career of his eldest son, John Adey, who would accompany him. The prime example of their co-operation is Sheringham, Norfolk.

The final end of hostilities brought fresh imports of wheat, and, despite the Corn Laws, prices fell. A period of agricultural depression set in. Many landlords were obliged to give rent rebates in order to keep their tenants. Hence those who might have harboured the desire probably no longer had the means for landscape gardening. Repton was pessimistic:

It is not, therefore, to be wondered at, that the art of landscape gardening should have slowly and gradually declined. Whether the influence of returning peace may revive its energies, or whether it is hereafter to be classed among the '*artes perditae*' [the lost arts], the Author hopes its memory may be preserved a little longer in the following pages[11].

The fact was that the days of large-scale place-making were indeed virtually

64 Cheeseburn Grange, design for the grounds.

The design for remodelling the grounds of a villa was made by the young Newcastle architect, John Dobson, in 1813. Concern about the approach is evident from the pencil sketching of drives on the plan.

over. The chief occupation of landscape gardeners from Regency times onwards was to provide grounds for villas; and, furthermore, as the popularity of villas was spreading into the urban middle classes they became smaller and smaller. Repton had himself found this:

It seldom falls to the lot of the improver to be called upon for his opinion on places of great extent, and of vast range of unblended and uninterrupted property, like Longleate or Woburn: while, in the neighbourhood of every city or manufacturing town, new places, as villas, are daily springing up; and these, with a few acres, require all the conveniences, comforts, and appendages, of larger and more sumptuous, if not more expensive places. And these have, of late, had the greatest claim on my attention . . .[12].

The young Newcastle architect, John Dobson, found just the same to be true in his part of the country. As perhaps his first venture in a long and fruitful career he had been lucky enough to assist Sir Charles Monck in the rebuilding of Belsay Hall in an austere neo-classical style from about 1812. All his life he described himself as a landscape gardener. He laid out the grounds of one or two villas where he was able to apply the principles appropriate to Northumberland. These are that the fine views so often obtainable from the main fronts should be maintained, but the entrance should be moved to a side of the house where it can be protected from the weather by shrubberies and plantations. However he seems only to have had one commission for a truly extensive design—Bolam Lake and its wooded surroundings, carried out in 1816[13]. Dobson had the mortification of seeing his designs frustrated. In an affidavit of 1849 he described his disappointment that the progressive thinning that he had specified had been neglected, with consequent loss of timber value.

The more circumscribed the grounds of the villa, the more stereotyped was its layout. Repton tried to assure his villa-owning clients to the contrary:

It has often been hinted to me, when called on for my opinion concerning places of small extent, that I can hardly be expected to give to them the same attention as to those of many hundred acres. My answer has generally been, that, on the contrary, they often require more attention than larger places[14],

but the results spoke for themselves. Perhaps part of the blame could be laid at Loudon's door.

Back in England from his extensive tour of the Continent, Loudon undertook some foolish speculations with his money, and lost nearly all of it. Then, after settling in Bayswater, he began to collect materials for a monumental *Encyclopaedia of Gardening*. This work was to contain copious information upon virtually every aspect of gardening, including how to design and create flower gardens, shrubberies and plantations, and with a choice of styles of gardens and garden architecture. It was written for inexperienced gardeners and was a huge success when published in 1822.

The sales were a just reward for the phenomenal amount of work that Loudon had put into it. He divided it into three parts—The History of Gardening, The Science of Gardening and Gardening as Practised in Britain. Because France and Italy were still in the coils of war at the time of his earlier travels, he devoted six months to a visit to these countries in 1819, and so completed the material for his History. In order to supplement his knowledge for the latter two parts he must have read widely, as his book list is extremely lengthy. The *Encyclopaedia* was a sharp contrast to the expensive publications written by Repton with aristocratic purchasers in mind. Loudon had aimed his accurately at the middle classes, who, he had early recognized, were to be the source of most of his employment henceforth.

It was only in a few peculiar instances that a client would appear with the money and the acres traditionally put at the disposal of the landscape gardener. There was the Prince Regent who, unlike his father, could not resist building. A check was kept on his extravagance by the government. There were a few reckless private individuals too. Two in particular caused sensations. The first, George Spencer, the Marquis of Blandford, was notorious for his profligate expenditure on his planting at Whiteknights, Berkshire, all through the war years[15]. In 1804 his bill from the nursery of Lee and Kennedy exceeded £15,000[16]. By 1814 his expenditure on plants and books was causing financial embarrassment. This was temporarily relieved in 1816 by a loan from John Farquhar, an eccentric millionaire who had made his money in India from gunpowder, and then invested it wisely in England. Blandford succeeded as fifth Duke of Marlborough in 1817, but even his vast inheritance could not prevent his creditors forcing the sale of Whiteknights, its contents, plants, bridges and even the covered garden seats specially designed by J. B. Papworth.

Curiously, Farquhar came to the aid of other landscape gardening schemes that had outstretched themselves. Park Crescent in London, where Portland Street was supposed to tie in with the Regent's Park scheme, was blighted by the bankruptcy of a builder in 1815 until Farquhar took an interest in the

65   Whiteknights, the Dolphin Fountain.

The engraving was published in Mrs Hofland's *Descriptive Account ... of Whiteknights* (1819). The barrel seats are of china. Hop and honeysuckle grow up the arch, through which is seen the conservatory. China roses, scarlet sage, dahlias and geraniums grow within the hexagon treillage.

speculation four years later[17]. A few years after that Farquhar was heard of in connection with the second great sensation, the sale of Fonthill Abbey.

William Beckford had neglected his financial affairs and at the same time he had spent vast sums on the Abbey and the grounds. Eventually in 1822 he decided to put the place on the market. He had always kept the public outside the Barrier, and much speculation and rumour resulted[18]. Beckford stage-managed the sale magnificently. He had a guide book made which ran through six editions in 1822, which opened with the advertisement:

The curiosity of the public has long been excited respecting the spacious buildings and improvements, together with the various ornamental collections that have been preparing for many years at Fonthill; but the Tourist and Virtuoso have hitherto waited in vain for that degree of perfection which the Proprietor required, before he opened his domains to general view. It being now announced, that admission may be gained by tickets ...[19].

Christie's sold 72,000 copies of the catalogue announcing that the sale was due to commence on 8 October. Tourists and virtuosi flocked to see what had hitherto been legend only. Then, just two days before the sale, it was announced that everything had been purchased by private treaty. The purchaser turned out to be Farquhar who had paid £330,000.

Although Farquhar was not typical of the landed gentry, he shared his Indian background with Colonel Cockerell, the creator of Sezincote, Glouces-

tershire, and his banking connections with Thomas Hope, of Deepdene, Surrey. Men like these now constituted most of the small band of big spenders on architecture and gardens. Perhaps it is a significant indicator of the times that the nobility's most noted representative as a maker of gardens in the period shortly after Waterloo, Charles Talbot, fifteenth Earl of Shrewsbury, and the creator of Alton Towers, Staffordshire, shared with Farquhar a reputation for eccentricity.

66 Alton Towers, panoramic view.

The pagoda and the conservatory across the valley were built by J. B. Papworth and Robert Abraham by the early 1820s. J. C. Loudon disliked the astonishing medley of buildings and gardens, but published an account and this engraving in his *Encyclopaedia of Gardening* (1834).

Picturesque Taste

Loudon's *Country Residences* (1806) had been the last substantial contribution to the controversial literature on picturesque improvement. The theorizing had by then moved into different fields. Richard Payne Knight developed his ideas on colour and taste generally in his *Analytical Inquiry into the Principles of Taste* (1805). In this he built upon the work of Archibald Alison and others of the Scottish School of aesthetics, and thereby popularized them in England. Meanwhile Price's ideas on architecture promoted a growing awareness of the Picturesque amongst architects. Both Price and Knight lived on for many years afterwards: Price died in 1829 having received a baronetage for his lengthy parliamentary services the year before: Knight died in 1824, being even better remembered as a scholar of early Greek texts and as a collector of bronzes, coins and gems, than he is for his theories on visual perception[20].

The only contribution to picturesque improvement from either Price or Knight after 1801 was a new edition of all Price's essays in 1810. He explained in an apologetic tone that this contained some new material, but that its purpose was chiefly to polish and summarize what he had written before[21]. The chief combatants had already perceived that it was time to desist. One reason was that the picturesque theorists were generally acknowledged as the victors (actually they never had any serious opposition); and perhaps another

67 Dr Syntax in search of the Picturesque.

This etching and others by Thomas Rowlandson mocking the vogue for the picturesque was published in *The Poetical Magazine* between 1809 and 1811. Here, the nag, Grizzle, is about to pitch the doctor into the lake.

is that there were far more serious problems engaging the minds of the public in the mid-1800s, such as the war and prices.

The reading public was indeed somewhat tired of the whole debate. Its very seriousness had made it slightly ridiculous. When Doctor Syntax, a caricature of the theorists of the picturesque, appeared before the public he provided the much needed comic relief. The instigator was Thomas Rowlandson, who offered a series of his inimitable drawings to the *Poetical Magazine* from 1809 to 1811. William Combe, who had previously worked on such topographical works as Boydell's *The River Thames* (1794), was asked to supply the letterpress to accompany the drawings. Combe never spoke to Rowlandson, but he managed to weave a light-hearted tale around them so successfully that his excruciating verse was all part of the fun. When the whole collection was reissued in 1812 as a book entitled *The Tour of Doctor Syntax in Search of the Picturesque* it was a huge success.

Combe chose William Gilpin to be the model of his own hero. Doctor Syntax was a curate whose hopes of church preferment were low, and who had taken up the profession of a schoolmaster to make ends meet. One evening he had a brilliant idea:

> I'll make a *tour*—and then I'll *write it*.
> You well know what my pen can do,
> And I'll employ my pencil too:
> I'll ride and write, and sketch and print,
> And thus create a real mint;
> I'll prose it here, I'll verse it there,
> And picturesque it ev'ry where.

Requiring no further prompting, his avaricious wife straightaway packed him off on his nag, Grizzle.

Syntax's odyssey to the Lakes was alternately disaster and happy fortune. He fell into the water sketching a ruined castle and lost his money at York races, but was fortunate enough to obtain a recommendation from Squire Hearty to 'Lord C******' (evidently Frederick Howard, fifth Earl of Carlisle, well known for his interest in the arts). This noble lord appointed himself Syntax's patron after the tour of the Lakes had been completed, and through his influence Syntax persuaded a bookseller to print his book. Not only did he receive a lot of money from it, but his fame was prodigious. Combe's text ends with the good Doctor obtaining his church preferment—a vicarage in the Lakes.

Actually Syntax's story does not follow Gilpin's very closely, as Gilpin did not publish his tours until many years after both his travels and his preferment. But this did not matter, as the book was not aimed at any one person but at the seriousness with which the picturesque debate was conducted. Hence Syntax was also made the mouthpiece of Uvedale Price's maxims. In one passage he sketches farm animals but refuses to draw a pretty young girl, declaring:

> The beams of beauty I disclaim;
> The Picturesque's my only aim.

Further satire on picturesque taste was provided by Thomas Love Peacock in his *Headlong Hall* (1816). In this, Repton is parodied as Marmaduke Milestone, Esquire (alluding to Knight's strictures on this subject). In one passage Milestone is with the Headlong family, showing them a sketch with a lift-up flap in his red book for Lord Littlebrain's park:

MR. MILESTONE.—This, you perceive, is the natural state of one part of the grounds. Here is a wood, never yet touched by the finger of taste; thick, intricate, and gloomy. Here is a little stream, dashing from stone to stone, and over-shadowed by these untrimmed boughs.
MISS TENORINA.—The sweet romantic spot! How beautifully the birds must sing there on a summer evening!
MISS GRAZIOSA.—Dear sister! How can you endure the horrid thicket?
MR. MILESTONE.—You are right, Miss Graziosa: your taste is correct—perfectly *en règle*. Now here is the same place corrected—trimmed—polished—decorated—adorned. Here sweeps a plantation, in that beautiful regular curve: there winds a gravel walk: here are parts of the old wood, left in these majestic circular clumps, disposed at equal distances with wonderful symmetry: there are some single shrubs, scattered in elegant profusion: here a Portugal laurel, there a juniper; here a laurustinus, there a spruce fir; here a larch, there a lilac; here a rhododendron, there an arbutus. The stream, you see, is become a canal: the banks are perfectly smooth and green, sloping to the water's edge: and there is Lord Littlebrain, rowing in an elegant boat.
SQUIRE HEADLONG.—Magical, faith!

Peacock treated Richard Payne Knight with some sympathy, but reviewers who merely proposed new terms were treated as pedants. Sir Patrick O'Prism and Mr Gall, representing these characters, were engaged in debate with Mr Milestone:

'Sir,' said Mr. Milestone, 'you will have the goodness to make a distinction between the picturesque and the beautiful.'
'Will I?' said Sir Patrick, 'och! but I won't. For what is beautiful? That which pleases the eye. And what pleases the eye? Tints variously broken and blended. Now, tints variously broken and blended constitute the picturesque.'
'Allow me,' said Mr. Gall. 'I distinguish the picturesque and the beautiful, and add to them, in the laying out of grounds, a third and distinct character, which I call *unexpectedness*.'
'Pray, sir,' said Mr. Milestone, 'by what name do you distinguish this character when a person walks round the grounds for a second time?'
Mr. Gall bit his lips, and inwardly vowed to revenge himself on Milestone, by cutting up his next publication.

Jane Austen when a young woman had been deeply interested in the picturesque, and references to it abound in her novels. Evidently she was not persuaded that sense should be abandoned to sensibility, and she had laughed at the rage for Gothic novels. Nevertheless she seems to have been a sincere admirer of William Gilpin[22], and to have been acquainted with the travel-guide literature for the Lake District and Derbyshire.

She was also mildly disrespectful of improvers. Perhaps this was because she had seen the mania affect one of her own family. In 1806 the Austens visited Mrs Austen's cousin, the Rev. Thomas Leigh, at his rectory at Adlestrop, in Gloucestershire. Leigh had, a few years before, called in Repton to advise upon a new drive, which provided access to his rectory rather than to the mansion house, but which was an ornament to both. No doubt Thomas took great pleasure in discussing his improvements. While the Austens were at Adlestrop the word came that Thomas had unexpectedly inherited Stoneleigh Abbey, Warwickshire, and so he and his cousins went to inspect it. It turned out to be old-fashioned in many ways, with a courtyard in front of the house, the walls of which blocked the views to the River Avon from the approach drive. Here was a much more exciting opportunity to carry out improvements. Repton was once more called in and produced a red book dated 1809.

Jane almost certainly had this episode in mind when writing *Mansfield Park* (1814)[23] although she could not use the character of her middle-aged cousin in a story about young people. His place is taken by the youthful but dull James Rushworth, Adlestrop by Compton, and Stoneleigh by Sotherton Court.

He [Rushworth] had been visiting a friend in a neighbouring county, and that friend having recently had his grounds laid out by an improver, Mr. Rushworth was returned with his head full of the subject, and very eager to be improving his own place in the same way . . .

'I wish you could see Compton,' said he, 'it is the most complete thing! I never saw a place so altered in my life. I told Smith I did not know where I was. The approach *now* is one of the finest things in the country. You see the house in the most surprising manner. I declare when I got back to Sotherton yesterday, it looked like a prison—quite a dismal old prison . . . I must try to do something with it, but I do not know what. I hope I shall have some good friend to help me.'

'Your best friend upon such an occasion,' said Miss Bertram, calmly, 'would be Mr. Repton, I imagine.'

'That is what I was thinking of. As he has done so well by Smith, I think I had better have him at once. His terms are five guineas a day.'

Rushworth continued to bore the rest of the party with the subject and presently reflected that Repton would certainly have the avenue down. At this point the book's heroine, Fanny Price, remarked:

'Cut down an avenue! What a pity! Does it not make you think of Cowper? "Ye fallen avenues, once more I mourn your fate unmerited."'

Evidently Jane Austen was not much in favour of calling in improvers, for Fanny's favourite cousin soon after remarks:

'Had I a place to new fashion, I should not put myself into the hands of an improver. I would rather have an inferior degree of beauty, of my own choice, and acquired progressively.'

Pride and Prejudice (1813) was originally written in 1797, when Gilpin was at the height of his popularity. The heroine, Elizabeth Bennet, is made to think when first viewing Darcy's country mansion:

It was a large, handsome, stone building, standing well on rising ground, and backed by a ridge of high woody hills;—and in front, a stream of some natural importance, was swelled into greater, but without any artificial appearance. Its banks were neither formal, nor falsely adorned. Elizabeth was delighted. She had never seen a place for which nature had done more, or where natural beauty had been so little counteracted by an awkward taste.

These sentiments would have been typical of Gilpin, and further indications that Jane Austen had studied his principles occur when she makes a joke with the rules of composition. A party was four strong, but the path was wide enough for three only. Elizabeth Bennet runs off from her companions saying:

'You are charmingly group'd and appear to uncommon advantage. The picturesque would be spoilt by admitting a fourth. Good bye.'

If Jane Austen's references to the picturesque had already lost some of their topicality when her books were published, Uvedale Price's views on uniting architecture and gardening, on flower gardens and on American gardening were brought to fruition in Regency days. We also find Nash's and Wyatt's ideas for irregular Gothic villas expanding upon their success.

Buildings were beginning to be seen as an opportunity to create new focal points in the English landscape. Many of the nobility wished to emulate Wyatt's great spire at Fonthill. In 1800 John Henry Manners, fifth Duke of Rutland, commissioned Wyatt to rebuild Belvoir Castle to complement its commanding position[24]. Wyatt died in 1813 before the project was completed and in 1816 his creation was partly burnt down. It was eventually completed in 1825 under the control of the duke's chaplain, the Rev. Sir John Thoroton. In the meantime the extensive domain had been transformed by the Duchess, a daughter of the fifth Earl of Carlisle, to provide a picturesque setting.

At the other end of the scale, and not far removed from a folly, was the rebuilding of Stafford Castle. The Jerninghams, remotely descended from the Barons Stafford, were proud of the role of the castle in Staffordshire's later medieval history. Edward Jerningham had the site cleared of vegetation and a survey of the remaining foundations undertaken in 1815. He then set about reconstruction in the castle style of the reign of Edward III, which was thought to be authentic[25]. The money ran out, but a suite of rooms on three storeys at the west end, flanked by two of the intended four octagonal corner towers, was made habitable by 1817 and is a prominent landmark, as intended. Jerningham occupied the place only occasionally and so there was no need for extensive gardens. He left the ancient trees surrounding the castle just as they were to provide a picturesque approach.

Curiously, then, gardening authors were already weary of debate in the 1810s, at the very time when the picturesque was still gathering force in architecture. The youthful George Johnson concluded in 1829 that:

After studying the writings of the several partizans, I have been able to draw but one conclusion, which is, that the principles of Knight and Price are correct if impartially considered, and have been acted upon by the general consent of modern designers; nor can there be a greater proof of this position than that in his maturer practice, Repton acted upon them himself[26].

Late in his life Loudon wrote of Repton along the same lines:

Though at first an avowed defender and follower of Brown, he gradually veered round with the change effected in public opinion by the *Essays on the Picturesque*: so that, comparing his earlier works of 1795 and 1803 with his *Fragments on Landscape-Gardening* published in 1817, he appears by the latter much more of a disciple of Price, than a defender of his 'great self-taught predecessor'[27].

George Johnson, born only in 1802, must have wondered how the

68 Belvoir Castle.

In this painting of 1816 J. M. W. Turner captures the spirit of the new castle – a picturesque building on a wooded hill to be seen from the country round about.

Picturesque Debate could ever have been so passionate. An impartial reading of Repton's earlier works would have shown that his differences with Price were not so much as to the correctness of Price's principles, but as to their applicability in landscape gardening. Moreover Repton had unfailingly expressed his views in a mild and inoffensive manner. The affair had been fuelled by Price's and Knight's appetite for controversy, and when they had apparently won the battle they had nothing left to do but to attack each other over their scarcely perceived differences. Perhaps Loudon was a bit ashamed of having taken the side against Repton so ardently. Surely his own objective had not been so much to establish the truth but rather to pull down the leader of his profession so that he could take his place? When his own views had changed considerably, he paid amends to Repton, recounting how Brown's style had given way,

not, however, as may be supposed, to the Picturesque School (which though adopted in many instances, in some part of an estate, yet, in very few cases was exclusively employed), but to what may be called Repton's School, and which may be considered as combining all that was excellent in the former schools, and, in fact, as consisting of the union of an artistical knowledge of the subject with good taste and good sense[28].

As if to signify their reconciliation publicly, Loudon eventually brought himself round to edit *The Landscape Gardening and Landscape Architecture of the*

Late Humphry Repton, Esq (1840). One might read Repton's text and Loudon's commentary and receive virtually no impression that the Picturesque Debate had ever been.

Gardening as an Art of Taste

Though emphasis varied over time and between individuals, the generally understood theories of improvement since Alexander Pope's time aimed to achieve the proper relationship of Art to Nature; and usually, since Nature is divine art and the exemplar to mankind, there could be only one true standard of taste. However theoretical writers like Burke, Cradock and Price had sown the seeds of doubt amongst the public. The Rev. Archibald Alison flatly contradicted the traditional view, and considered that beauty derived from the association of ideas only, and so might vary from person to person. The implication was that taste is not an objective matter, and no man can deride that of another.

Uvedale Price's theories were able to undermine the ideology of Nature in improvement, but unfortunately they proved not to be an alternative. The rapid reversal of Lancelot Brown's reputation had left many improvers confused, whilst the promoters of new styles could not form a united front except to agree that picturesqueness was to be sought for. Reactions to this unsettled state of affairs ranged from the feeling that a complete rejection of all recent standards of taste was justified to the other extreme—hoping that a diversity of styles could provide mental satisfaction in place of an ideology.

The bluntest rejection of all modern ornamental gardening came from William Cobbett. Heedless of the warnings about Sir William Temple's taste by Horace Walpole and his generation, Cobbett looked back with nostalgia at the canal at Moor Park that he had known in his youth:

SIR WILLIAM TEMPLE had one of his own constructing in his gardens at MOOR PARK ... I have stood for hours to look at this canal, for the good-natured manners of those days had led the proprietor to make an opening in the outer wall in order that his neighbours might enjoy the sight as well as himself ... I have travelled far since, and have seen a great deal; but I have never seen anything of the gardening kind so beautiful in the whole course of my life[29].

Humphry Repton gave quite the opposite response. Following from his work at Bulstrode and Woburn, he went to the extreme when asked to advise upon the eight acres of flattish ground to be laid out as pleasure grounds at Ashridge, Hertfordshire. In the Ashridge red book of 1814 he recommended gardens of as many different forms as he could think. Repton had by this time suffered 20 years of public abuse, and a number of years of severe physical pain. Betraying the spirit of a broken man, he referred to Ashridge as 'the youngest favourite, the child of my age and declining years'. He appears to have lost confidence in his own taste, his answer being to resort to novelty:

Every part of a modern pleasure-ground is alike; and, unless varied by views into the adjoining country, we soon tire of the sameness of gravel walks, in serpentine lines, with broad margins of grass, and flowers, and shrubs, everywhere promiscuously mixed and repeated; and, therefore, I ventured boldly to go back to those ancient trim gardens, which formerly delighted the venerable inhabitants of this curious spot, as appears from the trim box hedges of the monk's garden, and some large yew-trees still growing in rows near the site of the monastery[30].

He claimed 15 different kinds of garden in his plan. Amongst them were a winter garden, an arboretum, an American garden, and a rock garden. There were also some gardens of his own invention, including an imaginative

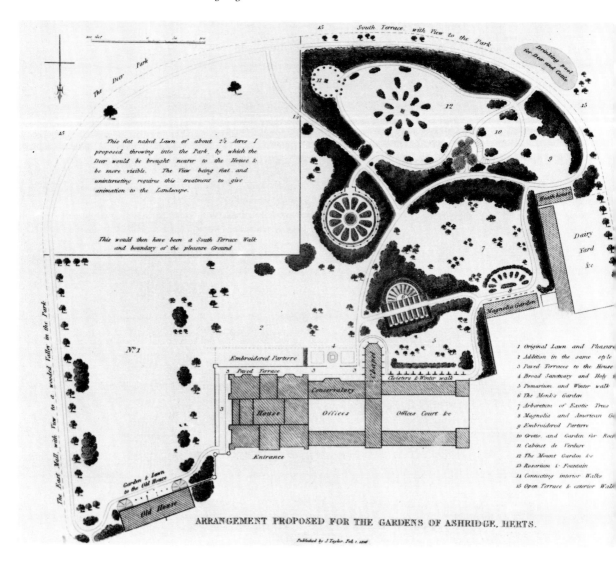

Within the plan, the following labels appear:

South Terrace with View to the Park

Drinking Pool for Deer and Cattle

The Deer Park

This flat naked Lawn of about 2½ Acres I proposed throwing into the Park, by which the Deer would be brought nearer to the House & be more visible. The View being flat and uninteresting requires this treatment to give animation to the Landscape.

This would then have been a South Terrace Walk and boundary of the pleasure Ground.

Heath house

Dairy Yard &c

Magnolia Garden

The East Wall with View to a wooded Valley in the Park

N° 1

Embroidered Parterre

Paved Terrace

Conservatory

Chapel

Cloisters & Winter walk

House   *Offices*   *Offices Court &c*

Entrance

Garden & Lawn to the Old House

Old House

1 Original Lawn and Pleasure
2 Addition in the same style
3 Paved Terraces to the House
4 Broad Sanctuary and Holy
5 Pomarium and Winter walk
6 The Monk's Garden
7 Arboretum of Exotic Trees
8 Magnolia and American G
9 Embroidered Parterre
10 Grotto and Garden for Rock
11 Cabinet de Verdure
12 The Mount Garden &c
13 Rosarium & Fountain
14 Connecting interior Walks
15 Open Terrace & exterior Walk

ARRANGEMENT PROPOSED FOR THE GARDENS OF ASHRIDGE, HERTS.

Published by J Taylor, Feb. 1 1816

69   Ashridge, design for the gardens.

Repton's recollection of the plan in his red book of 1813 when he wrote his *Fragments* (1816). He had designed a similar collection of gardens at Woburn in 1804, but those at Ashridge were 'my youngest favourite'.

reconstruction of a monk's garden and a circular rosary, each with a fountain, and an embroidered parterre 'with beds raised to meet the eye'.

Repton was conscious that:

the novelty of this attempt to collect a number of gardens, differing from each other, may, perhaps, excite the critic's censure.

but

I will hope there is no more absurdity in collecting gardens of different styles, dates, characters, and dimensions, in the same enclosure, than in placing the works of a Raphael and a Teniers in the same cabinet.

In any age when an ideology of improvement was strong, he would undoubtedly have met severe ridicule, but actually he met none. Indeed, had he lived to see Loudon's *Encyclopaedia of Gardening* he would have been agreeably surprised to see Ashridge noticed favourably[31]. Repton's young critic had come to recognize the limited use of picturesque principles and now agreed with Repton's view that:

The scenery of nature, called landscape, and that of a garden, are as different as their uses; one is to please the eye, the other is for the comfort and occupation of man: one is wild, and may be adapted to animals in the wildest state of nature; while the other is appropriated to man in the highest state of civilization and refinement[32].

Loudon also agreed that a garden

may be laid out with all the variety, contrast, and even whim, that can produce pleasing objects to the eye.

The growing diversification of style was accompanied by a revival of interest in the garden at the expense of the park. Indian, Italian, French and cottage styles of gardening appeared at a bewildering rate. At length, even Loudon, that arch disseminator of styles, was surfeited, and at the close of his career he looked back with some nostalgia at the days of his youth, when one could owe allegiance to one true taste:

Gardening, as an Art of Culture, since the commencement of the present century, has made rapid progress; but, as an Art of Taste, it has been comparatively stationary[33].

Architecture and Sculpture Softened by Vegetation

The first of the new styles to come to the public's attention after the picturesque was the Indian. Since Robert Clive's time, the British in India had been consolidating their position, and many of the 'nabobs' returned home extremely rich, not through conquest but through commerce. Views of Indian architecture by William Hodges became available from the 1780s, and were the inspiration for a number of architectural works by George Dance[34]. Both men questioned the exclusive use of Greek and Roman architecture, pointing out that Egyptian, Indian and Moorish architecture had merits too. Evidently Dance persuaded Sir George Beaumont of the merits of the Indian style, for its first tentative use for a country house was in 1804 at Coleorton, Leicestershire, where corner turrets with small domes and finials gave a mildly exotic outline to an otherwise unremarkable exterior.

Humphry Repton's conversion to the Indian style seemingly came with the force and suddenness of a thunderbolt. In 1805 he was invited to Sezincote, Gloucestershire, where the Indian veteran, Charles Cockerell, with the advice of his architect brother Samuel Pepys Cockerell and the artist Thomas Daniell, was building a country house entirely in an Indian style. A distinctively Indian setting was required for the first time, and this was provided by the garden architecture designed by Daniell, which was carefully placed in relation to water and picturesque planting. Actually Repton had little to contribute to Sezincote, but his imagination was fired by what he had seen. Soon after, he wrote:

I cannot suppress my opinion that we are on the eve of some great future change in both those arts [gardening and architecture], in consequence of our having lately become acquainted with scenery and buildings in the interior provinces of India[35].

The notion of an Indian style of gardening is perhaps rather curious, and it should not be understood too literally. Hodges' and Daniell's prints had shown ill-kept and often abandoned Muslim or native Indian architecture in formal garden settings that were being invaded by overgrown plants. What Repton admired in them was not so much any distinctive style of gardening, but the 'richness of effect' in Indian architecture and the 'new sources of beauty and variety'[36] that he found in the prints. He was converted to the view that the

pleasure ground 'should appear to be the rich frame of the landscape'. Such phrases are familiar from Price's and Knight's comments on old Italian terrace gardens, and it is no surprise to find Repton also declaring that

in garden scenery, we delight in the rich embellishments, the blended graces of *Watteau*, where nature is dressed, but not disfigured, by art; and where the artificial decorations of architecture and sculpture are softened down by natural accompaniments of vegetation.

Perhaps it was pride that prevented him from acknowledging that he was converted to an enthusiasm for picturesque effects in gardens; otherwise it is hard to explain why he found it necessary to claim that he had been one of the first to recognize the merits of an Indian style of gardening. This never really existed; there were just the effects created by architecture, which happened to be Indian in style, in the setting of a luxuriant garden.

Repton was consulted about the Royal Pavilion at Brighton immediately after his small contribution at Sezincote. The magnificent domed stables already there provided an excellent justification for 'Indian gardening and architecture'. Normally, all objects of mere convenience or comfort, including flower gardens, would be removed from the principal view and placed less conspicuously. It is true that Repton had previously shown a liking for conservatories, and that he had recognized the value of terraces in providing an appropriate transition between the artificial neatness of the house and the parkland. He had also admired 'flower passages' such as that at Woburn, and

70   Whiteknights, the seat.

Published in Mrs Hofland's *Descriptive Account . . . of Whiteknights* (1819), this view shows one of J. B. Papworth's garden buildings. From it one could see down the 1200-foot-long laburnum bower, and off to the left were the 'Chantilly Gardens'.

71   Brighton Pavilion. design for the grounds.

The engraving from Humphry Repton's *Design for the Pavillon* (1808) shows how he would have combined architecture with vegetation in a new 'Indian' style of gardening.

had designed a secluded regular flower garden at Valleyfield. However, his advocacy in his red book of 1806 (published as *Designs for the Pavillon* (1808)) of a new form of garden at the Brighton Pavilion, in which the barriers between the arts of gardening and architecture had been entirely broken down, was, as he pointed out, a considerable novelty; and marks the turning point in the fortunes of the geometric garden.

The Brighton Pavilion was the right place at which to try out his new system. The gardens 'were deemed by everybody too small to admit of any improvements' using conventional landscape gardening techniques designed to give the impression of unconfined extent. The belt of shrubs along the wall and the serpentine drive looked ridiculous in this tiny, but royal, estate. New expedients were required. Repton argued that gardening in the Natural Style would be 'confounding the character of a garden with that of a park'. Instead,

every residence of elegance or affluence requires its garden scenery, the beauty and propriety of which belong to art rather than to nature.

Repton proposed that the entire western, and larger, part of the grounds should be surrounded by a glazed corridor designed for use in the winter. Extensive flower beds adjacent to the corridor would turn it into an open 'flower passage' in the summer, with something of the character of a much elongated verandah. It would have linked the pavilion to an orangery (which could be transformed into an open 'chiosk' in summer), to the stables, to a pheasantry, and to an aviary. The chief feature within the enclosure was to have been a square pool on the axis of the stables, with an 'orchestra' along one side. Trees and shrubs were either to be left in position or planted amongst this profusion of Indian architecture (for the most part imitated from Daniell's aquatints) in order to soften its striking forms.

Although the Prince was delighted by Repton's ideas, he did not have the means to carry them out. When the project was revived in 1815, it was John Nash, Repton's one-time partner, who finally undertook it. Repton had been exasperated by broken promises, and he took little trouble to conceal his frustration at Nash's carrying out Indian designs that clearly owed much to inspiration by himself and his two architect sons. Perhaps, though, he should also have been flattered. If he had looked around to see how other architects were tackling the problem of settings for an increasing variety of styles, he would have seen the same formula being employed time and time again: trees and shrubs being intermixed with, and softening, new architectural forms.

At the time when Daniell and Cockerell were designing the Indian Sezincote, a number of country houses were being designed in a variety of neo-classical styles. They took different forms: Sir Charles Monck's Belsay Hall was an austere Greek Doric cube, without ornament from decoration or vegetation, but Thomas Hope's Italianate Deepdene had quite the opposite feel by the time that alterations were completed in the 1820s[37]. Like Nash, Hope was alive to the picturesque possibilities of an asymmetrical ground plan and varying roofline, and like Repton, he brought vegetation into the house and architecture into the garden.

Thomas Hope, the highly cultured son of a banking family, set down his views on the picturesque in an essay, *On the Art of Gardening*, published in the same year as Repton's *Designs for the Pavillon*, and the two men's view were remarkably similar. Hope complained that 'from the threshold of the still ever symmetric mansion one is launched in the most abrupt manner into a scene wholly composed of the most unsymmetric and desultory forms of mere Nature, totally out of character with those of the mansion'. His preferences were a fulfilment of Knight's prediction, in his *Analytical Inquiry* (1805), that 'another revolution in taste, which is probably at no great distance, will make them [i.e. the hanging terraces of the Italian gardens] new again'.

Hope admired the effects of

the suspended gardens within Genoa, and of splendid villas about Rome ... those striking oppositions of the rarest marbles to the richest verdure; those mixtures of statues, and vases, and balustrades, with cypresses, and pinasters, and bays; those distinct hills seen through the converging lines of lengthened colonades; those ranges of aloes and cactuses growing out of vases of granite and of porphyry scarce more symmetric by art than those plants are by Nature,

and he had a vision of recreating these effects in England:

... the cluster of highly adorned and sheltered apartments that form the mansion ... shoot out, as it were, into ... arcades, porticoes, terraces, parterres, treillages, avenues, and other such still splendid embellishments of art, calculated by their architectural and measured forms, at once to offer a striking and varied contrast with, and a dignified and comfortable transition to, the more undulating and rural features of the more extended, more distant, and more exposed boundaries.

Hope bought The Deepdene, near Dorking, in 1807. In its grounds was 'The Hope', an amphitheatre-shaped valley, around which the 9th Duke of Norfolk had planted whilst keeping the seventeenth-century garden of his ancestor, Charles Howard, with its caverns and alcoves. Above The Hope is a high ridge from which excellent views can be had in each direction. This formed the backdrop to the very elaborate architectural embellishments by the house and along the drives. The fullest expression of Hope's ideas came only in 1823 when he built an Italianate extension of asymmetrical ground plan at 45 degrees to the main house. This contained conservatories, in which the profusion of plants was quite astonishing, and sculpture galleries. The boundary with the garden was blurred by large glass doors and terraces which held pottery and stone vases, some containing aloes and around which strutted peacocks and other exotic birds.

Hope's sense of design was similar to that displayed by John Papworth, who rather pretentiously took the middle name Buonarotti in 1815, when he was deeply immersed in painting. Papworth was, though, a talented and inventive architect specializing in garden features of all kinds. One of the first of such architectural commissions was the series of elaborate garden seats for Whiteknights erected in 1815. Gothic, cedar and triangular seats were scattered throughout the grounds. The largest, called merely 'The Seat', could take a large party and stood opposite the 'laburnum bower', a 1200-foot-long treillage tunnel[38].

The next year he designed gateways, the Gothic summer-house, an aviary and other buildings for the Princess Royal's garden at Claremont, and made improvements to the pleasure garden as well[39]. This prestigious commission brought Papworth another—the King of Wurtemburg's palace and park at Cannstatt, on which he worked intermittently from 1817 to 1820, and for which he produced 'a design for converting the site of Belle Vue into a Park, Plantations, and Gardens, and improving the adjacent country, in a plan disposing the order of Planting'. Papworth was not given the opportunity to design any large English park comparable in extent to Cannstatt, but he did lay out grounds for a large number of the villas that he designed from 1819 onwards.

He was at Alton Towers in 1821 and 1822 attending to the Earl of Shrewsbury, and designed numerous features there, many in collaboration with Robert Abraham, including the conservatory, a Grecian Temple, the iron Gothic Temple, and garden seat, iron gates, a park entrance, the foundations to

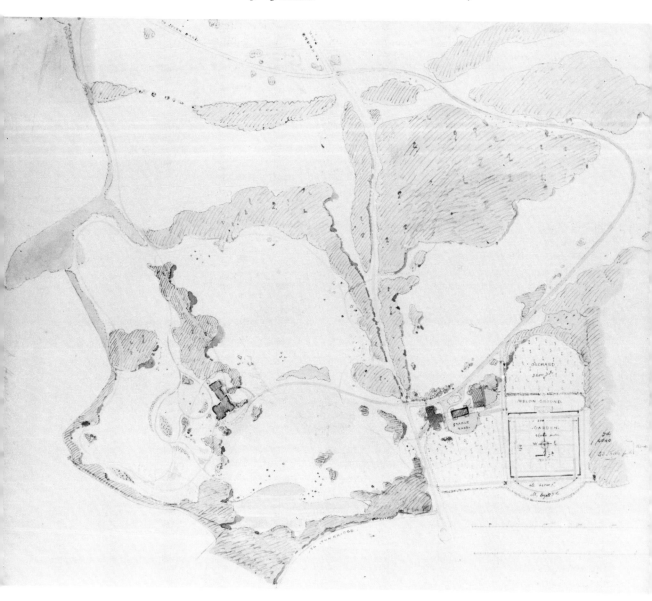

72   St Julian's, near Sevenoaks, design for the villa and grounds.

The design of about 1819 by J. B. Papworth was one of many villa designs that he made for places in the Home Counties.

Abraham's pagoda, and so forth. However nobody seems to have had an overall garden plan in mind, and Loudon, who visited in 1826 and 1831 remarked that 'though [the Earl] consulted almost every artist, ourselves among the number, he seems only to have done so for the purpose of avoiding whatever an artist might recommend'.

Papworth had been producing designs for Ackermann's *Repository of Arts* since 1813, and this led him to publish a collection entitled *Rural Residences . . . Interspersed With Some Observations on Landscape Gardening* (1818). He followed this up with *Hints of Ornamental Gardening* (1823).

Fashion [in gardens] is again adopting the aid of architecture and sculpture towards multiplying the means by which a judicious change and interest are created, in which she once abounded,

he wrote, and he himself was at its forefront. His designs for ice-houses, mausolea, tents, terraces and trellises in a variety of styles, sometimes Greek, sometimes Egyptian, sometimes Italianate, or even a mixture of these, capture the spirit of gay opportunism that pervaded Regency fashion.

The Display of Plants

Amongst his remarks on London Squares to the *Literary Journal* in December 1803, Loudon noted that,

The study of Botany is certainly the most delightful of studies:—it is peculiarly calculated for ladies, and is happily become very fashionable.

This remark that botany was a fashion is supported by the greatly expanded information for botanizers to be found in the printed travel guides of the early nineteenth century, and the vast improvement in horticultural illustration available to even the least energetic botanist. The first volume of William Curtis' *Botanical Magazine* was completed in 1787. This was composed of monthly issues of three hand-coloured engravings. The period after the Napoleonic War seemed propitious for others to start publishing, the best being the *Botanical Register* during the period 1815–1819, during which the artist Sydenham Edwards supplied over 300 superbly drawn colour plates.

Others besides Loudon observed that it was the ladies who developed a particular propensity for botany and horticulture. Prince Pückler-Muskau reflected in 1828 on their role in the revival of flower gardening:

it reflects honour on English women of rank, that most of them are distinguished for their taste and skill in this beautiful art. We should fall into a great mistake if we had hoped that any English gardener whatever were capable of producing such master-pieces of garden decoration ... These all owe their existence to the genius and charming taste for the embellishment of *home* which characterize their fair owners[40].

The purely scientific interest in plants was still chiefly restricted to their collection and classification, a field which Sir Joseph Banks had been leading. However the possibilities of increasing the interest and variety of already known species, through hybridization and selective breeding, were also being explored by amateurs and nurserymen alike. Probably the first experiments in hybridization had been undertaken by Thomas Fairchild, a nurseryman of Hoxton, Middlesex. About 1715 he crossed a carnation with the Sweet William. At various dates in the eighteenth century attempts were made to create new and more useful plants, and towards its end Thomas Andrew Knight, younger brother of Richard Payne Knight, was obtaining results from his experiments on fruit trees, which included hybridization[41].

Other hybridizations were for the improvement of the flower garden. In about 1802 John Champneys of Charleston, Virginia, crossed the musk rose with the China rose, which had been brought out of China only about a dozen years before. There was a very keen interest in roses in France at this date, and the new rose was sent there by an American nurseryman of French extraction, Philippe Noisette[42]. A host of hybridizations with the China rose followed in both France and England over the next few decades. Other breeders were meanwhile experimenting with the *Pelargonium* and the *Hippeastrum*. A watchmaker called Johnson was able to report that his hybrid *Hippeastrum* flowered in 1810. In about 1813 a nurseryman called Thompson created the pansy by crossing three *Viola* species, and towards the end of the same decade the hybrid rhododendrons commenced with *R. azaleoides*[43].

Some of the more prominent breeders and collectors banded together to form the Horticultural Society. The idea came from John Wedgwood, son of the famous potter, and who counted gardening as one of his many interests. He wrote to William Forsyth in 1801 suggesting that Forsyth should inform Sir Joseph Banks of the idea, but it was only in 1804 that the proposal was aired at a meeting of these three and four others at Hatchards, the bookshop in Piccadilly. Banks brought along William Townsend Aiton. Another gentleman gardener, the Rt Hon. Charles Greville, and two botanists also attended. Before long George Legge, the third Earl of Dartmouth of Sandwell Hall, Staffordshire, was attracted to the society as its first president, and so was Thomas Andrew Knight, who was its second president from 1810 for 27 years.

It is curious that the two Knight brothers should both have been so prominent in gardening, but with entirely different concerns. Thomas Andrew became the outstanding figure in the society, not only because of his unrivalled knowledge of physiology, but because he was a frequent and excellent contributor to the society's *Transactions*, begun in 1807. During his presidency an experimental garden was begun in 1818 on one-and-a-half acres of ground at Kensington, largely through the efforts of the secretary, Joseph Sabine. Four years later the plants were moved to a 33-acre site at Chiswick, leased to the society in perpetuity by William George Spencer Cavendish, sixth Duke of Devonshire. The gardens there rapidly usurped the predominant position in plant-collecting circles that Kew held till the death of Banks in 1820. In order to fill this garden with the plants of the world, Joseph Sabine organized expeditions to Bengal, China, Africa, the United States and so forth. Subscribers to the garden were able to share in its benefits. This proved to be an irresistible attraction to the country's horticulturalists. Membership of the society shot up from a few hundred to nearly a thousand in 1820, 1520 in 1822 and 2197 in 1824[44].

If critics found fault in Knight's running of the Horticultural Society, as Loudon did, they cited his unbending insistence that it was for the improvement of the useful and scientific parts of gardening only, with the consequent omission from the *Transactions* of any writings relating to landscape gardening, and in their excessively lavish production, which made them too expensive for ordinary gardeners. However most members' admiration for Knight continued undiminished. When George Johnson wrote his *History of English Gardening* (1829), he dedicated it to Knight and gave him adulatory notices, whilst making a point of Loudon's pretension in writing an encyclopaedia on gardening.

Many of the plants brought to Britain were tender and so could only be kept under glass. Glass was also useful for the propagation of hardy plants, particularly now that the fashion for flower gardens required great numbers. The pace of technical advances in glass-house construction quickened to meet the demands of collectors and gardeners. Knight pointed out to the Horticultural Society in 1805 that improvements in forcing houses were needed. A number of horticulturalists, including Loudon, responded with observations and ideas[45] However the greatest breakthroughs were to occur in the late 1810s; these were hot-water heating and the invention of the curvilinear glazing bar.

Hot-houses had been heated with steam experimentally since 1788, but the method had not proved to be markedly superior to the much older systems which used warmth from composting or from fires and smoke flues. Domestic hot-water heating had been invented in France before the Revolution, and sanction for its use in hot-houses from Knight in 1817 came at the moment when the emigré Marquis de Chabannes was writing pamphlets and offering his services to do just this[46]. The earliest system to be installed by Chabannes was at Sundridge Park, Kent, in 1816. A number of other gentlemen developed similar systems independently, and by the early 1820s there were several successfully in operation.

The invention of the curvilinear wrought-iron glazing bar began a revolution in the design of hot-houses themselves. Up till about 1820 the more imaginative designs, like that erected at Chiswick in 1813 with a cupola[47], still had to rest against a back wall for strength, and the wooden glazing bars were best kept short and straight. Loudon was intrigued by a paper read to the Horticultural Society in 1815[48] which proposed that the most efficient form of a hot-house is a hemisphere. This shape always presents a large surface of glass through which the sun's rays pass nearly at right-angles. The problem with such a shape, of course, was that glass and glazing bars were manufactured flat and straight. This challenged Loudon to design a wrought iron glazing bar that could be bent. He began experiments at his home in Bayswater with different forms of hot-houses, described in his *Remarks on the Construction of Hot-Houses* (1817) and *A Comparative View of the Common and Curvilinear Modes of Roofing Hot-Houses* (1818).

Much to his loss and their gain, Loudon disposed of the rights to his flexible glazing bar to W. and D. Bailey, who were already hot-house specialists[49]. By the time that he finished the *Encyclopaedia* in 1822, Loudon could include illustrations of his designs that Bailey's had sold. Most were still being built onto garden walls, and the favourite shape was the semi-ellipse. The first full dome may have been the small conservatory that Loudon placed in the centre of the façade of the 'double-detached villa' that he built for himself in Porchester Terrace, Bayswater, in 1823–24. Within a few years a new generation of graceful iron-framed conservatories stood free of supporting walls and as garden buildings in their own right.

73 A glasshouse made with curvilinear glazing bars.

J. C. Loudon invented a system of flexible iron glazing bars in the late 1810s. Here a simple early design for Lord St Vincent is illustrated in *The Green-House Companion* (1824).

The horticultural craze had a profound effect on pleasure grounds. For over half-a-century the flower garden had been banished to some secluded spot within the pleasure grounds in accordance with the precepts of the Natural Style. Even Marshall Conway's elaborate flower garden at Park Place was invisible from the house: so were Mason's English flower garden at Nuneham Courtenay, and Repton's formal flower garden at Valleyfield. When Repton advocated an extensive flower garden for the Brighton Pavilion in 1806 he asserted that of all the places he had seen he could name only five where the principal view was over flower gardens.

However changes were coming about even as Repton wrote this. Formal gardens were once again being planned adjacent to the more private rooms of mansions. In 1805 he himself had produced a scheme for the White Lodge in Richmond Park 'in the ancient formal style', which was later 'executed in every respect ... with the exception of the treillage ornaments'[50]. In the same year the Earl of Pembroke was agreeing to Wyatt's suggestion for Wilton that:

If that part which forms a Stage in front of the Library is to be devoted to a Flower Garden, a piece of good sculpture might be selected for the centre and a central walk start from the Library window[51].

'The Countess's garden, upon which the library opens, ... is laid out in the old French style', remarked Prince Pückler-Muskau in 1828, adding that 'the garden is extremely pretty and elegant'[52].

Although called 'French', gardens like Wilton were not *parterres* with box and coloured gravels: they were very much intended for the display of flowers, as were the 'mingled flower gardens'. The latter were often referred to as 'English gardens', in contradistinction to the formal styles. The art in them was to produce a gay effect from a variety of colours from at least February till October. This was achieved by the careful mingling of species so that as one set of species died away another began to bloom and so took its place. Such 'mingled flower gardens' were usually contrasted with the 'select flower gardens', which were the old-fashioned beds of single species for which the Dutch were renowned. These were largely discarded for the former, except by the florists for whom the select flower garden remained essential for the improvement of their hyacinths, tulips, pinks, auriculas and other florists' flowers.

Paradoxically the horticultural craze could be damaging to the effect of mingled flower gardens. To her sister enthusiasts, Mrs Maria Jackson of Somersall Hall, Derbyshire, wrote in her *Florist's Manual, or Hints for the Construction of a Gay Flower Garden* (1816) that:

The solicitude of those who wish to complete the superstructure must not be for rare species, but for new colour, so that the commonest primula which presents a fresh shade of red, blue, yellow, etc., ought to be esteemed more valuable than the most rare American plant which does not bring a similar advantage.

Loudon agreed, asserting in his *Encyclopaedia of Gardening* (1822) that:

It has frequently been observed that flower gardens have been on the decline for the last half century; and the cause of this appears to have been the influx of new plants during that period, by which gardeners have been induced, without due consideration, to be more solicitous about rarity and variety than well-disposed colours and quantity,

by which he seems to be saying that in his view nothing had yet surpassed the gaiety of Nuneham Courtenay flower garden.

There were other experimental forms of planting, the most notable of which was the 'massed flower garden' at Dropmore. Lady Grenville's gardens and conservatories there were already noted for a 'choice collection of exotics' in

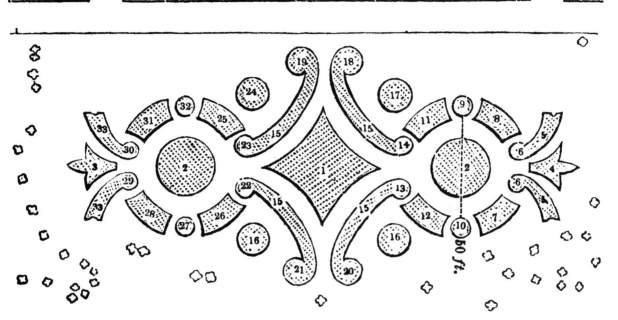

74 Dropmore, plan of the flower garden.

74 Dropmore, plan of the flower garden.

Lady Grenville's 'massed flower garden' was a complicated geometrical shape with each bed containing plants of a single colour only. The intensity of colour and the extended period of display were admired by J. C. Loudon when he visited in 1827.

1813[53], and by the time that Loudon visited her in 1827[54] the flower garden outside the library was famous. It consisted of a relatively complicated geometric *parterre*, in which separate beds contained only one colour each. This was achieved by massed planting with a succession of species, so that when one died down, it was replaced by the next which was of the same colour. This massed planting gave more intense colour, and the whole effect, with the beds being of different colours, was that of a brilliant pattern. It was not easy to maintain this effect, as there had to be extensive plungeing and removal of pot-grown plants which made this form of planting the most labour intensive.

Many Regency flower gardens continued the tried expedient of beds cut into the turf of the pleasure ground. Low wickerwork fencing often surrounded simple beds and kept their edges neat. This looked highly artificial, or 'polished', but such 'baskets' complemented the moveable tubs and pots and the trellis-work of the more architectural gardens; and they were particularly effective with the taller and more luxuriant species and with rambling roses. In time, more permanent materials came to be used and James Mean reported in the 1817 edition of *The Practical Gardener* that:

where round or oval parterres stand on a ground of lawn, it is a prevailing fashion to surround them with what are termed baskets. These are commonly made either of wood or cast-iron.

Those shown by Papworth in his books appear to have been wooden.

Lady Holland's garden at Holland House was an early example of an 'Italian' garden. It was also particularly noted for its dahlias. Some seeds of this Mexican plant had been sent to the Royal Gardens in Madrid in 1789. John Stuart, Viscount Mount Stuart, then ambassador to Spain, obtained some, but his stock failed after two or three years; the same happened to a nurseryman in 1802, and to Lady Holland herself in 1804. However in 1815 she was successful with seeds from France, and these showed signs of doubling. These became the progenitors of the huge variety of dahlias that soon appeared. The

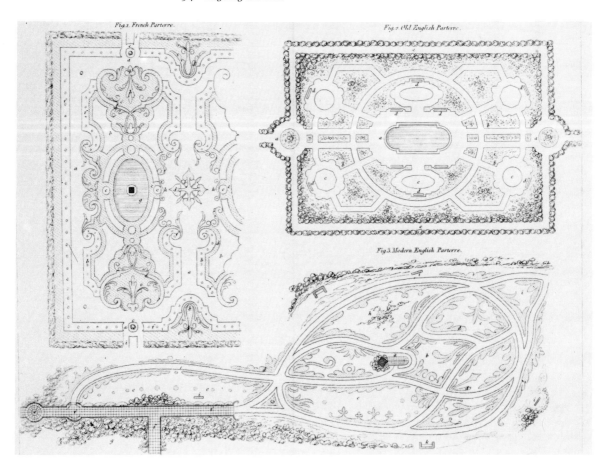

Fig.1 French Parterre.

Fig.2 Old English Parterre.

Fig.3 Modern English Parterre.

75   Loudon's designs for parterres.

A plate from J. C. Loudon's *Hints . . . on Pleasure Grounds* (1812). Publishing such designs would have been unthinkable only a decade previously.

Holland House gardens were famous for them for another 50 years at least[55]. The gardens were described in 1820 thus:

The gardens adjoining the house are laid out in various pleasing designs, among which a rosary of a circular form is particularly worthy of notice, and on the west, a parterre, laid out in various scrolls and devices in the Italian Style[56].

Where the garden was small or adjacent to the house, it was desirable to form the borders into some geometric pattern such as scrollwork, volutes or fans. From the start, the French-inspired patterns predominated, showing that, in spite of the wars, the English continued to be interested in French taste and vice-versa. Hence we find the Marquis of Blandford naming one of his woodland gardens at Whiteknights 'the Chantilly garden'[57], whilst the Duc d'Orléans imported turf from Epsom Downs for his gardens at Chantilly[58]. 'Italian' gardens were not so very different from the 'French', but they might have had gravel paths, statuary and terracing. There was even sometimes a 'Dutch' garden consisting of straightforward rectangular beds.

The Holland House rosary reminds us of the strong interest in roses at that date in Europe, especially in France. The Empress Josephine had a superb collection at the Chateau de la Malmaison, near Paris[59], and even the war did not prevent her from introducing 'Hume's Blush' tea-scented China roses (*Rosa indica fragrans*) from China in 1809. Men like Sir Abraham Hume of Wormleybury, Hertfordshire, after whom this rose was named, and Gilbert

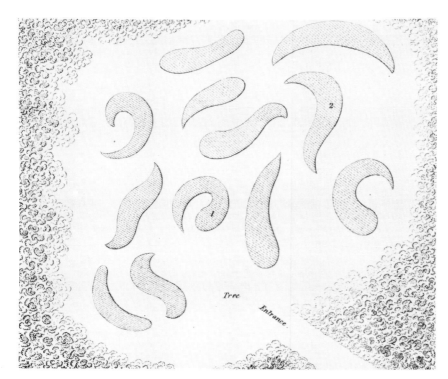

This somewhat
unimaginative illustration
of beds in turf was published
in Maria Jackson's *Florist's
Manual* (1822). No wonder
that J. C. Loudon looked
back to the Nuneham
Courtenay flower garden.

Slater of Low Layton, Essex, who was instrumental in introducing other China roses in the early 1790s, led the fashion in England.

The first English book to include designs for these geometric gardens was Loudon's *Hints on the Formation of Gardens and Pleasure Grounds* (1812), produced after he quitted farming and before his Continent travels. He had clearly caught up with the prevailing taste extraordinarily rapidly, and even, perhaps, surpassed it in his elaborate designs for English, French and Dutch *parterres*. The next book on flower gardening was *The Florist's Manual* (1816) by Maria Jackson. In the second edition of 1822, she gave some somewhat unimaginative designs for both beds-in-turf and geometric flower gardens.

New ways to display shrubs were also being found. The term 'American' no longer always implied savage or wild; in the nineteenth century, following Dr Fothergill's example, an 'American garden' was a garden for shrubs from America, and more specifically those naturally growing in bog-earth. Uvedale Price was an early exponent of them. In discussing the picturesque qualities of rocky banks in his *Essay on Artificial Water* (1798), he suggests:

Many of the choice American plants of low growth, and which love shade, such as kalmeas and rhododendrons, by having the mould they most delight in placed on the north, on that sort of shelf which is often seen between a lower and an upper ledge of rocks, would be as likely to flourish as in a garden.

American gardens followed such advice in generally, though not always, attempting to be naturalistic in layout. However, they were first and foremost collections of American plants, and so also needed to be laid out to display the range of species:

the most suitable way is to follow the natural orders, or genera attending, at the same time, to keep the higher sorts farthest from the walk or side from which the group or border is to be chiefly viewed. This arrangement has an excellent effect in an American shrubbery, where the low species of heaths and other bog under-shrubs which are introduced, supply the place of herbaceous plants[60].

Planting designs could be obtained from the more enterprising nurserymen. Foremost amongst them were John Kennedy, partner of the firm of Lee and Kennedy of Hammersmith, and his son Lewis. The firm produced designs for rosaries in 1809, and John made a plan for a flower garden in front of a greenhouse at Stow Hall, Norfolk, in 1812. Father and son were at Malmaison in 1810–11, after which Lewis commenced a highly successful career as a designer of geometric gardens and park landscapes in the Whiteknights mould until he concentrated upon land stewardship in the 1820s.

Like Loudon, Lewis Kennedy prepared *Notitiae* for his clients[61]. He was an excellent watercolourist and his green vellum volumes compare well to Repton's red books. The volume for Oddington, Gloucestershire, dated 1813, proposed trellis works. Another, for Chiswick, is dated 1814, and gives a large and elaborate semicircular design for an Italian garden, 'in the style of Le Notre' in front of the new conservatory. Around 1820, at the height of his reputation, he made American gardens at Trent Park, Middlesex, and at Wanstead, Essex.

The collecting instinct was showing itself amongst tree enthusiasts. About the turn of the century a number of arboriculturalists became more interested in complete collections than in profit or picturesque effects from planting. Repton's term 'arboretum', used in 1804 in his red book for Woburn, was widely adopted. Loudon wrote in *A Treatise on Country Residences* (1806):

a small botanic garden or botanic parterre, may contain a large collection of all, or several, of the different families of vegetables, as an *arboretum, frutecetum, harbarium* . . .

Such arboreta were arranged according to the Linnaean or some other system on the mown lawns of pleasure grounds.

One of the earliest was that of George Annesley, Viscount Valentia, who succeeded in 1816 as the second Earl of Mountnorris. It was commenced soon after 1796 when Valentia lost his wife to another man. Evidently he had an enquiring mind; he was a member of the Royal and the Linnean Societies, and from 1802 till 1806 he travelled in the East Indies.

He built up a magnificent collection of American oaks, maples, caryas and conifers on the lawns to the north of Arley Castle, then in Staffordshire, over 20 years[62]. During roughly the same period the Marquis of Blandford was assembling a collection of native and exotic trees and shrubs at White-knights[63], and Repton's plan for Ashridge, illustrated in the *Fragments* (1816), included an 'arboretum for exotic trees'.

More specialized collections of conifers, which became known as 'pinetums', were a variation on the theme. Perhaps the most famous during the 1820s was that assembled at Dropmore from about 1800 by William Wyndham Grenville, Baron Grenville, which eventually covered fifty acres. Lysons, in *Magna Britannia* (1813), reported that:

The pleasure-grounds were formed out of a common, have been planted with a great variety of forest-trees; one division contains almost every species of the fir,

and in 1827, Loudon made a lengthy schedule[64]. In the north of England Sir Charles Monck had another very complete pinetum at Belsay in the 1820s[65].

The Cottage Garden

The English nobility's propensity towards retreat to hermitages or cottages was never more in contrast with real rural conditions than during Regency times. The plight of the rural poor had become desperate. Prices were high during the Napoleonic Wars, and afterwards an agricultural depression brought extensive unemployment and a lowering of wages. The traditional buffer against starvation, the villager's rights on common land, had been removed in most parishes by the Enclosure Acts. The cost of Poor Law relief rose to a peak in 1818 and remained high throughout the 1820s. If any of the poor were tempted to poach, they risked murderous battles with gamekeepers, and transportation if apprehended.

The idealized image of the cottage garden seemed immune from all this. Uvedale Price spoke for most men of taste in remarking that,

A cottage, with its garden pales, and perhaps some shrub, or evergreen, a bay or a lilac, appearing through, and fruit-trees hanging over them; with its arbour of sweet-briar and honeysuckle, supported with vine or ivy—is an object which is pleasing to all mankind[66].

This connection of flower gardening to cottages was real enough—indeed florists' flowers were largely the preserve of the industrial labouring classes—but it led improvers into self-delusion. Many who were genuinely concerned for the poor measured their success by the state of the cottage gardens. A well-kept garden was taken not only as a sign of frugality and industry, but of happiness and contentment as well.

This was one reason why the gardens and settings of lodges, estate cottages and almshouses built at this time were given unprecedented attention. Repton, for example, paid far more attention to this aspect of improvement than any previous layer-out of grounds. Of particular note was Blaise Hamlet, designed in 1810 by John Nash and George Stanley Repton[67]. John Scandrett Harford wanted to provide almshouses. Nash suggested that an irregular disposition of picturesquely designed cottages around a central green would be a welcome change from the usual arrangement of a terrace displaying the benefactor's coat of arms, and could help the old people overcome their distaste of receiving charity.

The ten rustic cottages were built in 1812. The green was simple: the only embellishment besides a few trees was a large sundial. Hedges between the cottages and the green and between each other, were kept well tended, as were the gardens. Ivy, woodbine, honeysuckle and jasmine were planted to envelop the cottages. Nobody who saw Blaise Hamlet could avoid the feeling that it answered a most romantic image, and before long it found its way onto the tourist itineraries[68].

Blaise Hamlet so exactly answered the images of rural bliss held by the well-to-do, that it was not long before certain of them took to building 'cottages' in the same style. Such *cottages ornées*, as they were called, were full residences rather than just retreats. For example Nash went on to convert and enlarge the thatched cottage in Windsor Great Park, once Thomas Sandby's, into the Prince Regent's Royal Lodge in 1813[69].

Generally the *cottage ornée* appealed to 'men of study, science or leisure', as Papworth described them. He produced a number of designs for his books. Thatching, rustic verandahs, and climbing plants are much in evidence, although some could more properly have been described as villas. One of the villas in Regent's Park, Albany Cottage, was built as a *cottage ornée* in the early 1820s to the designs of C. R. Cockerell[70]. This kept to the already established pattern of verandah overlooking the lawn, and a luxuriant and varied shrubbery enveloping house and lawn.

William Wordsworth also advocated the cottage garden, but for more philosophical reasons. He accepted the scientific knowledge of his day, which

77 Regent's Park, Albany Cottage.

This *cottage ornée* was built in the early 1820s with a verandah, and surrounded by profuse and odiferous vegetation. The print is from Thomas Shepherd's *London and its Environs* (1829).

78 Lowther, design for the park of 1807.

The detailed plan by John Webb showed the alterations he suggested, including 'rides and wild walks in the park and demesne' and various estate buildings.

apparently belittled mankind in the vast, ordered system of the universe. To Wordsworth it was obvious that it was not created merely as a setting for the exploits of Man. He therefore had set himself the task of shaping a poetic vision which held the majesty of the universe in almost religious awe, but which found dignity in Man's enjoyment of his temporary abode. The powerful impressions of Nature gained in his native Lake District reinforced a conviction that the human soul benefits from communion with Nature.

There was a lesson here for improvers:

Laying out grounds, as it is called, may be considered as a liberal art, in some sort like poetry and painting; and its object, like that of all the liberal arts, is, or ought to be, to move the affections under the control of good sense; that is, those of the best and wisest: but, speaking with more precision, it is to assist Nature in moving the affections, and, surely, as I have said, the affections of those who have the deepest perception of the beauty of Nature[71].

Little wonder, then, that he had once considered himself endowed with the qualifications of only three callings—those of the poet, art critic and landscape gardener[72].

Wordsworth's views on 'that practice, by a strange abuse of terms denominated "ornamental gardening"' were strongly held. Superficially his distaste of the display of pomp echoed Knight's during the memorable dispute with Repton over milestones. But his reason for advocating modesty was not

primarily a rejection of pride, but that nothing 'can be considered as making amends for violation done to the holiness of Nature'. He fervently hoped that the landscape gardening as then practised, with its high-handed subjugation of Nature, was on the decline.

His own maxim for improvement, conveyed to Sir George Beaumont in 1805, was

the distinction made by Coleridge which you mentioned, that your house will belong to the country, and not the country be an appendage to your house.

He particularly objected to the practice of painting houses bright white. He advocated local materials and craftsmanship so that a house might quite literally grow out of its surroundings. In the laying out of grounds he delighted in small pathways through woodland, giving the impression that Man is just an unobtrusive observer.

To his great satisfaction he found that Sir William Lowther, Viscount Lonsdale, the new owner of the greatest house in Westmorland and a good friend of Sir George Beaumont, preferred to introduce such features to calling in a landscape gardener like Repton. Wordsworth, in the same letter to Sir George Beaumont in 1805, reported that:

The present lord seems disposed to do something, but not much. He has a neighbour, a Quaker, an amiable, inoffensive man, and a little of a poet too, who has amused himself, upon his own small estate upon the Emont, in twining pathways along the banks of the river, making little cells and bowers with inscriptions of his own writing, all very pretty as not spreading far. This man is at present Arbiter Elegantiarum, or master of the grounds, at Lowther, and what he has done hitherto is very well, as it is little more than making accessible what could not before be got at.

The man was Thomas Wilkinson of Yarnwath[73]. Although only of the yeoman class, he had a surprising circle of friends and acquaintants, one of whom was Edmund Burke. His poetry, like his gardening, did not amount to very much, but, like Stephen Duck beforehand, he found himself the object of much attention, especially from ladies who found his Cumberland accent fascinating. Evidently Lord Lonsdale's acceptance of this form of gardening was not a passing fancy, for when John Webb came to draw up a plan for Lowther in 1807, the suggested improvements were merely a pleasure ground immediately south of the house, and 'Rides and Wild Walks in the Park and Demesne'[74].

Wordsworth had a few opportunities to express his own taste. Perhaps the first was the winter garden that he improved for Lady Beaumont during his stay on the Coleorton estate during the winter of 1806–7. There was a grove of hollies near the hall. Wordsworth much preferred to see such indigenous species in a garden than 'foreigners', and created a deliberately old-fashioned atmosphere with an arbour and indigenous evergreen trees and shrubs, ivy, an ancient cottage, and beehives. In the summer of 1807 he took a house called Allen Bank, overlooking Grasmere, in order to house his enlarging household. He much despised the taste of the Liverpool lawyer who had just built the house, but must have been appeased by being allowed to lay out the parkland below the house with forest trees[75].

Wordsworth's most famous garden was that at his home from 1813 till his death, Rydal Mount. In fact it became a place of pilgrimage, even for royalty, during Victorian times[76]. This would have seemed extraordinary to the eighteenth-century tourist. The garden was only four-and-a-half acres on the side of a mountain, consisting merely of a small ancient mount in front of the house with a view of Windermere, an irregular and sloping lawn and kitchen garden to the west, and three crudely constructed terraces above the lawn[77].

However, the garden did seem to capture the 'sentiment' of the Lake District. Everything was unassuming, and accidents of nature such as the poppies growing between paving slabs were treasured. The feature most worthy of notice, though, was the upper terrace. This consists of 14 steps which lead onto the upward sloping walk to a prospect seat. A door at the side led out onto a continuation of the sloping terrace. This walk wound up and round the hillside and gave delightful views to Rydal Water below and access onto Wordsworth's much loved fells above.

Landscape Gardening in the Metropolis

Private parks were still being designed in small numbers in Regency times. Sheringham was Repton's only design for a large park, as opposed to garden, after his carriage accident of 1811. A new house was required near to the Norfolk coastline. Repton placed it in a protected position behind a well-wooded hill, and made an extensive vista in the other direction over grazing land[78]. In contrast to some of his earlier layouts, Sheringham is notable for the grandeur of the landscape, with its contrasts of sea, wooded hill and grazing land, rather than for the grandeur of the house.

John Webb produced a scheme for Woolley Park, Yorkshire, in 1811, and in 1816 found himself modifying Repton's arrangement of meres at Tatton. He was still working in 1827, but most of his work after 1810 seems to have been on villas. Loudon also had a few parks to design after 1810 including those at Hope End, Herefordshire, where Edward Moulton-Barrett had converted the

79 Bullmarsh Court, design for the park.

The design is from J. C. Loudon's 'Report on Bullmarsh Court' of 1818. The forest-like planting typifies his style of 'picturesque improvement'.

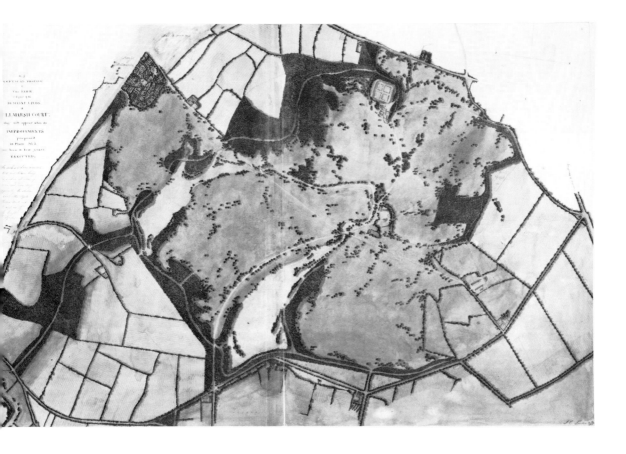

house to a 'Moorish' style in 1810–12[79]: Ditchley, Oxfordshire, in 1811: and Bullmarsh Court, Berkshire, where 'the effect intended to be produced on Bullmarsh Heath is that of a forest partially cleared' in 1818[80].

However, the chief interest of landscape gardening was that it was acquiring a new use—in urban parks. Between 1811 and his disgrace at the hands of the Select Committee on Buckingham Palace in 1831, Nash remoulded Marylebone Park as Regent's Park, relaid out St James's Park and transformed Buckingham House into Buckingham Palace with new gardens[81]. In addition, he remodelled the Royal Pavilion at Brighton and its grounds. Although he might not have been a very original landscape gardener, Nash proved throughout these improvements that he knew how and where to use landscape gardening. Nor was he without assistance in this quarter. Humphry Repton's youngest son, George Stanley, was Nash's chief assistant throughout the 1810s, and a former assistant, James Morgan, was his partner as architect to the Office of Woods and Forests. W. T. Aiton often helped with the planting.

Marylebone Park was originally a 554-acre park enclosed by Henry VIII. It was disparked in Cromwellian times and eventually it was just let by the Crown for grazing. Its possibilities for raising the revenue of the Crown Lands were recognized by John Fordyce, an elderly Scot occupying the office of Surveyor-General of Land Revenues. Looking forward to 1811 when the last lease would run out, Fordyce wrote to the Treasury in 1793 that 'a general plan should be formed for the Improvement of the whole of it'. He persuaded the Treasury to offer up to £1000 for any successful plans, but the response was disappointing. He died in 1809, but not before describing his vision of how Marylebone Park should be developed for high-quality housing. He foresaw that a new road would have to be cut through Marylebone and Soho to give access to Westminster (this idea became Regent Street), how a new water supply would have to be arranged, and how part of the development should be a new market area.

On Fordyce's death the Office of Woods and Forests merged with the Office of Land Revenues, and so Nash and Morgan found themselves architects to the Office of Woods, Forests and Land Revenues, and the architects from the office of Land Revenues became its 'surveyors'. Both partnerships were asked in 1810 to draw up plans for development of the park. Nash's scheme was to recreate a feeling of parkland with planting and ornamental water, and to place terraces and villas within it. He proposed that building plots should be planted and the trees only cut down when building was about to commence. A pair of panoramas were produced, possibly by George Stanley Repton, giving a somewhat rosy impression of views within the development. The overall impression was not dissimilar to that of Georgian Bath. Its rival consisted of straightforward gridiron streets and squares changing to villas further north.

The Prime Minister himself advised Nash not to worry so much about cramming as many houses onto the land as possible, but 'to form another [plan] with fewer buildings and a larger extent of Park'. His amended scheme kept a great double circus near the centre of the park, and the peripheral development, but a large amount of housing was omitted from the northern part. This allowed the parkland to unite with the countryside beyond at Primrose Hill, and the ornamental water to be more convincing as a river. Nash, always the opportunist, warmed to these alterations, and before long he was telling the Treasury that 'I have been able to form a Combination perfectly to my satisfaction'. It was to most other people's satisfaction as well, including the Prince Regent's. In October 1811 the Treasury gave the go-ahead, and a year later split the long promised £1000 award between Nash and Morgan.

Morgan was managing the planting, digging and road-making in the park in 1812. This included the dense planting around the sites of intended villas, which would not only screen the villas from each other but would 'present from without one entire Park compleat in unity of character and not an assemblage of Villas and Shrubberies like Hampstead ...'. 14,500 trees were planted on the building sites and in the parkland by competing nurserymen, and these plantations and the roads were finished by 1816. The bed of the ornamental water was still being dug at this date but was completed soon after.

The developers were slow to come; the first villa was built only in 1817, and the terraces awaited the opening of Regent Street. Eventually, in 1826, the Commissioners of Woods, Forests and Land Revenues called a halt to the building programme. Just eight villas had been built. Otherwise the interior of the park was entirely undeveloped. Any more development, the Commissioners felt

would so far destroy the Scenery, and shut out the many beautiful views towards the villages of Highgate and Hampstead, as to render it very advisable to reduce the number of Sites to be appropriated for Villas, and also to leave open the Northern Boundary of the Estate, formerly intended to be built upon.

Hence, then, extensive landscape gardening became open space within a city for the first time.

Nash's proposals for Marylebone Park aroused the Prince's admiration, and by 1812 he enjoyed the Prince's confidence. Over the next few years he undertook work for him at the Royal Lodge, Windsor, and at the Royal Pavilion, Brighton. His Indian designs for the latter were obviously inspired by Humphry Repton's ideas nine years before, but Nash's choice of gardening style was clearly not. He made no attempt to create appropriately Indian garden features, but formed a perfectly conventional pleasure ground the diminutive size of which, as Repton had explained, hardly provided an appropriate degree of grandeur or privacy for a Royal residence.

When the Regent became King George IV in 1820 he set his heart on a great metropolitan palace. After many delays it was agreed that Buckingham House should be extensively rebuilt. With the rebuilding from 1825 went a remodelling of the gardens. A lake was dug and the spoil went towards the making of a mound around the southern boundary. There were also some extensive shrubberies along the northern boundary. George IV had neglected Kew Gardens; but it is said that he asked William Townsend Aiton to lay out these gardens at Buckingham Palace[82].

Carlton House became redundant and was demolished when the palace became habitable. The proposal to rebuild with some magnificent terraces precipitated an order from the Treasury in 1827 to improve St James's Park. It still had its seventeenth-century straight canal, and was virtually unplanted except for its old avenues. Nash planned to restore the Mall as a salubrious promenade and to improve the appearance of the parkland. The canal was serpentinised with a large island at the eastern end, and clumps were planted at the water's edge and in the open parkland. The Mall and Birdcage Walk remained (and the Mall widened to bring its centreline onto the axis of the palace). Nash chose the trees and the planting was superintended by his gardener from his home at East Cowes, on the Isle of Wight.

Whether or not Nash had seen Lancelot Brown's scheme for improvement of St James's of over half a century before, the designs were noticeably similar. St James's Park was one of the last schemes of landscape gardening to be executed, almost an anachronism, for garden design was otherwise now firmly in the hands of the plant collectors and the geometric gardeners.

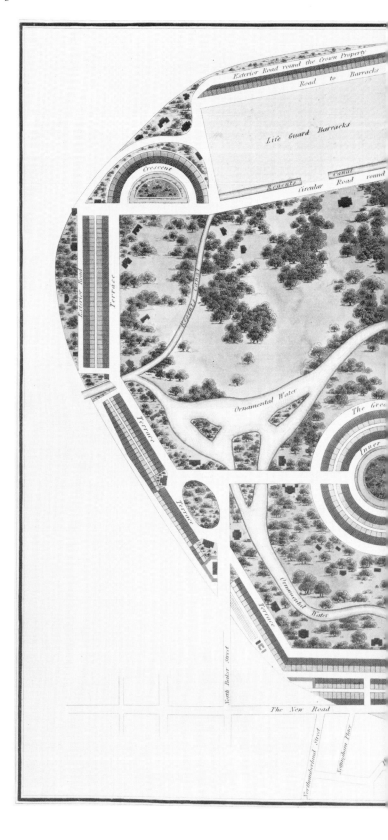

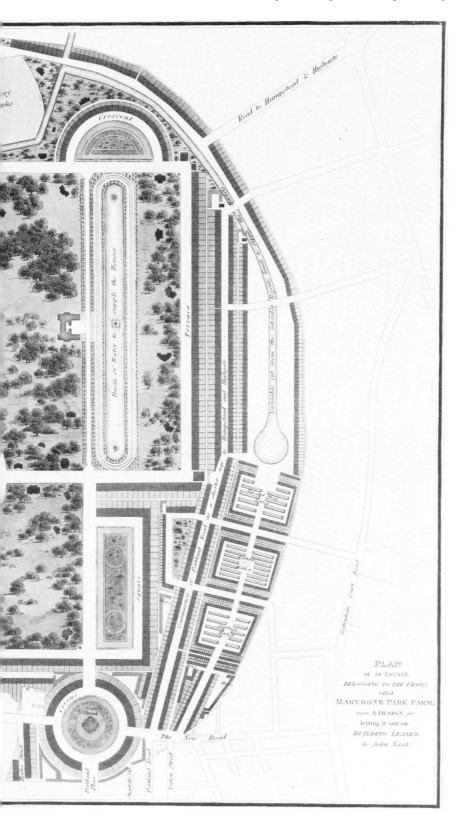

Notes

Where names introducing the notes are printed in small capitals, the reader should refer also to the Bibliography for further information.

Chapter 1

1 SPENCE 1966; all comments from Pope or Southcote reported by Spence that follow in this chapter are from Spence's *Anecdotes*.

2 HUSSEY 1967, pp. 114–31.

3 MACK 1969, pp. 37–40.

4 HILL A. 1753, letters dated 1 November 1733, 30 May 1734 and 8 June 1734.

5 Manning, Owen & Bray, William: *The History and Antiquities of the County of Surrey*, Vol. I, 1804, pp. 562–3; *Journal of Garden History*, Vol. I, No. 3, 1981, pp. 215–38, which notices other references.

6 'Il Penseroso' is the title of a melancholic poem by John Milton.

7 BROWNELL 1978, p. 210.

8 Brogden, William Alvis: 'Stephen Switzer: "La Grand Manier"' in WILLIS 1974.

9 The fullest study on Switzer to date is Brogden, William Alvis: 'Stephen Switzer and the Garden Design in Britain in the Early Eighteenth Century', Ph.D. thesis, Edinburgh, 1973.

10 This phrase is Switzer's own invention. Notwithstanding the confusion of genders, it shows his interest in French garden design at this period.

11 SWITZER 1718, pp. 45–6.

12 Bridgeman was already making alterations to Richmond in 1725 when he sent a detachment over to Pope's garden in Twickenham to form a theatre.

13 Scottish Record Office, GD 18/2110; Sir John Clerk of Penicuik, Midlothian, noticed in May 1733 that fields of corn were incorporated into the layout.

14 *Garden History*, Vol. IV, No. 3, 1976, pp. 50–64.

15 *Garden History*, Vol. IV, No. 1, 1976, pp. 30–53.

16 His reference to Richings and Dawley as 'now a doing' suggests a date in the late 1720s, but he refers to Robert Castell, who died in 1729, as 'lately deceased'.

17 In the 'Farther Account of Rural or Extensive Gardening' to be found at the end of *Ichnographia Rustica*, 2nd ed, 1742; for its date see note 16.

18 'A Dissertation on the Ancient and Modern Villas', in the June collection in Vol. 1.

19 *Garden History*, Vol. 9, No. 1, 1981, pp. 26–39.

20 KING 1974, pp. 27–60.

21 CLUTTON & MACKAY 1970, pp. 27–40.

22 Joseph Spence made a sketch plan of a section of Southcote's peripheral belt, and this is reproduced in SPENCE 1966, opposite p. 424.

23 *Garden History*, Vol. VII, No. 3, 1979, pp. 9–12.

24 MANWARING 1925, Chapter II.

25 BROWNELL 1978, pp. 10–17.

26 There is extensive mention in Pope's published correspondence about Sherborne in 1722 and Down Hall in 1725–26.

27 Pope to the Earl of Oxford, October 1724.

28　Pope to the Earl of Burlington, 4 April 1731: 'It has been above ten years on my
conscience to leave some testimony of my Esteem for your Lordship among my
writing'. Pope referred to this poem as his 'gardening poem', even though
garden design formed only a small part of the published whole.

29　HAZLEHURST 1980, p. viii.

30　WILLIS 1977, plate 80*a*.

31　HUSSEY 1927, pp. 56, 85–8.

32　WARTON 1756, 2nd ed, Vol. II, 1782, p. 185.

33　Prints by Highmore & Tinney of about 1745 show that Brown's predecessor,
George Lowe, was still clipping them, but prints of the 1780s show them as
having grown wild and huge.

34　WALPOLE 1785: 'Bridgeman . . . banished verdant sculpture . . . and though he still
adhered much to straight walks with high clipped hedges, they were only his
great lines'.

35　BROWNELL 1978, pp. 216–19.

36　BROWNELL 1978, p. 265.

37　*Correspondence of Frances, Countess of Hertford (Afterwards Duchess of Somerset) and
Henrietta Louisa, Countess of Pomfret, Between the Year 1738 and 1741*, 1805, p.
171.

38　Historic Manuscripts Commission Report No. 42, *Carlisle*, pp. 143–4.

39　BROWNELL 1978, p. 175.

40　Rocque, John: *Plan of the Cities of London and Westminster*, 1746.

41　Rocque, John: *An Exact Survey of the City's of London, Westminster . . . and the
Country Near Ten Miles Round*, 1746. Compare, for example, WILLIS 1977, plates
97*a* and 98.

42　Kent's sketch for the Chiswick cascade was copied onto Rocque's engraved plan of
1736, and was probably drawn about 1733, although not executed until 1738.

43　For Rokeby, see *Journal of the History of Architecture*, Vol. 10, 1980, pp. 38–50: for
Marble Hill, see WILLIS 1977, plate 71 (an engraving by Heckell and Mason
dated 1749).

44　The Serpentine was formed in 1730–31 by Charles Withers, Surveyor-General of
His Majesty's Woods (WILLIS 1977, p. 96): for Chiswick, see HARRIS 1979A,
plate 187*g*, which shows that the river was a serpentine even before Kent's
alterations of 1733–34.

45　HUSSEY 1967, p. 155.

46　HUSSEY 1967, p. 130.

47　TEMPLE W. 1692.

48　Ripa was in England in 1724, but whether Burlington acquired the set of prints at
that date is unknown.

49　For example at Hampton Court, Middlesex, and at Burghley House,
Northamptonshire.

50　Burlington had a number of Jones' masque designs in his collection.

51　Lang, Susan: 'The Genesis of the English Landscape Garden' in PEVSNER 1974,
p. 29.

52　MASON 1772, 2nd ed, 1783, note X on Book the First, pp. 210–11.

53　WALPOLE 1785: 'how common to see three or four beeches, then as many larches,
a third knot of cypresses, and a revolution of all three.'

54　CLARKE 1973.

55　WOODBRIDGE 1974, pp. 282–91.

56　Pembroke's irregular gardening at Westcombe House, Blackheath, predates
Kent's gardening—see HARRIS 1979A, plates 273*a–d*, although Switzer
dedicated a volume of SWITZER 1718 to Pembroke and so perhaps rural
gardening was being tried.

57　*Country Life*, 25 July & 1 August 1963, pp. 206–9, 264–7.

58　Batty Langley's 'new principles' were merely his own interpretation of the style
being advocated and developed from about 1716 by Burlington, Pope,
Bridgeman and Castel. To say 'nothing is more irregular in the whole, nothing
more regular in the parts' was the highest praise of this style: hence Pope's oft-
repeated theme of variety, and Langley's statement that 'Nor is there any thing

more SHOCKING than a STIFF REGULAR GARDEN'.

59 Numerous examples can be seen at suburban villas in Rocque, John: *An Exact Survey of the City's of London, Westminster . . . and the Country near Ten Miles Round*, 1746.

60 HAZLEHURST 1980; the Arc de Triomphe and the Trois Fontaines bosquets are described on pp. 111–16.

61 *Country Life*, 15 September 1977, pp. 670–1.

62 Brockwell, Maurice W. *Catalogue of the Pictures at Nostel Priory* (1915), p. 383 & plate XLV.

63 CLUTTON & MACKAY 1970.

64 *Country Life*, 15 March 1973, pp. 678–82.

65 WILLIS 1977, plate 24.

66 Castle Howard estate plan of 1727.

67 WALPOLE 1785, p. 55.

68 HUSSEY 1967, p. 157.

69 *Garden History*, Vol. IV, No. 2, 1978, pp. 22–5.

70 HUSSEY 1967, plates 227, 228.

Chapter 2

1 CONNER 1979, p. 49.

2 TEMPLE, W. 1692.

3 MASON G. 1768, p. 26: 'Little did SIR WILLIAM TEMPLE imagine, that in about half a century the CHINESE would become the fashionable taste of his country'.

4 CONNER 1979, p. 45.

5 HARRIS 1978.

6 COLVIN 1978, p. 549.

7 GODBER 1968, p. 137.

8 STITT 1970, p. 103.

9 KESWICK 1978, pp. 11, 203.

10 SPENCE 1751, printed in HUNT & WILLIS 1975, p. 269. The prints that Spence saw could either be those of the Yuan Ming Yuan, or else, as suggested by Patrick Conner in 'China and the Landscape Garden', *Art History*, Vol. 2, No. 4, December 1979, p. 434, they could be a set of Ripa's engravings of the Imperial Gardens at Jehol.

11 WALPOLE 1785, p. 47.

12 *The World*, No. 12, 22 March 1753.

13 MORRIS 1750, Preface.

14 *The World*, No. 117, 27 March 1755.

15 COLVIN 1978, p. 549.

16 Walpole to Richard Bentley, September 1753.

17 COLVIN 1978, p. 549.

18 Duncan Tovey (editor), *The Letters of Thomas Gray*, p. 247.

19 CLARK 1962, pp. 42–3.

20 EVANS 1956, pp. 155, 167–9.

21 WALPOLE 1784.

22 Walpole to the Earl of Strafford, 13 June 1781.

23 CONNER 1979, p. 68.

24 WALPOLE 1928, p. 36.

25 The series of guide book maps is reproduced in CLARKE 1973, pp. 558–65.

26 McCarthy, Michael. 'Eighteenth Century Amateur Architects and their Gardens' in PEVSNER 1974, pp. 33–5.

27 COLVIN 1978, p. 796.

28 HARRIS 1979A, p. 292; this shows a view of the north front of the Vyne from across the lake by Johann Henry Muntz, dated 1756.

29 Walpole mentioned Sir Henry Englefield's both in a letter to John Chute, 4 August 1753, and in WALPOLE 1785, p. 77.

30 CAMBRIDGE 1803, p. xi.

31 WOODBRIDGE 1971, p. 8.
32 GRAVES 1788, pp. 40, 48–50.
33 'Account of an Interview between Shenstone and Thomson', 1746, in *Edinburgh Magazine*, 1800.
34 KING 1978–80.
35 SPENCE 1966, note to anecdote 1069.
36 Introductory note to the Scolar press Facsimile of 1969.
37 SPENCE 1966, anecdote 1113.
38 CAMBRIDGE 1803, p. xxxvii.
39 Walpole to Sir Horace Mann, June 1753.
40 *The World*, No. 12, 22 March 1753.
41 *The World*, No. 6, 8 February 1753.
42 *The World*, No. 15, 12 April 1753.
43 *The World*, No. 26, 28 June 1753.
44 *The World*, No. 65, 28 March 1754.
45 *The World*, No. 15, 12 April 1753.
46 SPENCE 1966, anecdote 1078.
47 Pope, Alexander *Of Taste* (Epistle to Burlington), 1731, lines 62–4.
48 HERRING 1777, pp. 37–42.
49 Walpole to Richard West, 28 September 1739.
50 Walpole to Richard West, 28 September 1739.
51 Walpole to George Montagu, 19 May 1763.
52 Walpole to Richard Bentley, September 1753.
53 *Mrs Montagu, Queen of the Blues*, Vol. I, pp. 53–4.
54 The *Dialogue* was anonymous, but Gilpin's authorship is argued in Templeman, W. D. 'The Life and Works of William Gilpin' (1724–1804), Illinois Studies in Language and Literature, Vol. XXIV, Nos. 3–4, 1939, pp. 34–5.
55 Clarke, George. 'Heresy in Stowe's Elysium' in WILLIS 1974, p. 49.
56 Walpole to John Chute, 4 August 1753: the Temple of Modern Virtue was cleared away about 10 years later.
57 *Country Life*, 6 April 1972.
58 BROWN 1771.
59 GODBER 1968, pp. 132, 136.
60 WATERS 1975, p. 8.
61 CAMBRIDGE 1803, p. xi.
62 WATERS 1975, p. 13.
63 Hackfall was described many times, e.g. YOUNG 1770; GILPIN 1786; PENNANT 1804; and *The History of Ripon*, 1806.
64 Anon. *The Landscape*, 1748.
65 WOODBRIDGE 1971, pp. 11–12.
66 WALPOLE 1928, p. 43.
67 HODGES 1973, pp. 39–68.
68 In the absence of Hamilton's papers and correspondence this is inferred from the frequent statements by others that this was so, e.g. PRICE 1796; Mitford, John (editor) *Correspondence of H. Walpole and Rev. W. Mason*, 1851.
69 WALPOLE 1785, p. 75.
70 *The World*, No. 76, 13 June 1754.
71 *Country Life*, 19 November 1969.
72 *Garden History*, Vol. III, No. 3, 1975, pp. 50–7.
73 HARRIS 1979A, p. 320.
74 HADFIELD 1979, pp. 224–5.
75 CONNOR 1979, p. 189.
76 KING 1978–80, Vol. VII, No. 3, p. 29.
77 *Country Life*, 23 June 1960.
78 WOOD 1913, pp. 143–50.
79 *The Register of Premiums* 1778.
80 STROUD 1975, p. 42.
81 *Country Life*, 22 February 1979.
82 Petworth House Archives, receipted 14 August 1754.

83 STROUD 1975, p. 30.

84 Early references to Greening are by Richard Bradley in *New Improvements of Planting and Gardening*, 1731, p. 100, and by Daines Barrington in *Archaeologia*, 1769, p. 37, where he mentions that Greening measured a tree at Tortworth 'forty years ago'.

85 John Rocque's plan of Claremont dated 1738 is accompanied by an elevation of 'Mr Greening's house'.

86 *Landscape Design*, No. 133 February 1981, p. 28.

87 Robert Greening's drawings were on display at Wimpole in 1981.

88 PRO wills.

89 WRIGHT 1979.

90 KING 1978–80, Vol. VIII, No. 2.

91 COLVIN *et al.* 1980, pp. 27–8.

92 These are held in the Lancashire Record Office.

93 *Garden History*, Vol. I, No. 3, pp. 17–18.

Chapter 3

1 Blunt, Wilfred *In for a Penny: A Prospect of Kew Gardens*, 1978, p. 18.

2 Blunt, Wilfred *In for a Penny: A Prospect of Kew Gardens*, 1978, p. 19.

3 FIELD 1820, p. 47.

4 HENREY 1975, Vol. II, p. 90.

5 HARRIS 1970, p. 5.

6 BOSWELL 1791, under the year 1783.

7 BURKE 1756, Part IV, Section XXIII.

8 BOSWELL 1791, under the year 1769.

9 CONNOR 1979, p. 190.

10 Goldsmith, Oliver *Letters From a Citizen of the World to his Friends in the East*, 1762, letter 30.

11 HENREY 1975, Vol. II, p. 244.

12 HARRIS 1970, pp. 213–14.

13 'Plan of the Gardens of Kew, A.D. 1763': HARRIS 1970, plate 22.

14 WALPOLE 1928, p. 23.

15 HADFIELD 1979, p. 225.

16 HADFIELD 1979, p. 225.

17 *Ex inf.* John Harvey.

18 STROUD 1975, p. 122.

19 *Ex inf.* Hon. Mrs Jane Roberts, Royal Library, Windsor.

20 This and subsequent lists compiled from information in STROUD 1975.

21 LOUDON 1834, para. 1171.

22 TAIT 1980, pp. 70–85; Tait follows an error by Loudon in para. 362 of the 1828 edition of the *Encyclopaedia of Gardening* to the effect that 'Robertson, nephew of the King's gardener of that name', laid out Duddingston; this was corrected to 'Robinson' in para. 7618 of the same edition and para. 1220 of the 1834 edition. However, there WAS a Robertson—George, who made a plan for Bargany in 1774.

23 STROUD 1975, p. 125.

24 STROUD 1975, p. 206.

25 HARVEY 1974, p. 97.

26 Bedfordshire Record Office L30/9/17/139.

27 Their wills are in the PRO, Chancery Lane.

28 WRIGHT 1979, p. 14: biographical sketch by Eileen Harris.

29 HARVEY 1974, p. 97.

30 KING 1978–80, Vol. VIII, No. 3, 1980, p. 111.

31 Coates, Bryan E. 'The Work of Richard Woods, Landscape Gardener, in the West Riding of Yorkshire'. *Transactions of the Hunter Archaeological Society*, Vol. VIII, 1963, p. 298.

32 Firth, Ian J. W. 'Landscape Management: The Conservation of a Capability Brown Landscape—Harewood, Yorkshire' *Landscape Planning*, Vol. 7, 1980, p. 127.

33 *Country Life*, 5 January 1978, p. 20.

34 PRINCE 1967, p. 45.

35 STROUD 1975, p. 74.

36 WARNER 1801, p. 150.

37 Jackson-Stops, Gervase. *Claydon House, Buckinghamshire* (National Trust Guide Book), 1979, p. 26.

38 KING 1978–80, Vol. VIII, No. 3, 1980, p. 87.

39 LYSONS 1813, Vol. I, part III, p. 497.

40 *Country Life*, 14 September 1967, p. 596.

41 *Ex inf.* Keith Goodway.

42 Edwards, Ifor *Davies Brothers Gatesmiths*, 1977, p. 35.

43 Firth, Ian J. W. 'Landscape Management: The Conservation of a Capability Brown Landscape—Harewood, Yorkshire'. *Landscape Planning*, Vol. 7, 1980, p. 127.

44 Robinson, John Martin. 'A Catalogue of the Architectural Drawings at Carlton Towers, Yorkshire'. *Architectural History*, Vol. 22, 1979, p. 116.

45 LOUDON 1822, 1828 edition, para. 7640.

46 Society of Arts *Transactions*, Vol. II, 1784, p. 17.

47 Society of Arts *Transactions*, Vol. II, 1784, p. 11.

48 SPENCE 1966, anecdote 1120.

49 JOHNSON S. 1781, article on Shenstone.

50 Goldsmith, Oliver, *Essays*, 1765, essay XXI.

51 GILPIN 1786, Vol. I, p. 54.

52 SPENCE 1966, anecdote 1103.

53 LEES-MILNE 1976, p. 13.

54 WARNER 1801, p. 150.

55 Hodges, Alison. 'Painshill, Cobham, Surrey: The Grotto'. *Garden History*, Vol. III, No. 2, 1975, p. 23.

56 FAULKNER 1820, p. 121.

57 HODGES 1973, p. 61.

58 WATERS 1975, p. 16.

59 TEMPLE N. 1979, p. 43. Nigel Temple has given 1762 as the purchase date in private discussion.

60 McCarthy, Michael. 'Eighteenth Century Amateur Architects and their Gardens' in PEVSNER 1974, pp. 42–9.

61 Walpole, Horace *Memoirs of the Reign of George III*, Vol. III, 1845, p. 30.

62 Noble, Percy *Park Place, Berkshire*, 1905, p. 22 *et seq.*

63 EVELYN 1776, Vol. I, edition of 1801, pp. 95–6.

64 'Summary Abstracts of the Rewards bestowed by the Society from the Institution in 1754 to 1782 inclusive', in Society of Arts *Transactions*, Vol. I, 1783.

65 MAINWARING 1925, pp. 153–4.

66 BARR & INGAMELLS 1973, p. 54.

67 BATEY 1979, pp. 7, 25–8.

68 *Garden History*, Vol. V, No. 2, 1977, pp. 41–7.

69 *Country Life*, 22 June 1967, p. 1608.

70 Gray to Mr Palgrave, 6 September 1758.

71 Gray to Dr Thomas Warton, 18 October 1769; both above letters published in GRAY 1775.

72 *Garden History*, Vol. II, No. 2, 1974, p. 24.

73 HODGES 1973, pp. 48–56.

74 GILPIN 1782, p. 1.

75 GILPIN 1782, p. vi.

76 GILPIN 1786, Vol. I, p. 54.

77 HUSSEY 1967, p. 138.

78 HARRIS 1979B, pp. 39, 40, 41

79 BOSWELL 1791, under the year 1763.

80 *Victoria County History of Hertfordshire*, Vol. II, p. 271.

81 GILPIN 1786, p. xiv.

82 HENREY 1975, Vol. II, p. 524.

83 Batey, Mavis. 'Oliver Goldsmith: An indictment of landscape gardening', in WILLIS 1974, p. 58.

84 Harris, Eileen. 'Designs of Chinese Buildings and the Dissertation on Oriental Gardening', in HARRIS 1970, pp. 158–61.
85 Walpole to William Mason, 25 May 1772.
86 BOSWELL 1791, under the year 1781.
87 Harris, Eileen. 'Designs of Chinese Buildings and the Dissertation on Oriental Gardening', in HARRIS 1970, p. 161.

Chapter 4

1 Money for the pillar and its repair was raised by subscription. A plaque on it records that it was repaired in 1847 and 1896.
2 WOOD 1913, p. 332.
3 JOHNSON S. 1781, under MULL.
4 *Country Life*, 11 August 1977, p. 339.
5 Society of Arts *Transactions*, Vol. XXI, 1803, pp. 81–96.
6 Society of Arts *Transactions*, Vol. II, 1784, pp. 11–12.
7 *Country Life*, 6 April 1972, pp. 850–3.
8 These yards were mentioned by Lapidge in his will in the PRO (Prob 11, 1446, Fol. 582). They were later held by his son Edward, and are recognizably the same as those held by the Royal Gardeners from George London to Lancelot Brown.
9 *Gardener's Magazine*, Vol. IV, 1828, pp. 119. Lapidge's contract for Chiswick is in the Devonshire archives at Chatsworth.
10 *Country Life*, 26 May 1960.
11 STROUD 1975, p. 207.
12 Marshall, William. *The Rural Economy of the Midland Counties*, 1790, Vol. I, Preface; Vol. II, Advertisement.
13 TAIT 1980, p. 147, shows that White started working in Scotland in earnest from the early 1780s, whilst David Neave considers that almost all White's work was in Scotland from 1785.
14 Biographical information on Richmond is sadly lacking. Even his Christian name is unknown at present. However he was working at Lee Priory in 1780, and Repton mentioned 'the loss of Richmond' in a letter to the Rev. Norton Nicholls in 1788.
15 STROUD 1975, p. 207.
16 Essex Record Office, D/DE1 P27.
17 PRINCE 1967, p. 45.
18 STROUD 1975, p. 207.
19 *Ex inf*. Keith Goodway.
20 *Country Life*, 18 September 1975, p. 697.
21 STROUD 1975, pp. 92, 207.
22 *Landscape Design*, No. 129, February 1980, p. 27.
23 *Country Life*, 10 July 1958, p. 21.
24 LOUDON 1822, para. 2158.
25 *Country Life*, 11 March 1971, p. 558.
26 'Hird's Annals of Bedale' in *North Yorkshire County Record Office Publications*, No. 2, 1975.
27 *Ex inf*. John Harris.
28 Leeds City Council, Archives Department, HW 29.
29 National Library of Wales, Department of Prints, Drawings and Maps, Tredegar 577.
30 TAIT 1980, p. 85.
31 TAIT 1980, p. 150.
32 *Garden History Society Newsletter*, No. 17, May 1972, p. 13.
33 White's plan hangs in the hall at Belle Isle.
34 Blaikie, Thomas. *Diary of a Scotch Gardener*, 1931, p. 154.
35 *Gardener's Magazine*, Vol. II, 1827, p. 385; LOUDON 1834, paras. 255, 258 & 277.
36 This is stated in Gould's will, proved 1 February 1812, and now in the Lancashire Record Office.
37 *Country Life*, 29 December 1980, pp. 1598–1601.

38   STROUD 1975, p. 207.
39   *Ex inf.* Hon. Mrs Jane Roberts.
40   WARNER 1801, p. 210.
41   Britton, John. *Beauties of Wiltshire*, Vol. II, 1801, p. 221. 'N. Poussin' must surely be an error for Gaspar Poussin.
42   BRITTON 1801–8, Vol. I, p. 187, shows that the garden existed in 1801, and it was probably made in the time of Marshall Conway who died in 1795.
43   Noble, Percy. *Park Place, Berkshire*, 1905, pp. 61, 160 & 163.
44   *Country Life*, 29 December 1960, pp. 1598–1601.
45   *Country Life*, 21 February 1980, pp. 498–501.
46   Macaulay, Thomas Babington, Lord, *Critical and Historical Essays*, 1843, essay on Warren Hastings.
47   BATEY 1979.
48   SCOTT 1782, The Garden.
49   REYNOLDS 1797, Discourse XIII, 1786.
50   BOSWELL 1791, for 19 September 1777.
51   Johnson to Mrs Thrale, 13 November 1783.
52   REYNOLDS 1797, Discourse VIII 1778.
53   MASON W. 1772, edition of 1783, commentary by William Burgh on p. 138.
54   MASON W. 1772, edition of 1783, commentary by William Burgh on p. 146.
55   BARRINGTON 1785, p. 130.
56   REYNOLDS 1797, Discourse XIV, 1788.
57   REYNOLDS 1797, Discourse XIII, 1786.
58   CRADOCK 1826, edition of 1828, pp. xii, xviii.
59   LYTTELTON 1780, Letter the Twentieth.
60   *Westminster Magazine*, No. XCI, May 1780, p. 249.
61   FALCONER 1785, pp. 297–325.
62   WEST 1778, p. l.
63   WYNDHAM 1775, p. i.
64   CRADOCK 1777, p. 55.
65   GILPIN 1786, pp. i, vi.
66   Smith, Stuart. *A View From the Iron Bridge*, 1979, p. 5.

Chapter 5

1   PRICE 1795; there is a survey drawing by Emes, and in 1778 he was preparing a new kitchen garden; Merlin Waterson considers that the family tradition that Brown proposed to sweep away the terraces is likely to refer to proposals by Emes.
2   Clark, Michael & Penny, Nicholas. *The Arrogant Connoisseur: Richard Payne Knight 1751–1824*, 1982, pp. 32–49.
3   CARTER *et al.* 1982, pp. 5–14.
4   KNIGHT 1974, second edition, 1795, postscript.
5   CARTER *et al.* 1982, pp. 110–12.
6   REPTON 1795, Introduction.
7   MALINS 1978, Antony Red Book, 1792, under 'Ornamental Gardening'.
8   REPTON 1795, Chapter I.
9   REPTON 1795, Chapter I.
10   REPTON 1795, Chapter VI.
11   CARTER *et al.* 1982, Colour Plate 3.
12   REPTON 1795, Appendix.
13   *Gardener's Magazine*, Vol. IV, 1828, p. 119.
14   LOUDON 1822, paras. 7567, 2158.
15   STROUD 1975, p. 206.
16   *Country Life*, 15 July 1965, p. 159.
17   HARVEY 1974, p. 88.
18   *Proceedings of the Linnaean Society of London*, Vol. II, 1855, pp. 82–3, is Aiton's obituary and contains a list of the gardens he designed.
19   Lysons, David. *Environs of London*, 2nd edition, 1810.

20 *Ex inf.* Justin Meath-Baker, Landscape Architect.
21 LOUDON 1822, para. 2197.
22 BM Add MS. 36,278 G.
23 *Ex inf.* Keith Goodway, Lecturer, University of Keele.
24 *Ex inf.* Frederick Stitt, Stafford County Archivist.
25 *Essays in Staffordshire History*, Fourth series, Vol. VI, 1970, pp. 100–10.
26 *Landscape Design*, No. 129, February 1780, p. 27.
27 COLVIN 1978, p. 874.
28 *Ex inf.* Peter Goodchild, Institute of Advanced Architectural Studies, York.
29 Coxe, William. *A Historical Tour Through Monmouthshire*, 1801, p. 312.
30 *Country Life*, 21 April 1966, pp. 944–8.
31 Institute of British Geographers *Transactions*, New Series, Vol. 2, No. 2, 1977, pp. 319–21.
32 Marshall, William. *Planting and Rural Ornament*, 1803, p. 377.
33 CARTER *et al.* 1982, p. 114.
34 Society of Arts *Transactions*, vol. XVII, 1799, pp. 119–39.
35 *Country Life*, 30 September 1965, p. 819.
36 PRICE 1796–8, Essay on Decorations.
37 PRICE 1795.
38 REPTON 1794.
39 KNIGHT 1794.
40 KNIGHT 1794, Advertisement to the Second Edition, 1795.
41 CARTER *et al.* 1982, p. 153.
42 REPTON 1794.
43 CARTER *et al.* 1982, p. 39.
44 REPTON 1795, Appendix.
45 REPTON 1803, Chapter X.
46 PRICE 1795.
47 REPTON 1795, Chapter VII.
48 REPTON 1795, Chapter VII.
49 REPTON 1795, Chapter VII.
50 MALINS 1978, Red Book for Attingham, 1798, under 'Of Landscape-painting'.
51 *Garden History*, Vol. I, No. 2, February 1973, p. 23.
52 CRADOCK 1826, 2nd edition, 1828, p. xviii.
53 The first appendix dated 1798 answered the second edition of Price's *Essay*, whilst the undated second appendix was addressed to Price's three essays published in 1798. These appendices were bound into later copies of Mason's book.
54 *The Garden History Society: Newsletter* 5, Summer 1982, p. 4.
55 *Ex inf.* Christopher Jarvis, gardener at Warwick Castle.
56 COLVIN 1978, p. 554.
57 Allentuck, Marcia. 'Sir Uvedale Price and the Picturesque Garden: the Evidence of the Coleorton papers' in PEVSNER 1974.
58 BRITTON 1801–8, Vol. I, 1801, p. 268.
59 LEES MILNE 1976, pp. 36, 43, 56–9.
60 RUTTER 1822.
61 Society of Arts *Transactions*, Vol. XIX, 1801, preface, p. x.
62 Cumberland, George. *An Attempt to Describe Hafod*, 1796, p. 14.
63 Smith, James Edward. *A Tour to Hafod, in Cardiganshire*, 1810, p. 14.
64 Smith, James Edward. *A Tour to Hafod, in Cardiganshire*, 1810, p. 13.
65 TEMPLE, N. 1979, Chapter 5.
66 SUMMERSON 1980, pp. 20–2.
67 SUMMERSON 1980, pp. 33–7.
68 MALINS 1976, Red Book for Attingham, 1798, under 'The Park'.
69 REPTON 1803, Chapter III.
70 REPTON 1803, Chapter XIV.
71 REPTON 1803, Chapter VIII.
72 CARTER *et al.* 1982, p. 154.
73 REPTON 1803, Chapter XI.
74 REPTON 1803, Chapter X.

75 CARTER *et al.* 1982, p. 147.
76 Joyce, Henry *Woburn Abbey Guide Book*, 1974, p. 45.
77 REPTON 1816, fragment V.
78 Sanecki, Kay N. *Humphry Repton*, 1974, pp. 28, 33.
79 TAIT 1980, pp. 193–8.
80 LOUDON 1806, pp. 420, 565, 722 for Kingswood Lodge, p. 392 for Harewood,
      p. 644 for Farnley, p. 388 for Llanarth and pp. 248, 304 for Hopton Court.
81 LOUDON 1806, Vol. II, p. 715–16.
82 REPTON 1803, Chapter III.
83 LOUDON 1806, Vol. II, p. 399.
84 LOUDON 1806, Vol. II, pp. 437–9.
85 LOUDON 1806, Vol. II, pp. 703–8.

Chapter 6

1   REPTON 1816, fragment XXVII.
2   COBBETT 1830, for 1 August 1823.
3   Analysis of dates of most of his commissions can be made from the gazetteer in
      CARTER *et al.* 1982: though a number can be dated only by their first mention in
      Repton's publications.
4   REPTON 1816, preface.
5   Lewis, Lesley (editor). 'Hird's Annals of Bedale'. *North Yorkshire County Record
      Office Publication No. 2*, 1975, line 446.
6   See his lists of works in COLVIN 1978, p. 874.
7   Much of this account relies upon Jane Loudon's 'A Short Account of the Life and
      Writings of John Claudius Loudon' originally printed in *Self Instruction for Young
      Gardeners, &c . . .*, 1845, but reprinted a number of times recently.
8   LOUDON 1808.
9   REPTON, 1840, 'Biographical Notice of the late Humphry Repton, Esq.', written by
      a member of Repton's family.
10 REPTON 1816, fragment XXXV.
11 REPTON 1816, preface.
12 REPTON 1816, fragment XI.
13 WILKES 1980, p. 73.
14 REPTON 1816, fragment XVI.
15 SMITH 1957, p. 23.
16 HADFIELD 1979, p. 275.
17 SUMMERSON 1980, p. 73.
18 LEES-MILNE 1976, p. 43.
19 RUTTER 1822.
20 *Dictionary of National Biography*.
21 Price, Uvedale. *Essays on the Picturesque*, 1810, Vol. I, p. xviii.
22 Austen, Henry. 'Biographical Notice of the Author' published with AUSTEN, 1818.
23 *Garden History*, Vol. V, No. 1, p. 20.
24 *Country Life*, 6 December 1956, p. 1284.
25 *Victoria County History of Staffordshire*, Vol. 5, p. 84.
26 JOHNSON G. 1829, p. 269.
27 LOUDON 1834, para. 1186.
28 REPTON 1840, Introduction, p. vii.
29 COBBETT 1829, para. 318.
30 REPTON 1816, fragment XXVII.
31 LOUDON 1822, edition of 1825, para. 6076.
32 REPTON 1816, fragment XXVII.
33 REPTON 1840, Introduction, p. v.
34 CONNER 1979, p. 115–17.
35 REPTON 1806, 'Conclusion of the inquiry'.
36 REPTON 1808, 'Prefatory observations'.
37 WATKIN 1968, Chapter VI.
38 HOFLAND 1819, pp. 74 & 90.

39 Papworth, Wyatt. *John B. Papworth, Architect to the King of Wurtemburg*, 1879, p. 40.
40 PÜCKLER-MUSKAU 1832, Vol. II, p. 232.
41 See George Johnson's enthusiastic notice of Knight, and the list of his writings in JOHNSON G. 1829, pp. 271–3.
42 HADFIELD 1979, p. 292.
43 GORER 1975, pp. 78 & 82 and 'The Gardenesque Garden, 1830 to 1890' in HARRIS 1979C, p. 53.
44 JOHNSON G. 1829, pp. 331–3.
45 Loudon, J. C. *A Short Treatise on some Improvements Lately Made in Hot-houses*, 1805.
46 *Gardener's Magazine*, Vol. IV, 1828, pp. 28–31 & 63.
47 BERRY 1865, for 1 June 1813.
48 Mackenzie, Sir George. 'On the Form which the Glass of a Forcing-house ought to Have, in order to Receive the Greatest Possible Quantity of Rays from the Sun'. *Transactions of the Horticultural Society*, 1816.
49 GLOAG 1970, p. 51.
50 REPTON 1816, fragment XVI.
51 *Country Life*, 1 August 1963, p. 267.
52 PÜCKLER-MUSKAU 1832, Vol. II, p. 232.
53 LYSONS 1813, Vol. I, Part III, p. 689.
54 *Gardener's Magazine*, Vol. III, 1827, pp. 257–69.
55 LIECHTENSTEIN 1873.
56 FAULKNER 1820, p. 121.
57 HOFLAND 1819, p. 90.
58 COBBETT 1829, para. 315.
59 HADFIELD 1979, pp. 274 & 291. See also *Garden History*, Vol. V, No. 3, 1977, pp. 40–6.
60 LOUDON 1834, para. 5574.
61 Harris, John. *A Catalogue of British Drawings for Architecture, Decoration, Sculpture and Landscape Gardening 1550–1900 in American Collections*, 1971, pp. 127–8.
62 LOUDON 1838, Vol. I. pp. 250–3, 272 & 467, & Vol. II. p. 913.
63 HOFLAND 1819, pp. 74, 90.
64 *Gardener's Magazine*, Vol. III, 1827, pp. 257–69.
65 SELBY 1842, p. 392.
66 Price, Uvedale. *Essays on the Picturesque*, Vol. II, 1810, p. 142.
67 TEMPLE N. 1979, p. 80.
68 PÜCKLER-MUSCAU, 1832, Vol. II, p. 204.
69 SUMMERSON 1980, p. 95.
70 SAUNDERS 1981, p. 23.
71 Wordsworth, William, 'Of Building and Gardening and Laying out of Grounds' (a letter to Sir George H. Beaumont, 17 October 1805), appendixed to the 1906 reprint of the fifth edition of WORDSWORTH 1810, p. 144.
72 De Selincourt, Ernest, Introduction to the 1906 reprint of the fifth edition of WORDSWORTH 1810, p. xvii.
73 DE QUINCEY 1840, under 'Society of the Lakes—III'.
74 COLVIN *et al.* 1980, p. 37.
75 MOORMAN 1965, pp. 108–9, and *Cottage Gardener*, 18 November & 23 December 1875.
76 MOORMAN 1965, pp. 575–7.
77 The guide book for Rydal Mount, 1978, p. 10.
78 MALINS 1978, Sheringham Red Book.
79 LOUDON 1811, p. 98.
80 Tait, A. A. 'Loudon and the Return to Formality' in MACDOUGALL 1980, p. 70.
81 SUMMERSON 1980, Chapters 5, 9 and 12; and Summerson, John 'The Beginnings of Regents Park'. *Architectural History*, Vol. 20, 1977, pp. 56–62.
82 *Proceedings of the Linnaean Society of London*, Vol. II, 1855, p. 82.

Bibliography

Contemporary Works

ANGUS 1787–97: William Angus, *The Seats of the Nobility and Gentry in Great Britain and Wales*

AUSTEN 1814: Jane Austen, *Mansfield Park: A Novel*

AUSTEN 1818: Jane Austen, *Northanger Abbey*

BADESLADE & ROCQUE 1739: Thomas Badeslade & John Rocque, *Vitruvius Britannicus, Volume the Fourth*

BARRINGTON 1785: Daines Barrington, 'On The Progress of Gardening' in *Archaeologia*, Vol. VII

BERRY 1865: Mary Berry, *Extracts from the Journals and Correspondence of Miss Berry from 1783 to 1852.*

BOSWELL 1791: James Boswell, *The Life of Samuel Johnson, LL.D., comprehending an account of his studies and numerous works, in chronological order*

BRITTON 1801–8: John Britton, E. W. Brayley & J. Brewer, *The Beauties of England and Wales*

BROWN 1771: John Brown, *A Description of the Lake at Keswick*

BURKE 1756: Edmund Burke, *A Philosophical Enquiry into the Origin of our Ideas of the Sublime and Beautiful*

CAMBRIDGE 1803: G. O. Cambridge (editor), *The Works of Richard Owen Cambridge, Esq.*

CASTELL 1728: Robert Castell, *The Villas of the Ancients Illustrated*

CHAMBERS 1757: William Chambers, *Designs of Chinese Buildings, Furniture, Dresses, Machines, and Utensils*

CHAMBERS 1763: William Chambers, *Plans, Elevations, Sections and Perspective Views of the Gardens and Buildings at Kew in Surry*

CHAMBERS 1772: William Chambers, *A Dissertation on Oriental Gardening*

COBBETT 1829: William Cobbett, *The English Gardener*

COBBETT 1830: William Cobbett, *Rural Rides*

COMBE 1812: William Combe, *The Tour of Dr. Syntax in Search of the Picturesque*

COWPER 1782: William Cowper, *Poems by William Cowper of the Inner Temple, Esq.*

COWPER 1785: William Cowper, *The Task*

CRADOCK 1774: Joseph Cradock, *Village Memoirs*

CRADOCK 1777: Joseph Cradock, *An Account of Some of the Most Romantic Parts of North Wales*

CRADOCK 1826: Joseph Cradock, *Literary and Miscellaneous Memoirs*

DALTON *c.*1758: John Dalton, 'A Descriptive Poem: addressed to Two Ladies, at their return from viewing the mines near Whitehaven' in *A Collection of Poems* edited by George Pearch (1768)

DE QUINCEY 1840: Thomas de Quincey, *Recollections of the Lakes and the Lake Poets*

DUCK 1755: Stephen Duck, *Caesar's Camp; or, St. George's Hill; a Poem*

EVELYN 1776: Alexander Hunter (editor), *Silva, or, a Discourse of Forest-Trees*

FALCONER 1785: Dr William Falconer, 'Thoughts on the Style and Taste of Gardening among the Ancients' (read 1782) in *Memoirs of the Literary and Philosophical Society of Manchester*

FAULKNER 1820: Thomas Faulkner, *The History and Antiquities of Kensington*

FIELD 1820: Henry Field, *Memoirs, Historical and Illustrative, of the Botanick Garden at Chelsea*

GILPIN 1748: William Gilpin (attributed), *A Dialogue upon the Gardens of the Right Honourable the Lord Viscount Cobham, at Stow in Buckinghamshire*

GILPIN 1782: William Gilpin, *Observations on the River Wye, and Several Parts of South Wales, &c. Relative Chiefly to Picturesque Beauty; Made in the Summer of the Year 1770*

GILPIN 1786: William Gilpin, *Observations, Relative Chiefly to Picturesque Beauty, made in the Year 1772, on Several Parts of England; Particularly the Mountains, and Lakes of Cumberland, and Westmoreland*

GILPIN 1789: William Gilpin, *Observations, Relative Chiefly to Picturesque Beauty, made in the Year 1776, on Several Parts of Great Britain; Particularly the High-lands of Scotland*

GILPIN 1791: William Gilpin, *Remarks on Forest Scenery, and Other Woodland Views, (Relative Chiefly to Picturesque Beauty) Illustrated by the Scenes of New-Forest in Hampshire*

GILPIN 1792: William Gilpin, *Three Essays: on Picturesque Beauty; on Picturesque Travel; and on Sketching Landscape*

GIRARDIN 1777: Marquis René-Louis de Girardin, *De la Composition des Paysages*

GRAVES 1772: Richard Graves, *The Spiritual Quixote, or the Summer's Ramble of Mr. Geoffry Wildgoose, a Comic Romance*

GRAVES 1779: Richard Graves, *Columella; or the Distressed Anchoret, a Colloquial Tale*

GRAVES 1788: Richard Graves, *Recollections of some Particulars in the Life of the Late William Shenstone*

GRAY 1775: William Mason (editor), *The Poems of Mr. Gray*

HEELY 1777: Joseph Heely, *Letters on the Beauties of Hagley, Envil, and The Leasowes*

HERRING 1777: *Letters from the Late Reverend Dr. Thomas Herring*

HILL A. 1753: *The Works of the Late Aaron Hill, Esq.*

HILL J. 1757: John Hill, *Eden: or, a Compleat Body of Gardening*

HOFLAND 1819: Mrs Barbara Hofland, *A Descriptive Account of the Mansion and Gardens of Whiteknights, Seat of the Duke of Marlborough*

HOPE 1808: Thomas Hope, 'On the Art of Gardening' in *Review of Publications of Art, No. II*

HUTCHINSON 1774: William Hutchinson, *An Excursion to the Lakes in Westmoreland and Cumberland, August 1773*

JAGO 1767: Richard Jago, *Edge-Hill; or, the Rural Prospect Delineated and Moralised*

JOHNSON G. 1829: George W. Johnson, *A History of English Gardening*

JOHNSON S. 1775: Dr Samuel Johnson, *A Journey to the Western Isles of Scotland*

JOHNSON S. 1781: Dr Samuel Johnson, *The Lives of the Most Eminent English Poets*

JOHNSON S. 1816: Dr Samuel Johnson, *A Journey into North Wales, in The Year 1774*

KAMES 1762: Lord Kames, *Elements of Criticism*

KNIGHT 1794: Richard Payne Knight, *The Landscape, A Didactic Poem*

LOUDON 1803: John Claudius Loudon, 'Hints respecting the manner of laying out the grounds of the Public Squares in London, to the utmost picturesque advantage' in *Literary Journal*, Vol. II, No. 12

LOUDON 1804: John Claudius Loudon, *Observations on the Formation and Management of Useful and Ornamental Plantations; on the Theory and Practice of Landscape Gardening; and on Gaining and Embanking Land from Rivers or the Sea*

LOUDON 1806: John Claudius Loudon, *A Treatise on Forming, Improving, and Managing Country Residences; and on the Choice of Situations Appropriate to Every Class of Purchasers*

LOUDON 1808: John Claudius Loudon, *An Immediate and Effectual Mode of Raising the Rental of the Landed Property of England, and Rendering Great Britain Independent of Other Nations for a Supply of Bread Corn*

LOUDON 1811: John Claudius Loudon, *Designs for Laying Out Farms and Farm Buildings in the Scotch Style: Adapted to England*

LOUDON 1812: John Claudius Loudon, *Hints on the Formation of Gardens and Pleasure Grounds with Designs in Various Styles of Rural Embellishment*

LOUDON 1818: John Claudius Loudon, *Sketches of Curvilinear Hothouses*

LOUDON 1822: John Claudius Loudon, *Encyclopaedia of Gardening*

LOUDON 1834: John Claudius Loudon, *Encyclopaedia of Gardening, New Edition*

LOUDON 1838: John Claudius Loudon, *Arboretum et Fruticetum Britanicum*

LYSONS 1813: The Reverend David Lysons & Samuel Lysons, *Magna Britannia*

LYTTELTON 1780: William Combe?, *Letters of the Late Lord Lyttelton*

MALTHUS 1783: Daniel Malthus (translator), *An Essay on Landscape*—see GIRARDIN 1777

MARSHALL 1785: William Marshall, *Planting and Ornamental Gardening; a Practical Treatise*

MARSHALL 1795: William Marshall, *A Review of the Landscape, A Didactic Poem; Also of an Essay on the Picturesque*

MASON G. 1768: George Mason, *An Essay on Design in Gardening*

MASON G. 1795: George Mason, *An Essay on Design in Gardening, First Published in MDCCLXVIII. Now Greatly Augmented. Also a Revisal of Several Later Publications on the Same Subject*

MASON W. 1772: The Reverend William Mason, *The English Garden, a Poem*

MASON W. 1773: The Reverend William Mason (attributed), *An Heroic Epistle to Sir W. Chambers*

MATTHEWS 1794: Dr John Matthews, *A Sketch From the Landscape, a Didactic Poem*

MORRIS 1750: Robert Morris, *Rural Architecture*

PAPWORTH J.B. 1818: John Buonaroti Papworth, *Rural Residences*

PAPWORTH J.B. 1823: John Buonaroti Papworth, *Hints on Ornamental Gardening*

PEACOCK 1816: Thomas Love Peacock, *Headlong Hall*

PENN 1813: John Penn, *An Historical and Descriptive Account of Stoke Park in Buckinghamshire*

PENNANT 1804: Thomas Pennant, *A Tour from Alston Moor to Harrogate and Brimham Rocks*

PRICE 1794: Uvedale Price, *An Essay on the Picturesque*

PRICE 1795: Uvedale Price, *A Letter to H. Repton, Esq. on the Application of the Practice as well as the Principles of Landscape-Painting to Landscape-Gardening*

PRICE 1796–8: Uvedale Price, *Essays on the Picturesque, as Compared with the Sublime and the Beautiful*

PRICE 1801: Uvedale Price, *A Dialogue on the Distinct Characters of the Picturesque and the Beautiful*

PÜCKLER-MUSKAU 1832: Prince H. L. H. von Pückler-Muskau, *Tour in England, Ireland, and France in the Years 1828 & 1829*

PYE 1783: Henry James Pye, *The Progress of Refinement*

REPTON 1794: Humphry Repton, *A Letter to Uvedale Price, Esq. on Landscape Gardening*

REPTON 1795: Humphry Repton, *Sketches and Hints on Landscape Gardening*

REPTON 1803: Humphry Repton, *Observations on the Theory and Practice of Landscape Gardening*

REPTON 1806: Humphry Repton, *An Enquiry into the Changes of Taste in Landscape Gardening*

REPTON 1808: Humphry Repton, *Designs for the Pavillon at Brighton*

REPTON 1816: Humphry Repton, *Fragments on the Theory and Practice of Landscape Gardening*

REPTON 1840: John Claudius Loudon (editor), *The Landscape Gardening and Landscape Architecture of the Late Humphry Repton, Esq.*

REYNOLDS 1797: Edmund Malone (editor), *The Discourses of Sir Joshua Reynolds*

RUTTER 1822: John Rutter, *A Description of Fonthill Abbey, and Demesne, Wilts.*

SCOTT 1782: John Scott, *Poetical Works*

SELBY 1842: P. J. Selby, *British Forest Trees*

SHENSTONE 1764: Robert Dodsley (editor), *The Works in Verse and Prose of William Shenstone, Esq.*

SPENCE 1751: Joseph Spence, 'Letter to the Rev. Mr. Wheeler' in HUNT & WILLIS 1975

STEUART 1828: Sir Henry Steuart, *The Planter's Guide; or, a Practical Essay on the Best Method of Giving Immediate Effect to Wood by the Removal of Large Trees and Underwood*

SWITZER 1718: Stephen Switzer, *Ichnographia Rustica: or the Nobleman, Gentleman, and Gardener's Recreation.*

TEMPLE W. 1692: Sir William Temple, 'Upon the Gardens of Epicurus; or, Of Gardening, in the Year 1685' in *Miscellanea*

TRUSLER 1784: Dr John Trusler (attributed), *Elements of Modern Gardening: or, the Art of Laying Out of Pleasure Grounds, Ornamenting Farms, and Embellishing Views Round About our Houses*

WALPOLE 1784: Anon., *A Description of the Villa of Mr. Horace Walpole at Strawberry Hill Near Twickenham, Middlesex*

WALPOLE 1785: Horace Walpole, *Essay on Modern Gardening*

WARNER 1801: The Reverend Richard Warner, *Excursions From Bath*

WARTON 1756: Joseph Warton, *Essay on the Genius and Writings of Pope*

WATTS 1779–86: William Watts, *The Seats of the Nobility and Gentry*

WEST 1778: Thomas West, *A Guide to the Lakes*

WHATELY 1770: Thomas Whately, *Observations on Modern Gardening*

WHITEHEAD 1788: William Mason (editor), *The Works of William Whitehead, Esq.*

WORDSWORTH 1810: William Wordsworth, *A Guide Through the District of the Lakes*

WYNDHAM 1775: Henry Penruddocke Wyndham, *A Gentleman's Tour Through Monmouthshire and Wales, in the Months of June and July, 1774*

YOUNG 1770: Arthur Young, *Tour of the North*

Modern Historical Sources

BARR & INGAMELLS 1973: Bernard Barr & John Ingamells, *A Candidate for Praise: William Mason 1725–97 a Precentor of York*

BATEY 1979: Mavis L. Batey, *Nuneham Courtenay, Oxfordshire*

BROWNELL 1978: Morris Brownell, *Alexander Pope and the Arts of Georgian England*

CARTER *et al.* 1982: George Carter, Patrick Goode & Kedrun Laurie, *Humphry Repton, Landscape Gardener, 1752–1818*

CHASE 1943: Isabel Wakelin Urban Chase, *Horace Walpole: Gardenist*

CLARK 1962: Kenneth Clark, *The Gothic Revival*

CLARKE 1973: George Clarke, 'The Gardens of Stowe' in *Apollo*, Vol. XCVII, June 1973

CLUTTON & MACKAY 1970: Sir George Clutton & Colin MacKay, 'Old Thorndon Hall, Essex: A History and Reconstruction of its Park and Garden' *Garden History Society Occasional Paper No. 2*

COLVIN 1978: Howard Colvin, *A Biographical Dictionary of British Architects 1660–1840*

COLVIN *et al.* 1980: Howard Colvin, J. Mordaunt Crook & Terry Friedman, 'Architectural Drawings from Lowther Castle, Westmorland' *Architectural History Monographs: No. 2*

CONNER 1979: Patrick Conner, *Oriental Architecture in the West*

CONNOR 1979: T. P. Connor, 'Architecture and Planting at Goodwood 1723–1750', *Sussex Archaeological Collections*, Vol. 117

EVANS 1956: Joan Evans, *A History of the Society of Antiquaries*

GLOAG 1970: John Gloag, *Mr. Loudon's England*

GODBER 1968: Joyce Godber, 'The Marchioness Grey of Wrest Park' *The Publications of the Bedfordshire Historical Record Society*, Vol. XLVII

GORER 1975: Richard Gorer, *The Flower Garden in England*

HADFIELD 1979: Miles Hadfield, *A History of British Gardening*

HARRIS 1970: John Harris, *Sir William Chambers*

HARRIS 1978: John Harris, *Gardens of Delight—the Rococo English Landscape of Thomas Robins the Elder*

HARRIS 1979A: John Harris, *The Artist and the Country House*

HARRIS 1979B: John Harris, *A Country House Index*

HARRIS 1979C: John Harris (editor), *The Garden: a Celebration of one Thousand Years of British Gardening*

HARVEY 1974: John Harvey, *Early Nurserymen*

HAZLEHURST 1980: Franklin Hamilton Hazlehurst, *Gardens of Illusion: the Genius of André le Nostre*

HENREY 1975: Blanche Henrey, *British Botanical and Horticultural Literature Before 1800*

HERRMANN 1973: Luke Herrmann, *British Landscape Painting of the Eighteenth Century*

HODGES 1973: Alison Hodges, 'Painshill Park, Cobham, Surrey (1700–1800)' in *Garden History*, Vol. II, No. 2

HUNT & WILLIS 1975: John Dixon Hunt and Peter Willis, *The Genius of the Place*

HUSSEY 1927: Christopher Hussey, *The Picturesque: Studies in a Point of View*

HUSSEY 1967: Christopher Hussey, *English Gardens and Landscapes 1700–1750*

KESWICK 1978: Maggie Keswick, *The Chinese Garden*

KING 1974: Ronald W. King, 'The Ferme Ornée: Philip Southcote And Wooburn Farm' in *Garden History*, Vol. II, No. 3

KING 1978–1980: Ronald W. King, 'Joseph Spence of Byfleet' in *Garden History*, Vol. VI, No. 3, Vol. VII, No. 3 & Vol. VIII, Nos. 2 & 3

LEES-MILNE 1976: James Lees-Milne, *William Beckford*

LIECHTENSTEIN 1873: Princess Marie of Liechtenstein, *Holland House*

MACDOUGALL 1980: Elisabeth B. Macdougall (editor), 'John Claudius Loudon and the Early Nineteenth Century in Great Britain' *Dumbarton Oaks Colloquium on the History of Landscape Architecture VI*

MACK 1969: Maynard Mack, *The Garden and the City*

MALINS 1978: Edward Malins, *The Red Books of Humphry Repton*

MALINS & GLIN 1976: Edward Malins & The Knight of Glin, *Lost Demesnes: Irish Landscape Gardening, 1660–1845*

MANWARING 1925: Elizabeth Manwaring, *Italian Landscape in Eighteenth Century England*

MONTAGU 1924: Reginald Blunt (editor), *Mrs. Montagu, 'Queen of the Blues'*

MOORMAN 1965: Mary Moorman, *William Wordsworth: The Later Years 1803–1850*

PAPWORTH W. 1879: Wyatt Papworth, *John B. Papworth, Architect to the King of Wurtemburg*

PEVSNER 1974: Nikolaus Pevsner (editor), 'The Picturesque Garden and its Influence Outside the British Isles' *Dumbarton Oaks Colloquium on the History of Landscape Architecture II*

PRINCE 1967: Hugh Prince, *Parks in England*

SAUNDERS 1981: Ann Saunders, *The Regents Park Villas*

SMITH 1957: Ernest Smith, *A History of Whiteknights*

SPENCE 1966: James M. Osborn (editor), *Observations, Anecdotes, and Characters of Books and Men*

STITT 1970: Frederick B. Stitt, 'Shugborough: The End of a Village' in *Essays in Staffordshire History*, 4th Series, Vol. VI

STROUD 1962: Dorothy Stroud, *Humphry Repton*

STROUD 1975: Dorothy Stroud, *Capability Brown*

SUMMERSON 1980: Sir John Summerson, *The Life and Work of John Nash, Architect*

TAIT 1980: Alan A. Tait, *The Landscape Garden in Scotland*

TEMPLE N. 1979: Nigel Temple, *John Nash & the Village Picturesque*

WALPOLE 1928: Horace Walpole, 'Journals of Visits to Country Seats' in *Walpole Society*, Vol. 16

WATERS 1975: Ivor Waters, *Piercefield on the Banks of the Wye*

WATKIN 1968: David Watkin, *Thomas Hope and the Neo-Classical Idea*

WIEBENSON 1978: Dora Wiebenson, *The Picturesque Garden in France*

WILKES 1980: Judge Lyall Wilkes, *John Dobson, Architect & Landscape Gardener*

WILLIS 1974: Peter Willis (editor), *Furor Hortensis*

WILLIS 1977: Peter Willis, *Charles Bridgeman and the English Landscape Garden*

WOOD 1913: Sir Henry Trueman Wood, *A History of the Royal Society of Arts*

WOODBRIDGE 1971: Kenneth Woodbridge, *The Stourhead Landscape*

WOODBRIDGE 1974: Kenneth Woodbridge, 'William Kent's Gardening: The Rousham Letters' in *Apollo*, Vol. C

WRIGHT 1979: Eileen Harris (editor) Thomas Wright, *Arbours & Grottos*

Index of Names

Place Index

* These properties are listed in *Historic
Houses, Castles & Gardens in Great Britain
& Ireland 1983* (ABC Historic
Publications, Dunstable), which gives
brief details and times for visiting. Other
private properties, and public or royal
parks may also be open to the public.